La galerie

Monseigneur Le Marquis acheual

Aued van Scheel fecit   35

PORTRAIT OF A CAVALIER

PORTRAIT OF A CAVALIER

William Cavendish, First Duke of Newcastle

Geoffrey Trease

TAPLINGER PUBLISHING COMPANY
NEW YORK

First published in the United States in *1979* by
TAPLINGER PUBLISHING CO., INC.
New York, New York

Library of Congress Catalog Card Number: 79–4929

ISBN 0–8008–6418–2

For Marian

Contents

List of Illustrations

Between pages 96 and 97

Endpapers Newcastle schooling one of his horses at Bolsover *(Abraham van Diepenbeke, from La Méthode Nouvelle . . . .)* The Little Castle *(left)* links with the Cavendish Apartments, kitchens and other domestic quarters, and the Great Gallery of the Terrace Range.

Acknowledgements

My first thanks must be expressed to Lady Anne Cavendish-Bentinck for permission to quote material, some hitherto unpublished, from the Portland Papers deposited on loan in the Department of Manuscripts, British Library, and in the Manuscripts Department, University of Nottingham Library. I must similarly thank Sir Sacheverell Sitwell for allowing me to quote from his poem on Bolsover in *The Thirteenth Caesar*.

Of the countless people who have helped me in one way or another I must voice my special appreciation to three scholars, Dr P. R. Newman and Mrs H. M. Hughes (formerly Miss H. M. Cocking), who lent me the typescripts of their theses and offered me the full use of their material, and Dr Dolores J. Palomo, University of Washington, Seattle, who with equal generosity shared her thoughts about the poems in the Portland Papers.

I do not know the name of every librarian and archivist who has laboured behind the scenes to answer my queries. With apologies to the unnamed I must single out Mrs M. A. Welch, Keeper of the Manuscripts at the University of Nottingham, Mrs S. M. Cooke and Mr Stephen Best of the Local Studies Library in that city, Mr Adrian Henstock of the County Record Office there, Mr T. S. Wragg at Chatsworth, Mr A. G. Lee at St John's College, Cambridge, Mr Patrick Strong, Keeper of College Library, Eton, Mrs J. Radford at the Derbyshire County Library, Mr M. Y. Ashcroft, County Archivist of North Yorkshire, and Mrs V. J. Dawson, Finsbury Reference Librarian. I am also most grateful for the assistance given, by post or on personal visits, by the staff of the British Library, the Bodleian, the House of Lords Record Office, the Public Record Office, and the public library departments of Birmingham, Newcastle-upon-Tyne, Richmond, and my own Hereford and Worcester.

Acknowledgements

For other help I am indebted to Sir Anthony Wagner, then Garter King of Arms; Sir Oliver Millar, Keeper of the Queen's Pictures; Mr Jacob Simon, Assistant Curator at the Ranger's House, Blackheath; Canon H. Ferraby, Rector of Handsworth, Sheffield; Colonel R. Mathews, Bursar at Welbeck College, for arranging my visit to the Abbey; Mrs K. White, Curator at Bolsover, for guiding me round the Castle, and Dr Rosalys Coope, for information about its decoration; Mr J. R. Bibby, for help with the local history of Northumbria; Mr Neil Burton, Department of Architecture and Civic Design, Greater London Authority, for help in dating the Clerkenwell house; Mr Robert Walker of Brussels, for checking further points at the Rubens House in Antwerp; Mrs Allardyce Nicoll for lending me books from the library of her late husband and my old friend; Professor David M. Vieth, University of Carbondale, Illinois, Professor Robert D. Hume, Pennsylvania State University, Professor Judith Milhous, University of Iowa, and Professor A. H. Scouten, University of Pennsylvania, for their courteous dealing with my queries in the same field, the seventeenth-century theatre; and Mr David Durant, for supplementing in correspondence the help already derived from his published work. Coming last to my own family, I must thank my niece, Jill Polak, for her hospitality, for driving us to Bolsover and Hardwick, and for help and suggestions with my researches; my cousin, Dick Trease, and his wife Joan for hospitality which greatly assisted my research at Nottingham; and my wife Marian, for her patience, enthusiastic interest and encouragement through all the stages of the book, during which time His late Grace has been a constant, and cheerfully accepted, member of the household.

December 1978   GEOFFREY TREASE

Northern England: the area of Newcastle's Civil War campaigns.

CAVENDISH FAMILY TREE (simplified)

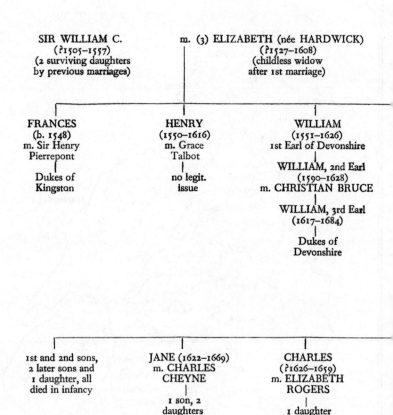

SIR WILLIAM C.
(?1505–1557)
(2 surviving daughters
by previous marriages)

m. (3) ELIZABETH (née HARDWICK)
(?1527–1608)
(childless widow
after 1st marriage)

FRANCES
(b. 1548)
m. Sir Henry
Pierrepont

Dukes of
Kingston

HENRY
(1550–1616)
m. Grace
Talbot

no legit.
issue

WILLIAM
(1551–1626)
1st Earl of Devonshire

WILLIAM, 2nd Earl
(1590–1628)
m. CHRISTIAN BRUCE

WILLIAM, 3rd Earl
(1617–1684)

Dukes of
Devonshire

1st and 2nd sons,
2 later sons and
1 daughter, all
died in infancy

JANE (1622–1669)
m. CHARLES
CHEYNE

1 son, 2
daughters

CHARLES
(?1626–1659)
m. ELIZABETH
ROGERS

1 daughter
died in infancy

NOTE: The revived Newcastle title became extinct again in 1711, when Margaret's husband died. The Cavendish estates later passed, via their daughter, to the Dukes of Portland.

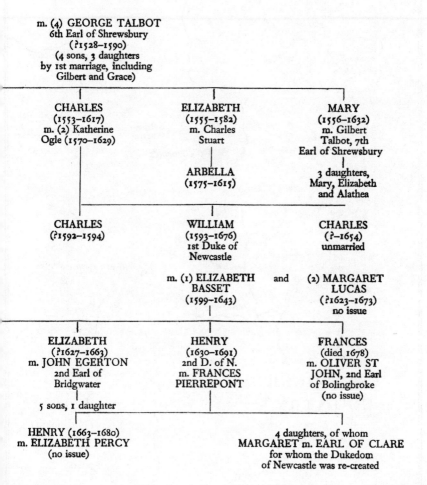

m. (4) GEORGE TALBOT
6th Earl of Shrewsbury
(?1528–1590)
(4 sons, 3 daughters
by 1st marriage, including
Gilbert and Grace)

CHARLES
(1553–1617)
m. (2) Katherine
Ogle (1570–1629)

ELIZABETH
(1555–1582)
m. Charles
Stuart

MARY
(1556–1632)
m. Gilbert
Talbot, 7th
Earl of Shrewsbury

ARBELLA
(1575–1615)

3 daughters,
Mary, Elizabeth
and Alathea

CHARLES
(?1592–1594)

WILLIAM
(1593–1676)
1st Duke of
Newcastle

CHARLES
(?–1654)
unmarried

m. (1) ELIZABETH
BASSET
(1599–1643)

and

(2) MARGARET
LUCAS
(?1623–1673)
no issue

ELIZABETH
(?1627–1663)
m. JOHN EGERTON
2nd Earl of
Bridgwater

HENRY
(1630–1691)
2nd D. of N.
m. FRANCES
PIERREPONT

FRANCES
(died 1678)
m. OLIVER ST
JOHN, 2nd Earl
of Bolingbroke
(no issue)

5 sons, 1 daughter

HENRY (1663–1680)
m. ELIZABETH PERCY
(no issue)

4 daughters, of whom
MARGARET m. EARL OF CLARE
for whom the Dukedom
of Newcastle was re-created

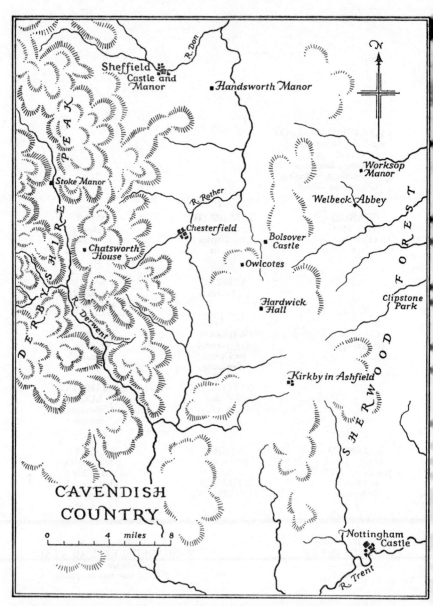

Cavendish Country: the main North Midland seats of the Cavendish family, both branches, with the neighbouring Talbot properties. The Duke of Newcastle's other estates were widely scattered from Somerset to Northumberland.

ONE

Elizabethan Boy

'A PALACE', wrote Nikolaus Pevsner, 'which looks as if it stood in North Italy or Prague.' Instead, incongruously, it dominates from its sandstone precipice a wilderness of railway sidings in an English Midland city. Who on earth, one wonders, could have set out to plant such an improbable castle at Nottingham in the equally improbable year of 1674?

An equestrian statue stands over the doorway, so battered by the Reform Bill rioters who fired the building in 1831 that it might as well depict a fragmented centaur from the Parthenon. And not altogether inappropriately, for the unrecognisable cavalier is the one of whom Ben Jonson wrote in *Underwoods*:

> When first, my Lord, I saw you back your horse,
> Provoke his mettle and command his force
> To all the uses of the field and race,
> Methought I read the ancient art of Thrace,
> And saw a Centaur past those tales of Greece,
> So seem'd your horse and you both of a piece!

This was no mere flattery of a patron, for William Cavendish, later Duke of Newcastle, was unquestionably one of the outstanding horsemen of his period.

He was, however, much besides. A writer himself, he befriended authors ranging from Jonson to Dryden. He could talk painting with Van Dyck and science with Hobbes and Descartes. Turned man of action by the Civil War, he held the North of England with viceregal powers. At eighty he began the building of this castle – to his own design. Even in that era of versatility such a man invites closer scrutiny than he has ever yet received.

His wife's classic biography, published in his lifetime, does not say when he was born or where. 'Mad Madge of Newcastle' had no patience with prosaic detail. Even *The Dictionary of National Biography*, misled by Arthur Collins, the eighteenth-century chronicler of noble families, gives the year wrongly as 1592. Luckily we still have the parish register of Handsworth, a Yorkshire village now part of Sheffield, and know that on 16 December 1593 Thomas Legge, the rector, 'christened Willm Cavendish sonn of Sir Charles Cavendish'. In those days of appalling infantile mortality baptism was prompt. Most likely William was born only weeks or even days before that date. His parents had married on 11 July 1591, and had already a son, Charles. William was a much favoured baptismal name, to the great confusion of later researchers. It was the name of our subject's grandfather, uncle, and cousins – at Chatsworth the William Cavendishes followed each other monotonously – and as all crop up in the documents of the period the price of accuracy is eternal vigilance.

When our particular William arrived, his father was forty-one. He had been married before, briefly and childlessly, and then after nine years as a widower had married Katherine Ogle, daughter of Lord Ogle, last in a line of Northumbrian border barons. She was about twenty-three at William's birth. The marriage was happy. Her elder sister, Jane, had earlier married Sir Charles's stepbrother, Edward Talbot, so that Katherine, though she had come far from home, was scarcely a lonely exile in the south.

She bore this second child at Handsworth Manor, a house of which only a large stone or two can be traced near Finchwell Road. It had been lent by another of Sir Charles's stepbrothers, Gilbert Talbot, seventh Earl of Shrewsbury. Having just inherited Sheffield Castle and several other mansions, Gilbert had a surplus. Not that Sir Charles was homeless: he had Stoke Manor, up the Derwent Valley from Chatsworth, remote from the world in general but inconveniently close to his iron-willed mother. For he was the youngest son of Bess of Hardwick, a relationship so significant to the new-born infant that she demands, as she did when alive, immediate attention.

Then nearing seventy, William's formidable grandmother was still handsome, dark-eyed, reddish-haired, and as outspoken as her old friend, Elizabeth I. In her native Derbyshire, indeed, she was a kind of queen, her accumulated estates requiring no fewer than seventeen bailiffs. That accumulation was wickedly explained by Horace Walpole:

> Four times the nuptial bed she warm'd,
> And every time so well perform'd,
> That when death spoiled each Husband's billing
> He left the widow every shilling. . . .

Three marriages had been childless. It was to her second husband, that earlier William Cavendish, an eminent public servant, that she had borne three sons and five daughters in ten years. She had gone on to a third and a fourth marriage, productive only of property. Her master stroke had been the bargain with her final suitor, George Talbot, sixth Earl of Shrewsbury and one of the richest men in England. A widower, he had seven children, but she was equal even to that complication.

A contract preserved at Chatsworth embodies her conditions. The Earl's second son (and, as it proved, his heir) was Gilbert, then fourteen. He must marry, before Easter, Bess's third daughter, Mary Cavendish, aged twelve. If Mary died before then, or 'before carnal knowledge betwixt them', he would marry her next sister, Elizabeth. If anything happened to Gilbert, Mary would be transferred to a younger brother. Similarly, Bess's eldest son, the eighteen-year-old Henry, must wed the eight-year-old Grace Talbot; and again, if either died before consummation, the survivor would be matched with whatever appropriate substitute remained. As things turned out, the original couples were duly married within five weeks and both unions were later consummated, so that young Charles Cavendish was never called upon. The essence of the contract was, needless to say, a generous settlement of properties, Bess and her new husband retaining a life interest. But none of these watertight arrangements could guarantee the success of their own marriage, which was to end in estrangement and separation. This early family history is vital to an understanding of the interlocking relationships that were to shape young William's early life. Though born the younger son of a younger son, an unpretentious country gentleman, he was always potentially something more.

His father was the most likeable of Bess's three boys. Brought up in the merged Talbot and Cavendish family, he quickly became devoted to his slightly older stepbrother Gilbert, now also his brother-in-law. Gilbert was quarrelsome, Charles easy-tempered. Any trouble he became involved in sprang usually from loyalty to Gilbert. Loyalty, the constant thread running through William's career, was first learnt from parental example.

How long he remained cradled at Handsworth is unknown and unimportant, for it was certainly a brief period, and to a baby one ceiling must look much like another. It was in this manor that the sixth Earl, his marriage with Bess having broken down, had consoled himself with a mistress. Gilbert, as heir, was still enmeshed in tiresome litigation with her over valuables she alleged she had been given by his father. He had also to cope with Bess in her triple role of widow, stepmother and mother-in-law. She had her life-interest and looked indestructible. As their wrangles intensified over the years, Charles's friendship with Gilbert cost him his mother's approval, and in consequence William saw less of his redoubtable grandparent than he would otherwise have done.

In 1597, the year that Bess made a stately entrance with musicians playing into her new Hardwick Hall, Gilbert passed over to Charles the lease of Welbeck, a former Premonstratensian abbey lying in a hollow in Sherwood Forest. It was attractively close to Gilbert's own favourite residence, Worksop Manor, a superlative showpiece erected by his father, and well away from Bess's two Derbyshire seats at Hardwick and Chatsworth. She, however, was not so preoccupied with her new house that she could not in that same year (possibly as a dig at Gilbert) encourage her son to build on his own account. She gave him four hundred pounds. By all means let him live on the fringe of Sherwood. But this building, it may be noted, was begun at Kirkby-in-Ashfield, only a few miles from Hardwick. For a dramatic reason it was never finished.

On the morning of 9 June 1599 Sir Charles, who was staying at Kirkby to supervise the work, mounted a 'little nag' and rode to the site with his wife's kinsmen, Harry and Launcelot Ogle, and a groom. Nearing the brick-kiln – when the Cavendishes built they made their own bricks, quarried their own stone and felled their own timber – he noticed about twenty horsemen on a distant hillside. He took them for a hunting party led by his Newstead neighbour, Sir John Byron, but when they wheeled and came galloping towards him he recognised Sir John Stanhope. Gilbert had an old feud with the Stanhopes and Charles had been drawn into it. Years ago in London he had challenged Stanhope to a duel, but Sir John had turned up in an excessively padded doublet, and when Charles objected to so much defensive upholstery the fight had been called off. Now the prospect of having him as neighbour had stirred Sir John to action.

The odds were absurd. Charles, though a brave little man, set spurs to his horse and made for the shelter of the building site. His mount fell, however, and before he could get his foot out of the stirrup his pursuers were upon him. Two pistols were fired. One bullet hit him in the thigh, the other shot peppered him with pellets. He defended himself vigorously with his rapier, supported by the Ogles, who had a Borderer's relish for an affray. Though so heavily outnumbered, they unhorsed six of their attackers, killed two and badly wounded two more. This improbable-sounding cloak-and-sword scenario is documented in the State Papers and by that tireless letter-writer, John Chamberlain. Some workmen came running up, and

John Stanhope, who was the hindmost during all the fight, was now the foremost in running away, carrying all the rest of his hirelings with him. . . . They left behind them six good geldings, whereof some are worth twenty pounds apiece, two or three cloaks, two rapiers, two pistols, one sword and dagger, and some of their hats, all which are safely kept by Sir Charles.

Charles, 'hurt also in the head and in the hand', was assisted to the house where he was staying. His wife was there. William may not have been – he spent a good deal of time at Worksop with his Aunt Mary and Uncle Gilbert, who had no sons – but he must soon have heard the whole story, exciting enough to an impressionable five-year-old, for his father's main wound was slow to heal, and the Chesterfield surgeon could not extract the bullet. Six months later Queen Elizabeth sent down her own surgeon, Mr Clowes, who was (in a wince-provoking phrase) to 'meddle with his probe'. Writs were issued from Greenwich Palace. Both parties were warned to keep the peace.

As a result, Charles abandoned Kirkby in favour of Welbeck, where he commissioned some new building, finished in 1604. Gilbert also gave him an option on Bolsover, a dilapidated twelfth-century castle in Derbyshire. Unlike Welbeck, which Evelyn called 'a noble yet melancholy seat . . . environed with woods', Bolsover enjoyed a splendid skyline position on a limestone ridge. This appealed to Charles, who also, when in Nottingham, would glance wistfully at that other ruin so superbly crowning its tawny cliff. He could not rebuild Bolsover until his mother died. Bess had no need of the crumbling fortress, so near Hardwick that it was visible from her fine new home, but she jealously guarded her life-interest in the coal-pits surrounding it.

William's earliest memories were thus chiefly of Welbeck. He never knew his elder brother, Charles, who had died a few months after his own arrival. When a third boy was born he too was christened Charles. He was stunted in physique. John Aubrey called him 'a little, weak, crooked man', but Clarendon wrote that 'in this unhandsome or homely habitation there was a mind and soul lodged, that was very lovely and beautiful'. Sir Charles was an enlightened parent, never seeking to force his sons into a particular mould. To William he could impart his mastery of fencing and horsemanship and his delight in strenuous country activities. Charles junior, equally loved, should have intellectual opportunities. 'Nature,' says Aubrey, 'having not adapted him for the court nor camp, he betook himself to the study of the mathematics, wherein he became a great master.' He and William were always devoted to each other. Again, the streak of loyalty gleams through a lifetime.

Even by Elizabethan standards it was a particularly musical home. That great madrigal composer, John Wilbye, dedicated his first collection to Sir Charles in 1598. The boys must have grown up to the sweet strains of *Stay, Corydon* and *Flora gave me fairest flowers*. The foundations were laid to make William later, in Clarendon's phrase, 'amorous in poetry and music'.

If it was all harmony at Welbeck there was plenty of discord elsewhere in the family, as William, when old enough to sort out the ramifications, became well aware. Bess was always at odds with her eldest boy, 'my bad son, Henry', who opposed her in everything and whose scandalous life caused him to be remembered a century later as 'the common bull of Derbyshire and Staffordshire'. Quite different was William, her favourite and submissive shadow, who only in his forties was allowed a home of his own and then only three miles away at Owlcotes, still under her eye. He had a son, also William, three years older than his Welbeck namesake.

As to the Cavendish aunts, two of Bess's five daughters had died young. Mary had married Gilbert and was now Countess of Shrewsbury. Frances had married Henry Pierrepont of Holme Pierrepont near Nottingham, and their son would one day be Earl of Kingston, starting one of several noble dynasties that sprang from Bess's far-sighted matrimonial investments. Her other daughter, Elizabeth, had been dead for years, but she had left the family an intractable problem.

In arranging her marriage, Bess had for once gone too far. She had infuriated Queen Elizabeth by matching the girl with a Stuart, Charles, Duke of Lennox, Darnley's brother. The marriage had been brief, both partners dying young, but leaving a daughter, Arbella Stuart, who until James of Scotland had children came next after him in the logical succession to the English crown. By the time her Welbeck cousin was old enough to grasp the implications her political significance had been diminished by the birth of Prince Henry, but in that conspiratorial period she was still a piece on the board, a pawn, yet a potential queen.

That Arbella was something special must have been evident to William. Probably he saw little of the unhappy, tempestuous girl eighteen years his senior. Before he was born she had often stayed with his father, and had gone to court with him in 1587. Aunt Mary had taken her there the next year, when her high-and-mighty ways had offended the Queen. Thereafter, forbidden the court, she had been passed round various relatives, ending as the semi-prisoner of her apprehensive grandmother. Bess knew that Arbella must not mix with the wrong people, still less marry until the Queen's pleasure was known. Even a small boy could not have been unaware of these things. Talk of the great world filtered through to the house in the forest. Bess, though she went no more to London, was as nearly an old personal friend of the Queen as any subject could presume to be. Uncle Gilbert, though sometimes in hot water, was a grandee of indisputable importance. Even Sir Charles, unambitious and home-loving, had travelled widely, sat in Parliament, and hobnobbed with the mighty. Any Cavendish counted.

William's maternal relatives loom more faintly. Lord Ogle died when he was three and, though his grandmother lived on, Northumberland was a remote world. The barony went into abeyance for lack of a male heir, the estates (subject to Lady Ogle's life-interest) were divided between the two daughters. Jane, as elder, received the larger portion and moved with her husband, Edward Talbot, into Bothal Castle, set deep in the ravine of the Wansbeck where that river winds down from Morpeth to the North Sea. William's mother had spent her own childhood there amid 'fair gardens and orchards, wherein grows all kind of herbs and flowers, and fine apples, plums of every kind, pears, damsons, nuts, wardens, cherries too, the black and red, walnuts, and also liquorice very fine', but there is no record of his going north, as a child, to sample these delights himself. He would hear also of Ogle Castle, the earlier family seat amid the wild moors inland. But even if his mother entertained him with tales of his swashbuckling border ancestors, she could scarcely have outdone the current melodramas of the Cavendishes. Just after his ninth birthday there was an incident at Hardwick, the repercussions of which must have vibrated at Welbeck.

On 10 March 1603 Uncle Henry arrived at the gates of Hardwick, with thirty or forty armed riders lurking in the background, to remove Arbella from his mother's custody. Bess and her servants stood firm. Henry was admitted alone, but Arbella was not allowed to leave with him. This drama set messengers posting up and down the London road. In no time the Queen's commissioner arrived to take statements from all concerned. He ruled that Arbella should move to Bedfordshire, under the supervision of the Earl of Kent. Bess bowed to his arbitration, but cut both her rebellious relatives out of her will.

Four days later came an event of wide national importance: before dawn on 24 March the Queen died. Soon James was hastening southwards, and by 20 April Gilbert was playing host at Worksop to the shambling new sovereign with his broad Scots speech. It is unlikely that William and his parents missed the chance to be there.

Queen Anne and Prince Henry followed later. Prince Charles, only two and a half, was thought too delicate to make the journey, but in July of the next year he too stopped at Worksop. Gilbert summoned his nephews from Welbeck. William's account to his father was dutifully composed in schoolroom French: '*Monsieur et Père Jay pence que cestoit mon debuoir de vous escrire . . .*' or, since the original can be tiresome in its seventeenth-century spelling:

I thought it my duty to write to you by the bearer what honourable entertainment my Lord Duke and his company have received at Worksop, and how my brother and I received much honour, comporting ourselves so well that the Scottish noblemen were astonished, principally in the French language, in which his governor is perfect, as also are several noblemen of his suite, with whom we had a good deal of conversation. I will end by begging you to inform yourself further of this, and likewise by most humbly kissing the hands of my Lord my uncle and my Lady my aunt, to whom I offer thanks for the honour that they do me, in considering me fit to entertain such a prince, and in this assurance I remain your very humble and obedient son, William Cavendish.

We do not know what civilities actually passed between the stammering toddler from Scotland and the confident English boy. But, however superficial the encounter, William had been face to face for the first time with the ill-starred prince whose future was to have so profound an effect upon his own.

TWO

Youth of Promise

How DID William acquire the French of which he was so proud?

His uncles had been at Eton, but the College records say nothing of
Sir Charles or his sons. There were, of course, schools at Mansfield and
at Nottingham, where Sir Thomas Hutchinson sent John, the famous
Roundhead colonel-to-be, but the Cavendishes were beginning to prefer
private tutors. Uncle William's children were instructed first by Bess's
chaplain and later by the future philosopher, Hobbes. Of the heir to
Welbeck the antiquary William Oldys wrote in *Biographia Britannica*
that Sir Charles,

discovering, even in his infancy, the strongest marks of an extraordinary
genius . . . was extremely careful of them, and took all imaginable pains to
have him instructed, as well in sciences as in languages; so that, at an age when
most young gentlemen are but entering on knowledge, he might be truly said
to have acquired a large stock of solid learning, which was adorned with an
easy and polite behaviour, that, except on proper occasions, entirely concealed
the scholar under the more taking appearance of the fine gentleman.

The impression that emerges is of a happy and secure boyhood in an
affectionately united family. There was study, but none of that Tudor
cramming that pressed the almost infant nose into Greek and Hebrew.
There was much music, riding through Sherwood glades, jollity indoors
and out, as may be fairly deduced from a memorandum William long
afterwards submitted to the exiled Charles II, advising him when
restored to wipe out Puritan prohibitions and revive Merrie England.
Clearly harking back to the pleasures of his own youth, William wanted
'all the old holidays, with their mirth and rites set up again'. Besides re-
opening the London playhouses, 'there should be players to go up and
down the country'. Nostalgically he called for 'May games, morris
dances, the Lord of the May, the Lady of the May, the Fool and the
Hobby Horse . . . also the Whitsun Lord and Lady . . . carols and wassails

at Christmas, with good plum porridge and pies, which now are forbidden as profane ungodly things'. He hoped to see again, after Sunday evening service, the lads and lasses dancing round the maypole to the bagpipe, 'refreshed with their ale and cakes'. He was unmistakably echoing Sir Toby Belch: 'Dost thou think, because thou art virtuous, there shall be no more cakes and ale?' He had been eight when *Twelfth Night* was written.

In those years he was developing the deep love of Welbeck that always drew him back. Sir Charles, who had sat in several of Elizabeth's Parliaments, went to none of the King's. More than ever he was content to be the country gentleman, training William in the responsibilities that would one day be his.

To some of the family the old Queen's passing brought more changes. Gilbert's lavish hospitality at Worksop had pleased James, and he was soon given several high-sounding appointments. Arbella reappeared at court, the new disorderly Whitehall of buffoonery and childish games, deep drinking and sexual deviation. 'This most ridiculous world', she described it acidly. 'If ever there were such a virtue as courtesy at the court,' she wrote to Uncle Gilbert, 'I marvel what is become of it.' She could detect it only in James's long-suffering queen, who welcomed her company. So Arbella masked her disgust, attended the coronation next in precedence to Her Majesty, accepted an increased allowance from James, and settled down in her own apartments, with a small separate household, in the rambling rabbit-warren of Whitehall. She spent much time with the royal children, was friendly with the powerful Cecil, and was a connection of immense potential value to all her relatives.

In the spring of 1605 she came down to Hardwick to make her peace with her grandmother. The King had given her a blank patent for a peerage. With Bess's approval, she would insert Uncle William's name. Bess could not resist the offer, and her favourite son duly became Baron Cavendish of Hardwick, though it cost him £2000, for James was finding the sale of titles an excellent source of income. Arbella was thus forgiven; but Gilbert, and by association Sir Charles, remained in disfavour with Bess, so the Welbeck boys probably saw little of their grandmother. Reconciliation came in December 1607, when Sir Charles, with Gilbert and Mary, spent a whole day at Hardwick. Bess was confined to her room, but her mind was still lively. Soon, however, it was evident that she was going downhill, and on 13 February she died.

All the Cavendishes, except Henry, seem to have attended her funeral

at Derby. Henry, of course, had long been disinherited. Nearly everything went to her second son. Sir Charles got nothing, but to show there
was no ill-feeling she left each of his boys 2000 marks to buy land.
Presumably he respected her wishes, and it was on some other occasion
that young William spent a legacy on a horse, a dog and the services of
'a singing boy', whereas a more prudent relative put his share into land.
'If any son of mine put money into land before he was twenty,' declared
Sir Charles contemptuously, 'I'd disinherit him.'

It was probably at the following Michaelmas, 1608, that William, then
approaching his fifteenth birthday, went up to Cambridge. He entered
St John's, of which college his Aunt Mary was a munificent benefactress,
having just doubled its size by building a second court. William qualified
as 'noble' under the somewhat elastic regulations and was exempt from
any tedious academic tests. His college contemporaries included a tall,
severe-looking Yorkshire lad, Tom Wentworth, later Earl of Strafford.

Cambridge had long lost the intellectual vitality of early Tudor days,
when St John's alone contained men like Ascham, Cheke and the young
William Cecil. Learning had too often degenerated into pedantic
quibbles. Some of the syllabus was still medieval. Bright boys came up,
forced on beyond their years, and then wilted with disillusionment. In
this atmosphere William's tutors, says the Duchess, 'could not persuade
him to read or study much, he taking more delight in sports, than in
learning'. Sir Simonds d'Ewes, coming up to St John's ten years afterwards, complained that 'swearing, drinking, rioting and hatred of all piety
and virtue . . . did abound there and in all the university'. William had
no more taste for such mindless amusements than he had for arid scholarship, and the Duchess may have been thinking of him when she wrote
of a nameless student in *Nature's Pictures*: 'At last considering with himself that he was buried to the world and the delights therein, conversing
more with the dead than the living, in reading old authors . . . he left
the University.' Certainly William had soon had enough. It was not
unusual to leave without graduating. Wentworth did the same, but
whereas he and many others proceeded to the Inns of Court and studied
law, William characteristically followed his own bent and went to the
Royal Mews.

In all matters equestrian France was by now leader of European fashion.
Pluvinal de la Baume, after six years at the famous Pignatelli school near
Naples, had established an academy under royal patronage at the Louvre.
One of his foremost disciples, St Antoine, had been sent over by Henri IV
to instruct Prince Henry in the new standards by which, henceforth,

a good cavalier was to be judged, with much emphasis on ceremonial style and those complicated evolutions still to be seen at the Spanish Riding School in Vienna.

In London the lessons took place on the royal tiltyard, now Horse Guards Parade, and were shared by other aristocratic adolescents. From the start William was fascinated by the artificialities of the *haute école*. Racing, so popular with the Stuarts, he took up only late in life, and hunting was never a passion. It was the *manège*, or dressage, that absorbed him, with its ballet-like techniques, *capriole* and *courbette*, *volte* and *demi-volte*, *levade* and *passade*, and all related questions of breeding, training, diet and veterinary care. 'I have practised', he wrote in old age, 'ever since I was ten years old, have rid with the best masters of all nations, heard them discourse at large and tried their various ways; have read all the Italian, French and English books and some Latin ones and in a word all that had been writ upon that subject good and bad.' Whatever his Cambridge record, he was clearly anything but illiterate. He read critically, had no automatic reverence for print, and, while warmly appreciating literature in its imaginative forms, felt that in the practical affairs of life first-hand experience was more important. 'I would not have you too studious,' he told the future Charles II as a boy, 'for too much contemplation spoils action . . . therefore take heed of too much book.' He shared the views, as well as the riding lessons, of the athletic Henry. 'I know what becomes a prince. It is not necessary for me to be a professor, but a soldier and a man of the world.'

When Henry was to be invested as Prince of Wales, William was among the twenty-five well-born youths chosen to attend him. To mark the occasion, all would be created Knights of the Bath. A week of celebrations was planned for June 1610.

It began with the Prince's journey down-river from Richmond Palace to Chelsea, where he was welcomed by the Lord Mayor and then escorted, to the strains of fife, drum and trumpet, by a flotilla of ornate barges and two synthetic sea-monsters. One was a gigantic dolphin, from whose back a stout little Amphion (played by the eminent actor, Richard Burbage) declaimed flattering verses. The other, a whale, bore one of the leading boys from Shakespeare's company as Corinea, Queen of Cornwall. At Whitehall Stairs the Prince landed amid thunderous gun-salutes and was conducted to the privy chamber where his parents awaited him.

Thus far William had been a mere spectator. Two days later, parading with the other candidates for knighthood at Durham House, he walked in the procession along the Strand. At the palace, after a service in the Chapel Royal, they were given dinner in the Guard Chamber, between the King's Presence Chamber and the great hall. Here they were to sleep, soldier-like, on pallets on the floor. Before that, however, they had to take the initiatory bath, and twenty-five red-canopied tubs stood ready in an adjacent apartment.

After, one might imagine, a somewhat restless and murmurous night, the youths rose, donned grey-hooded gowns, and in this unwonted monkish attire filed into the chapel to take the oath. Then, blossoming into crimson taffeta and white sarsenet, they returned to Durham House, so that they could ride back to the palace through admiring crowds to the thrilling blare of trumpets. There James was waiting to bestow the accolade. William knelt with the rest and rose again 'Sir William'. Next came the dedication of his sword in the chapel. Emerging, he faced the ritual challenge of the aproned royal chef, threatening to hack off his new gold spurs. He paid the customary coin and passed on.

The morrow was Prince Henry's great day. The new knights assembled under the lofty beamed roof of Westminster Hall. William observed Uncle Gilbert among the earls carrying the regalia. Gilbert, nowadays a martyr to gout, bore the coronet. The heralds checked details, marshalled the procession, and led the way. The new Knights of the Bath followed, then the earls, Henry last. The King was on his throne in the Parliament House, little crook-backed Salisbury ready to receive the letters patent from Garter King of Arms. There was much bowing, the letters were read, and James invested his son with the regalia. That night, while the proud father supped quietly in his privy chamber, Henry presided over a banquet with the newly dubbed knights.

The next evening came Samuel Daniel's masque, *Tethys' Festival*, with spectacular effects by Inigo Jones. From an ornate proscenium arch hung a curtain, painted with clouds, which rose to reveal Milford Haven with distant vessels gliding to and fro. One contrivance succeeded another. It was the sort of opulent show in which the Jacobean court delighted. The Queen and her ladies took part, and Prince Charles, now nine, appeared as Zephyr, in a brief robe of green satin, with silver wings, an aureole of finest lawn and a floral garland, with a ring of little girls as naiads to attend him. A night to remember. Doubtless William remembered it when, over twenty years later, he was planning for Charles a similarly lavish entertainment.

On the following afternoon there was tilting, at which William himself was now an expert, especially in 'running at the ring', when the contestant charged between two high posts and tried to carry off, on his lance-point, the metal ring that dangled from the crossbar.

The week concluded with a mimic sea-battle on the Thames in front of the palace. Two merchantmen were assailed by a Turkish corsair, with a Turkish fortress looming in the background on the Lambeth bank. The corsair was of course defeated, the fortress blown up. The June night blazed with fireworks, a splendid climax to the celebrations.

If a trifle worn by the week's excitements, the sixteen-year-old Sir William Cavendish, K.B., must have tumbled into bed with a certain sense of satisfaction and confidence in his own future. His gold-spurred foot was on the ladder, and if he wished to climb there were some influential hands to help.

That was 6 June. Before the month was out, his too-often frustrated Cousin Arbella had secretly married William Seymour, the suitor expressly forbidden her by the King. Within days her disobedience was known and she was in custody. For the few remaining years of her tragic existence she was in no position to help anyone.

THREE

The Mission to Savoy

IT WAS TIME for a young gentleman to see something of the wider world. Early in 1612 a convenient opportunity arose when Sir Henry Wotton went out to Savoy on a diplomatic mission. 'I shall have with me, for gentlemen of quality,' he wrote to a friend, 'Sir Robert Riche . . . Mr Francis Haward, son to my Lord William, and Sir William Candishe . . . a young gentleman very nobly bred, and of singular expectation; some other gentlemen there are of meaner note. . . . Our whole troop together, when we shall pass the mountains, will be about fifty horse.' William's brother was among those of 'meaner note'.

The Cavendish boys landed at Boulogne with the main party on 18 March. Rich was to join them in France. Sir Peter Saltonstall, one of the royal equerries, had gone ahead with part of the King's gift to the Duke of Savoy, ten horses extravagantly caparisoned, to travel by easy stages and await Wotton at Lyons.

The mission's object was to discuss a possible match between Prince Henry and the Duke's daughter. Charles Emmanuel badly needed an ally. His duchy was sandwiched between the northern Italian dominions of a hostile Spain and a France whose attitude, since the assassination of his brother-in-law, Henri IV, had become unpredictable. James, while wanting Savoy's friendship, did not mean to make unnecessary enemies elsewhere. It would be Wotton's task to impress upon the Duke the splendour of England, or rather Great Britain, as James preferred to say. Wotton had been chosen for his diplomatic skill and experience. He was spoken of, that winter, as the likely successor to the failing Salisbury as Secretary of State.

Sir Charles was fortunate in finding such a man to take his sons on their first trip abroad. Wotton, now nearing his mid-forties, had spent most of his adult life on the Continent. While he could turn out a gracefully phrased Latin oration when required, he was more remarkable for his idiomatic grasp of French and other languages, which had

enabled him in his earlier days to perform prodigies of impudent daring as
an intelligence agent in a variety of disguises. He was outstanding in the
breadth of his interests and the depth of his knowledge, and with that
intellectual zest went a love of good company and witty conversation.
Above all, he liked the young.

What did they talk of during those spring days as they rode through
Picardy and Champagne and Burgundy? Their mission, presumably
Would Prince Henry like the Savoyard girl? What was Turin like as a
city? Wotton, of course, had been there. There must have been times
when it seemed to the boys that Wotton had been everywhere. He could
tell them about the Duke too, a devious intriguer who for over thirty
years had worked to enhance the status of his precarious duchy. And it
would be surprising if Wotton did not entertain his young companions
with reminiscences of his cloak-and-dagger period. How he had once
'entered Rome', when it was dangerous for an English Protestant to do
so,

with a mighty blue feather in a black hat, [so that] first, I was by it taken for no
English, upon which depended the ground of all. Secondly, I was reputed as
light in my mind as in my apparel (they are not dangerous men that are so).
And thirdly, no man could think that I desired to be unknown, who, by wear-
ing of that feather, took a course to make myself famous through Rome in a
few days.

Wotton's ability as a raconteur was well described by Casaubon, remembering their time together in Geneva: 'Ah, what days those were,
when heedless of the lateness of the hour we passed whole nights in
lettered talk! I hanging on your stories of all you had seen of many men
and many lands. . . . Oh, that was life worth living, pure happiness! I
cannot recall those times without groaning in spirit.'

Wotton was much more, though, than a yarn-spinner. He loved music
and scientific speculation: William's own interest in science may have
owed something to him. Then there was architecture. Bess of Hardwick's grandsons were confronted daily with foreign novelties, and it
is scarcely likely that the future author of *Elements of Architecture* missed
the chance to expound to them his principle that every building should
be 'a sound piece of good art, where the materials, being but ordinary
stone, without any garnishment of sculpture, do yet ravish the beholder
(and he knows not how) by a secret harmony in the proportions'. How
far did William's impressions on this journey influence his own building
projects? One recalls Pevsner's Nottingham comparison, 'a palace which

looks as if it stood in North Italy'. After that summer, William was never to see Italy again.

There was probably talk of poetry. Perhaps it was Wotton who introduced him to the work of Donne, his close friend since Oxford days, whose influence shows in the imagery of William's own verses. Wotton himself wrote sparingly but with fastidious elegance – lines like 'You meaner beauties of the night' and the lapidary couplet 'Upon the Death of Sir Albert Morton's Wife':

> He first deceased; she for a little tried
> To live without him, liked it not, and died.

Morton, his nephew, was in the party, designated for the post of English Resident at Turin if all went well.

Of the others, perhaps the most interesting, when he joined them, was Robert Rich, later Earl of Warwick, 'one of the most best-natured and cheerfullest persons I have in my time met with', as his daughter-in-law was one day to testify. His was a complex personality, for, while inclining to the Puritans, he was (wrote Clarendon) 'of a life very licentious and unconformable to their professed rigour . . . of a pleasant and companionable wit and conversation, of an universal jollity, and such a licence in his words and in his actions that a man of less virtue could not be found'. No doubt he made his own contribution to the broadening of the young Cavendish minds. Thirty years later they were to find themselves on opposite sides, for it was his decisive action that secured the fleet's adherence to Parliament in the Civil War.

More of William's own age was Francis Howard, son of that 'Bauld Willie' whom Scott inaccurately depicted as 'Belted Will' in *The Lay of the Last Minstrel*. When the war came, Francis was to be a Cavalier colonel under William's command.

All that lay far ahead, unimaginable, as the cavalcade made its peaceful progress across France. After cold March winds the weather changed suddenly. At Troyes William went down with 'a little indisposition' brought on by the heat. They rested there a day and a half, Wotton 'being loath', he told Salisbury in a dispatch, 'to leave behind so sweet an ornament of my journey, and a gentleman himself of so excellent nature and institution'. They reached Lyons on the Wednesday morning of Easter week, just as planned, three weeks after leaving Boulogne. Equally prompt on schedule Sir Peter Saltonstall arrived, via Orléans, in time for dinner. 'Our meeting thus together,' wrote Wotton, 'in the place which we had determined with the difference of so few hours, we esteemed a good presagement of the rest.'

Now, though, there was an unforeseen delay. One of the horses intended for the Duke had lamed itself, treading on a vine-dresser's pruning sickle. The party waited, hoping for a quick recovery, then reluctantly decided to leave the animal behind. The others were in splendid condition and 'everywhere admired for delicate beasts'. The five-day halt had its compensations. Lyons was a fine city, its merchants' houses soaring like cliffs of shining white freestone from the cobbled streets. The Place Bellecour was lively with musicians and skittle-alleys. The shopgirls were famous among travellers for their good looks.

This was the threshold of Savoy. The shortest route to Chambéry was a precipitous track, unsuitable for horses, over the Col d'Aiguebelette. The party had to take the longer road. Once inside the Duke's territory, their reception, Wotton assured Salisbury, 'was full of circumstances of great respect'. Outside Chambéry they were met by the Marquis de Lanz, who had ridden out with sixty cavaliers, an unprecedented courtesy. After ceremonious greetings and introductions the combined procession entered the town, passing up the main street to the castle on its commanding height.

The Marquis combined superb dignity with a courtesy that endeared him to all classes. He would 'put off his hat to the meanest artisans', a lesson not lost on William who later enjoined similar civility upon the future Charles II. On the following morning the Marquis broke precedent again, taking Wotton in his own coach for the first few miles towards Montmélian. There they saw an enormous fortress crowning a rock and were saluted by 'all the small and great artillery'. After an admiring trudge round the ramparts they were entertained 'with a very delicate banquet and music'. There was a second banquet at their lodgings in the town below. Wotton was accorded a guard of musketeers and arquebusiers outside his chamber. 'Nearer pomp than necessity', he observed. After breakfast the Marquis walked the first quarter of a mile with him and there was an exchange of farewell compliments.

The ninth of May saw them at Lanslebourg, below Mont Cenis, by which they must cross the Alps into Piedmont. It was a well-trodden road, used by mule-trains, and presented no problems.

The most exhausting element in their journey was now the hospitality. Elaborate welcomes were prepared in every town, a banquet every few miles. It was too much even for the hardened Wotton. At Rivoli he collapsed with a high temperature and – nightmare for a diplomat – was unable to meet the Duke who had ridden forth in person to greet him. It was two days before he was fit to complete the journey.

Turin was *en fête* for the English. William and his young companions enjoyed a giddy month of banquets, balls and concerts, agreeably diversified with riding and hunting. The Duke was all amiability, delighted with the splendid horses and the diamond-crusted sword sent him by James. He was particularly gracious to William, who was accorded a place beside him at some of the feasts.

In public Wotton put on one of his most polished performances, charming everybody with his wit and producing blushes and giggles from Princess Maria, Henry's potential bride. In private, matters were going less easily. Both rulers wanted the alliance, but James was less keen on the marriage, which Charles Emmanuel saw as the cornerstone. The month ended with a tournament in the piazza, Wotton seated in a coach opposite that of the Savoy princesses, so that he could study them once more. Their portraits were given him for the King. For himself and his suite there were appropriately graded gifts. William, the Duchess records in her biography, received 'a Spanish horse, a saddle very richly embroidered, and . . . a rich jewel of diamonds'. Charles Emmanuel wanted to keep him, promising 'he would not only confer upon him the best titles of honour he could, but also give him an honourable command in war, although my Lord was but young . . .'. Wotton, however, would not leave William behind without his parents' consent.

He had planned to show the young men more of Europe and, though a projected visit to congratulate the newly elected Emperor was now cancelled, he was not going to deprive them of their sightseeing. On 15 June the party left, by way of Asti, for a short stay in Milan.

Then it was time to turn homewards, but by another route. They crossed Switzerland and started down the Rhine from Basle. The valley was perilous country, full of bandits who, as that indefatigable tourist Coryat had just written, 'seldom rob any man but forthwith they cut his throat'. He had been shocked by the numerous gallows and execution-wheels lining the river, 'a doleful spectacle for any relenting Christian to behold'. Whatever William's reaction at the time, the Duchess records his considered view 'that in cases of robberies and murders, it is better to be severe than merciful; for the hanging of a few will save the lives and purses of many'. No desperado hindered his own passing. The English party was too formidable to invite attack.

By mid-July they were past Cologne and on 27 July they reached London. Wotton dallied a week before setting off to report to the King, then on a Midland progress at Belvoir Castle. Most likely the Cavendishes rode north with him.

The sequel is quickly told. Wotton made a favourable report. Henry rode up post-haste from Richmond, nearly a hundred miles in two days of a heat-wave. Princess Maria's portrait stirred his enthusiasm, but there were many pros and cons, and soon, taking his cue from his elders, he became more circumspect. In October, when other foreign brides came under consideration, he drafted an objective assessment of their advantages. His father must decide. 'Your Majesty may think that my part to play, which is to be in love with any of them, is not yet at hand.' He was never called upon to play it. A week or two later, after a heavy supper and a swim in the autumnal Thames, he was taken ill with a fever and died on 6 November.

So the Savoy mission came to nothing. So – though for quite other reasons – did Wotton's hopes of succeeding Salisbury as Secretary of State. For William Cavendish, however, the journey had not been wasted. He had been sent abroad to learn more of the world and its ways, and he had certainly done so.

FOUR

Heir Apparent

HOME AGAIN, William seems to have settled happily. He did not, as his father had done and many youths still did, seek military experience as a gentleman-volunteer abroad. He was the heir and, save for his crippled younger brother, the sole hope of continuing the Welbeck family. James I's dissolute court made scant appeal, nor would this have been an auspicious moment to seek advancement. Prince Henry was dead. Wotton was in eclipse, his recommendation no asset. Arbella languished in the Tower, and Aunt Mary too, for her suspected connivance in the elopement. Uncle Gilbert, though innocent and at liberty (so far as his chronic gout permitted), came no more to the council table and exercised no influence.

Had Bess been still alive and match-making, William might have been occupied with marriage. Cousin William, at eighteen, had been married to the twelve-year-old Christian Bruce – and then smartly dispatched on the grand tour with his tutor until that attractive red-headed child was a little older. Charles and Katherine Cavendish, however, were not inclined to such cold-blooded arrangements. Just as William had not been forced into an arbitrary mould as a boy, he was not now to have a 'suitable' marriage imposed upon him. Against the network of animosities presented by the Cavendish and Talbot families in general, Welbeck shines out in cheerful contrast. The Duchess's testimony sounds credible: 'His natural love to his parents has been so great, that I have heard him say, he would most willingly, and without the least repining, have begg'd for his daily relief, so God would but have let his parents live.'

Though in no haste to wed, he was never deficient in normal instincts. 'Cupid, I've served thee this many a year,' he wrote in old age, and the verses of his own daughter Jane, long afterwards, suggest that he had a way with women:

> Maid, wife, or widow, which bears the grave style,
> Newcastle but name him, I know then she'll smile;
> From thence you may follow this track in her face,
> So read by their eyes, they will run Cupid's race. . . .

But no scandals are recorded. He did not take after bad Uncle Henry. We must make what we can of the Duchess's verdict: 'In short, I know him not addicted to any manner of vice, except that he has been a great lover and admirer of the female sex; which whether it be so great a crime as to condemn him for it, I'll leave to the judgment of young gallants and beautiful ladies.' Himself a 'young gallant', nearing nineteen on his return from Savoy, William must have been acquiring the character she depicts.

His homecoming coincided with the start of his father's long-cherished project to transform Bolsover Castle. As Sir Charles was now in his sixtieth year it was of obvious concern to his heir. William, in any case, was not without the Cavendish passion for building.

The ruinous Norman fortress had been granted to the Talbots only some sixty years before. Now Bess was dead, Gilbert could keep his promise to his brother-in-law. As an interim measure, he gave him a thousand-year lease, and William came home to find his father's plans taking confident shape. The surviving building accounts date from December of that year, though the purchase of the freehold, along with half a dozen adjacent manors, was not completed until the following August. It made Sir Charles owner of a considerable territory, straddling the two shires from Chesterfield to Welbeck.

In Bolsover he acquired a site rather than a home. The crumbling keep perched at one end of a precipitous ridge, with the usual inner and outer bailey between it and the little town. His idea was to sweep away the keep and build an entirely fresh castle, a fanciful structure conceived rather in the romantic spirit of the *Faerie Queen* than with any eye to defence, a more durable version of those flimsy structures erected for the elaborate masques and tournaments of that age. 'Bolsover is like nothing else in England,' wrote Mark Girouard. 'By an unlikely miracle [it] has survived into this century as an almost untouched expression in stone of the lost world of Elizabethan chivalry and romances. . . .'

In itself it was not to be a large building. It is known today as 'the Little Castle' to distinguish it from the more extensive range of apartments that were gradually added along the escarpment running due south.

Sir Charles was fortunate in having the services of the remarkable

Smythson family. Old Robert Smythson, an architect of originality and imagination, had been tempted north from Longleat many years before. He had been concerned with George Talbot's flamboyant Worksop Manor and with Bess's new Hardwick Hall, as well as Wollaton outside Nottingham. At Welbeck he had prepared an ambitious rebuilding plan, of which only a small part was realised. By this time he was seventy-seven, with only two years to live, and it seems certain that the Smythson who actually supervised the job (and whose expenses appear in the accounts, fourpence per meal, and a shilling a day for his horse) was his son John. John had less flair for grandiose plans, and more interest in the design of decorative detail. Girouard suggests that the old man was fully consulted, and that the plan of the Little Castle was 'one of the last products of his ingenious and experimental mind'. In which case, the Bolsover we see today brilliantly enshrines the complementary talents of father and son – indeed, two fathers and two sons, for the contribution of Sir Charles and William went far beyond the mere settling of the bills.

Self-sufficiency was the aim. Stone was cut and dressed in freshly opened quarries nearby, or brought from the abandoned site at Kirkby. Kilns were established to make plaster from the local limestone. Timber was hauled from Scarcliffe Park, just across the valley. Even the barrows, the wooden shovels, hods and hurdles were made by craftsmen on the estate. By April the Norman keep had gone, new foundations had been excavated and a well sunk, and the scaffolding was standing out bravely on the skyline. In the summer the site swarmed with women, boys and girls, doing lighter work for a few pence per day. The masons and other craftsmen earned about a shilling. By February 1614, when the accounts break off, there were more than fifty workers on the payroll.

William's own visits to the site – it was only a six-mile ride from Welbeck – were interrupted by other affairs that spring. James had dissolved his first Parliament three years earlier, unable to stomach the frank criticisms that some Englishmen felt free to express. Now need of money forced him to summon another, which he hoped would be more pliable, a 'Parliament of love'. In the countryside, where the few qualified electors did as they were bid by the dominant landowners, this seemed feasible. Thus Sir Charles Cavendish, though disinclined to attend Westminster himself, needed only a nod to ensure William's election as M.P. for the Nottinghamshire borough of East Retford. On 5 April, a foul day that marred the pageantry of the state opening, William stood with the rest and listened to a lengthy oration in that broad Scots voice. The King made many promises and assured them that they would always find him sympathetic and approachable. He then dismissed the Commons to choose their Speaker, and they all filed off to the old St Stephen's chapel, now secularised, with benches round its four sides and the Speaker's chair where once the altar had been.

Two-thirds of the members were, like William, taking their seats for the first time. John Eliot, a year his senior, was representing St Germans. John Pym, older, a lawyer with a grasp of finance, was making his debut as M.P. for Calne. John Hampden – another name of omen – was not yet in Parliament. Among those who were William saw various familiar faces, young and old: Tom Wentworth, his Cambridge contemporary, and Wotton, ebullient as ever, eager to talk his way back into favour by supporting the King's policies.

Even Sir Ralph Winwood, appointed principal Secretary of State only a week before, was as new as William. When he stood up to propose the Speaker whom James wanted he was at some disadvantage, for he had never heard anyone else speak in Parliament. However, his 'somewhat strange' delivery 'in a kind of academical tune' mattered little, for the election was a formality and the King's man was unopposed. Winwood's newness proved a more serious handicap in the ensuing weeks, when he found himself unable to whip up the voting support for his master's requirements.

William soon saw that this was no 'Parliament of love'. There were too many lawyers, too many young men determined to have their say. Chamberlain's letters to Dudley Carleton give a good idea of those debates. 'Our Parliament goes on after the wonted manner, with many controversies and altercations. . . .' A month later, 'The House is full of business and many irons are in the fire, but yet we see no great matter dispatched, for hitherto they have been much troubled with disputes about elections and privileges. . . .' By late May William himself was on a select committee concerned with a breach of privilege. Another day, in a debate on imposts, Wotton made a 'mannerly and demure speech', justifying them by the practice of other countries, and William heard his old mentor scornfully answered by later speakers, 'that we were to be governed by our own laws, not by foreign examples'. Wentworth, the future royalist, was most vehement for the opposition.

William favoured monarchy not so much as the 'divine right' claimed by the Stuarts but as the most satisfactory way to govern a nation. With a stratified order of sovereign, nobility and solid landowners, people knew where they were. Let there be discussion, by all means, of art, literature and natural philosophy, but not of state business, except in the

Privy Council, the handful of grandees who met after Sunday morning service. Parliament should not meddle in questions outside its concern. Unfortunately the Council could not produce hard cash, and for mere advice the King increasingly turned to his favourites.

It was Parliament that held the purse-strings. Though James could not participate in their tiresome debates he could certainly interfere. When he could not persuade the Commons through his mouthpieces he would harangue them by personal summons to the Upper Chamber or send them a letter demanding that they came to grips with his financial problem. They, however, merely 'grew every day more fiery and violent in their speeches'.

When not scandalised, William was probably bored. With no taste for public affairs, he sighed for a little decisive action. Happily his morning attendance at the House, and an occasional afternoon committee meeting in the Painted Chamber, left ample time for other occupations. He was sure of his welcome at the palace, where his boyhood connections were now reinforced by his status as a King's man in Parliament. Bowls, tennis, cockfighting and other diversions were available in the royal precincts. One could cross the river to a bear-baiting or visit a playhouse. Supper came about half past five, a sociable meal which many followed with gambling. One had to be out of the palace before nine, when the gates were locked, the guard mounted and the password issued. For some young blades this meant only the opening of an even livelier session in their own lodgings, with gaming, drinking and whoring into the small hours.

How far William entered into these activities is not recorded. He was never a heavy drinker, and he certainly preferred music and conversation to cards and dice. The theatre, we know, was a life-long interest. Shakespeare, for whose writings he was to develop a deep admiration and to transmit it to the Duchess, had by this date retired to Stratford. It was Ben Jonson who, living in Westminster, at the height of his powers as court masque-writer and public playwright, dominated the scene. Life and soul of a brilliant, fashionable circle, in himself an aggressive, dogmatic yet somehow attractive personality, he was irresistible. Perhaps Wotton brought them together. Their friendship was well developed three years later, by which time William had swallowed all Ben's literary theories and become a Jonsonian for life.

That summer, however, his stay in London was not long. By 3 June James had lost patience and, in a peremptory letter to Parliament, threatened immediate dissolution unless his needs were met. This did not help. Speaker after speaker leapt to his feet indignantly. 'There was never known a more disorderly House,' reported Chamberlain, 'more like a cockpit than a grave council.' On 7 June James dissolved Parliament in a fury, tearing up with his own hands the eight bills that had been submitted for his assent. Not inappropriately was this remembered as 'the Addled Parliament'. William's first and last experience of the Commons coloured his political outlook ever afterwards. Yet it is fair to say that his poor opinion of the House was shared by most people at the time.

Home again, he found his father still happily occupied with John Smythson at Bolsover. The dream castle was gradually becoming a reality. The vaulted cellar and kitchen must have been well advanced, but there were to be three storeys above them. The work must have suffered a serious check in January, when, as a churchwarden recorded at Youlgreave, not twenty miles away, 'began the greatest snow which ever fell upon the earth, within man's memory . . . to the great admiration and fear of all the land, for it came from the four parts of the world'. There were ten successive falls, the last the heaviest, and though the thaw came in mid-March there was more snow throughout April, lying a foot deep on the moors on May Day morning, when 'instead of fetching flowers the youths brought in flakes of snow . . .'. Summer proved equally extreme. John Chamberlain smacked his lips over 'the best and fairest melons and grapes that ever I knew in England', but to the men sweating on the sun-baked site at Bolsover the long heat-wave may have been less enjoyable.

There were other worries for the Cavendishes besides the weather. Sir Charles had a tiresome land dispute with some Sherwood Forest tenants. September saw the death, still in the Tower, of the hapless Arbella. Aunt Mary, her detention no longer relevant, was released that Christmas, 1615, but Uncle Gilbert died in the following May. Bad Uncle Henry died that year also, leaving numerous children but none legitimate. The older generation was dropping away.

For that reason Gilbert had sensibly made William his executor, along with the old Secretary of State, Winwood. Gilbert's own sons had died young. William, who had spent so much time with his uncle in boyhood, was very close. The earldom, but little else, went to Gilbert's estranged younger brother Edward, married to Jane Ogle and living up at Bothal. The estates went to Gilbert's three daughters, and it was with them and their husbands, then or eventually the Earls of Pembroke, Kent and Arundel, that the young executor had to deal. He can have had little help from Winwood who, overworked and ailing, died in the following year. Chamberlain describes the post-mortem with ghoulish gusto: 'his heart withered almost to nothing, his spleen utterly rotten, one of his kidneys clean gone, the other perished, his liver full of black spots, his lungs not sound, besides divers other defects'. So far as the administration of the late Earl of Shrewsbury's estate was concerned, William may have managed better on his own.

This business, and pleasanter affairs, must have called him to London more than once in 1616. He distinguished himself in 'running at the ring' when young Charles became Prince of Wales in November. The court festivities were somewhat muted, the King having no heart to repeat the glories of Henry's investiture. There was nothing muted about the Lord Mayor's banquet, however. William was presumably invited with the other Knights of the Bath, who were 'entertained at Drapers Hall with a supper and a play, where some of them were so rude and unruly and carried themselves so insolently divers ways but specially in putting citizens' wives to the squeak' that the proceedings broke up in disorder.

It was most likely this year that William met Ralegh, released from the Tower in March. Perhaps Jonson brought them together. Two scraps of their talk William quoted long afterwards. Ralegh told him that in the West Indies 'there were the finest shaped horses, and the finest colours in the world', which the ignorant natives killed for their skins. And one wonders if the old explorer was gently teasing the young stay-at-home when he remarked, 'There are stranger things in the world than between Staines and London.' The friendship had little chance to develop. The next year, Ralegh left on his fateful last voyage.

By then William had other matters on his mind. Sir Charles died on 4 April 1617.

He was laid to rest in Bolsover church, his alabaster effigy in armour under an arched canopy with pillars of white and blue marble and six coats of arms quartered. The splendour of the memorial is set in perspective, however, by Jonson's verses:

> Sons, seek not me among these polished stones,
> These only hide part of my flesh and bones ...
> Let such as justly have outlived all praise,
> Trust in the tombs, their careful friends do raise ...
> It will be matter loud enough to tell
> Not when I died, but how I lived – farewell.

FIVE

His Lordship

OVERNIGHT William had become, at twenty-three, a personage. His brother had not been forgotten: 'His father', says Aubrey, 'left him a good estate, the revenue whereof he expended on books and on learned men.' In due course Charles, who never married, got John Smythson to build him Slingsby Castle on his Yorkshire estate near Malton. Their mother, co-heiress to the Ogle lands in Northumberland, where she later retired, was well provided for. To William therefore came Welbeck and Bolsover and a complex of other estates, far and near, even the St Loe properties in the West Country derived from his grandmother's childless third husband.

An early concern was the completion of the Little Castle. What stage had been reached at Sir Charles's death is uncertain. The ground floor, with its pillared and vaulted hall and parlour, must have been built, for the hall chimney-piece, the only one that is an integral part of the structure, bears the date 1616. But how far the upper storeys had proceeded, and whether a start had been made on the forecourt, with its battlemented pavilions and broad staircase, we do not know. Before work was resumed that summer, William dispatched his architect on a lengthy visit to London, where Inigo Jones, fresh from his Italian travels with the Arundels, was building the Queen's House at Greenwich and where, as William knew, many fresh ideas were stirring. Smythson returned with a full sketchbook, the results of which are traceable in the work he subsequently carried out at both Bolsover and Welbeck. Though he never fully absorbed the palladian principles – and William, with his eclectic architectural tastes, did not encourage him to – Smythson was one of the first to disseminate Jones's influence north of the Trent.

While Smythson sketched balcony windows, scroll-sided gables and rusticated gateways, William's eye ranged in other fields. It was time, his mother said, to find a wife. He did so, as her eventual successor assures us, 'both to his own good liking and his mother's approving'.

Elizabeth was the only child of William Basset, of Blore in Stafford-shire. At nineteen she was already the widow of the Earl of Suffolk's third son. In the Ranger's House at Blackheath is a portrait of her in mourning, probably by William Larkin, showing a dark-haired, dark-eyed girl, with regular features in an oval face rising from a vast circuit of lace ruff. She looks small. William himself was not very tall.

Elizabeth had over three thousand pounds a year, and some seven thousand in cash. William had a formidable rival in Kit Villiers, young brother of the King's rising favourite who would soon be Duke of Buckingham. But Kit was dim-witted, and no brighter for his heavy drinking. The girl preferred William. By 24 October 1618 Chamberlain could report: 'Sir William Candish hath married Henry Howard's widow, a great heir, that was much sought and pursued for Christofer Villers.' By the time Smythson was ready to install the elaborate fireplace of the parlour at Bolsover he was able to embody the Basset arms impaled by those of Cavendish, and the family crests, the Cavendish serpent and the Basset boar.

Though Elizabeth's Staffordshire estates were not irrelevant, there was real love in the match. 'God made him happy in marriage,' the Duchess testifies, adding magnanimously that her predecessor 'was a very kind, loving and virtuous lady'. After the marriage William 'lived, for the most part, in the country, and pleased himself and his neighbours with hospitality, and such delights as the country afforded; only now and then he would go up to London for some short time to wait on the King'. On such occasions his letters to Elizabeth began 'Dearest Heart' and he addressed numerous love poems to her.

It was in the summer preceding their marriage that Jonson, so formative an influence on William's literary taste, set forth on his famous walking tour to Scotland. Tantalisingly, his itinerary was burnt with much of his library, and it remains uncertain whether he stopped at Welbeck, though it would be a little strange if he did not, since it lay so convenient to the traditional road northwards. Two poems, praising William's horsemanship and fencing, were probably inspired by a visit to his home, but some phrases suggest a slightly later date. Having flatteringly declared that he almost wished himself a horse, Jonson continues:

> And surely had I but your stable seen
>   Before, I think my wish absolv'd had been.
> For never saw I yet the Muses dwell,
>   Nor any of their household half so well.

> So well! as when I saw the floor and room,
>   I look'd for Hercules to be the groom.

This reads like an allusion to the magnificent stables and riding-house built at Welbeck between 1623 and 1625. The other poem eulogises William as a swordsman:

> They talk of fencing, and the use of arms,
>   The art of urging and avoiding harms,
> The noble science, and the mastering skill
>   Of making just approaches how to kill. . . .
> I hate such measured, give me mettled, fire,
>   That trembles in the blaze, but then mounts higher!
> A quick and dazzling motion; when a pair
>   Of bodies meet like rarefied air! . . .
> All this, my lord, is valour: this is yours,
>   And was your father's, all your ancestors!

Before 1620 William was not a 'lord'. But even if precise dates are lacking – and the verses might have been written long after the original occasion – it is fairly safe to picture the burly, swarthy, pock-marked Jonson at some time during these years revelling in Welbeck's lavish hospitality, dogmatising on every topic under the sun, and treating his young host and hostess to a sonorous rendering of his own compositions. William was no mean reader, the Duchess tells us, but she had 'heard him say, he never heard any man read well but B.J.; and yet he hath heard many in his time'.

Another famous visitor is more definitely dated. In 1619 the King hunted in Sherwood for the second consecutive summer, and on 10 August the new mistress of Welbeck (whose first son must have been born uncomfortably close to that time) had the daunting honour of welcoming the royal party. James's obsession with the sport was notorious. He declared it vital to his health. The Council, at such seasons, should get on with governing the kingdom and not trouble him with business. Cost apart, he was not difficult to entertain. Heedless of the weather, he and his gentlemen were in the saddle until about four in the afternoon, after which they could have needed little but food and drink, though in gargantuan quantities. Once, at another place, his favourite hound Jowler was missing overnight and returned with this message tied round his neck: 'Good Mr Jowler, we pray you speak to the King (for he hears you every day, and so doth not us) that it will please his Majesty to go back to London, for else the country will be undone; all our provision is spent already, and we are not able to entertain him longer.'

At Welbeck, however, the hospitality was unstinted. William's estates offered some of the best sporting tracts of that legendary forest, now in the final era of its glory. His particular delight was Clipstone Park, not only containing, says the Duchess, 'the tallest timber-trees of all the woods he had' but 'watered by a pleasant river . . . full of fish and otters' and well stocked with deer, hares, partridges, and pheasants, 'besides all sorts of water-fowl'. Though not himself fervently addicted to the blood sports, he would always join in for social reasons. No doubt the King enjoyed his visit.

Charles was knighted that year, most likely on this occasion, for James was dubbing any gentleman with thirty pounds to pay the fee. The College of Arms could not keep pace with the new creations. To postpone calling another tiresome Parliament, he made the sale of titles a major source of income. In his whole reign he created 111 peerages, about seven times as many as Elizabeth in a period twice as long. Many, not all, were bought. Uncle William at Chatsworth had just paid £10,000 to become Earl of Devonshire.

His nephew was, for the moment, content with other signs of royal approval. In 1620 Prince Charles agreed to stand godfather to his second son, the first having died only a month before. The exact dates of Elizabeth's children are mostly unrecorded, but evidently her pregnancies followed one another at minimal intervals and to the prejudice of her health. This second boy was baptised on 20 May at their town house, then in Blackfriars, just downstream from Whitehall. Jonson wrote an interlude for performance, a somewhat crude script embodying appropriate allusions, with a Forester to represent Welbeck, a Mathematician (to stand for Uncle Charles) making optimistic astrological calculations for his small nephew's future, some broad crosstalk between a midwife Holdback, a wet-nurse Duggs, and a dry-nurse Kecks, and the obligatory compliments to the royal guest and godfather, now a reserved and dignified youth of nineteen. A convivial chorus of Blackfriars Watermen set the tone of the subsequent celebrations:

> They say it is merry when gossips do meet,
> And more to confirm it, in us you may see't,
> For we have well tasted the wine in the street,
> And yet we make shift to stand on our feet.

As soon as we heard the Prince would be here,
We knew by his coming we should have good cheer;
A boy for my lady! then every year,
Cry we – for a girl will afford us but beer.

Poor Elizabeth! The new Charles did not live long. It was two more years before she bore a child destined to reach maturity. It was a girl, Jane. And, whatever the Watermen sang, she was to be dearly loved.

Soon after the Blackfriars festivities William travelled up to his mother in Northumberland. Aunt Jane also was now a widow: Edward Talbot had not long enjoyed his Shrewsbury earldom. He had left no children, so William could expect in the fullness of time to inherit the reunited estates of his Ogle grandfather.

He was still busy with the winding up of Uncle Gilbert's affairs. The main beneficiaries were his three cousins and their husbands, of whom Alathea's, the connoisseur Earl of Arundel, was most active in concern. There was a complication over certain lands that Aunt Mary had wished William himself to have, and as sole surviving executor he was in a delicate position. While he was staying at Bothal Castle in September 1620, Arundel wrote asking him to a meeting at court on the twenty-fifth for a final settlement. The Earl's proposition may be deduced from a letter of 7 November from John Woodford to Sir Francis Nethersole, then English agent in Prague: to accommodate the disputes 'between the heirs of the late Earl of Shrewsbury and Sir William Cavendish', it had been decided 'as an expedient to create the said Sir William, at the request of the heirs above mentioned, Viscount Mansfield . . .'. The creation is variously dated as 29 October or 3 November. At least William achieved his peerage without a crude cash payment. Smythson was able to add the new crest, with its coronet, to both sides of the parlour chimney-piece at Bolsover.

William's introduction to the Upper House was not long delayed. A new Parliament was called in the New Year. For seven years James had managed to keep going without the insolent intervention of Westminster, finding his revenue not only by the sale of honours but by import duties, 'benevolences' or gifts extracted under pressure, and monopolies in trade and industry awarded to individuals in lieu of payment for their services. The high officers of state could not exist on salaries and pensions paid in arrears or not at all. By the end of 1620, however, his expedients were inadequate. What with the gradual inflation of the period and the prospect of a costly war to back his Protestant son-in-law in Germany, James had no alternative but to summon Parliament.

William rode up for the opening on 30 January. He found London locked in the grip of winter, the Thames frozen, with ice piled up in crags by wind and tide. Nevertheless, a vast crowd turned out to see the procession and two scaffolds collapsed, causing many injuries. 'The King went on horseback and was very cheerful,' noted Chamberlain, but 'from the church was carried in a chair to the Parliament House, being so weak in his legs and feet.' At fifty-four James was betraying signs of premature senility, though his frequent spells of depression were varied with flashes of his old sharpness and energy. That day he harangued his new Parliament on the merits of brevity, speaking for more than an hour.

William found the Upper House more congenial than the Lower, full of familiar faces, relatives or connections or at least men of his own class and sympathies. He was not a man of relentless political ambition. Anyhow Parliament, meeting so seldom, was hardly the place for that. The real arena was the court, and the atmosphere of James's court was not attractive.

Throughout the next six weeks he attended the debates regularly. 'Although my Lord love not business,' wrote the Duchess, 'especially those of State (though he understands them as well as anybody) yet what business or affairs he cannot avoid, none will do better than himself.' Though scarcely impartial, she presents a credible portrait of a conscientious, pragmatic, if sometimes autocratic, man. She goes on:

Neither is he passionate in acting of business, but hears patiently, and orders soberly, and pierces into the heart or bottom of a business at the first encounter; but before all things, he considers well before he undertakes a business, whether he is able to go through it or not, for he never ventures upon either public or private business, beyond his strength.

When she wrote that, life had long confirmed William in his caution, but even in 1621 he was no hot-head. The Cavendish motto suited him: *Cavendo tutus*, 'Safe by taking care.'

Parliament worked hard that winter, sitting before and after dinner, 'besides many conferences and committees', harried by daily communications from the King. William escaped before the end. Elizabeth was ill at Welbeck, and on 10 March he got leave 'to be absent from Parliament . . . but to send up his proxy to some fit person'. Attendance was otherwise compulsory, with fines for unauthorised absence. William gave his proxy to Buckingham, who collected them and exercised a block vote. In letters William took care to address the all-powerful favourite as 'my most Honourable Patron'. This was probably the occasion when he pleaded the same reason for absence from the tilting which always marked James's Accession Day, 24 March. An undated 'letter to my wife, on my being excused from tilting', runs:

> Sweet Heart,
>   The reason I in verse will tell
> Of my long stay, and therefore hearken well.
> I was importun'd much to try my force,
> This year at tilt, and there to run my course. . . .

After decrying the waste of time and money involved, he ends, with somewhat insensitive facetiousness:

> But, oh, now listen to the joyful news.
> Your cruel sickness, this year, did excuse
> Me from the tilting: therefore (do you hear?)
> Fail not I pray of sickness every year,
> And as I am a knight, with spurs all gilt,
> When I come home I'll run with you at tilt.

For the rest of 1621, certainly, he was at home with the ailing Elizabeth and supervising the work at Bolsover. The Little Castle was taking shape, a tall block with three turrets and a staircase tower, unusual for its period in its conscious resemblance to a Norman keep. On the first floor was the principal apartment, the Star Chamber, so called from its ceiling of gilded stars. The walls were to have painted panels of biblical characters, and that these were now being executed is proved by the date, 1621, on 'Moses'. Adjoining this state room was a small tapestry-hung chamber called, from its black-and-white slabbed floor, its marble vaulting and hooded fireplace of the same material, the Marble Closet. The rest of this floor was taken up by the master bedroom suite, including two retiring rooms, the Elysium Room, decorated by some unknown artist with a proliferation of pagan deities and philosophers, and the Heaven Room, in which the same hand portrayed Christ's ascension surrounded by angels and cherubs. Some of these cherubs were thoughtfully provided with music books containing Thomas Ravenscroft's contemporary composition, *Three Country Dances in One*. The second storey consisted of family and guest chambers grouped round an octagonal space under the handsome domed lantern that rose above the battlements of the flat roof.

If John Smythson's forte was décor, William had given him ample scope. The interior of the Little Castle was an exuberant medley of Gothic and classical elements, Doric and Ionic and Tuscan, with even, in some of the chimney-pieces, reminiscences of the Turkish Seraglio at Constantinople, a city which bad Uncle Henry had visited in 1589, though the connection seems tenuous. Pink alabaster and various coloured marbles were used liberally, and a golden stone which even today, comments P. A. Faulkner, 'gives a surprising effect of perpetual sunlight'. Appropriate allusion was made to William's personal enthusiasms: besides the music-carrying cherubs there were groups of instruments on brackets supporting one of the fireplace hoods, and the vault bosses of the ground-floor parlour were adorned with horses' heads.

With all this fascinating work in progress William must have felt well out of the wrangles at Westminster. Even the decorous Lords had been in uproar. Arundel had been briefly committed to the Tower, but released on the King's intercession. His letter to William suggests that any disagreement over the Shrewsbury will was now forgotten:

I am sorry that this accident of mine had that effect to my friends – especially far off – as to make them, out of their care to me, give themselves trouble. For myself I thank God it gave much ease and rest whilst I was in the Tower, and when I came out, it showed the King's constancy and favour to his servants that love him truly and made me see I had some true friends.

When Parliament resumed its sittings in November there is no record of William's attendance. Perhaps Elizabeth's health was still causing anxiety. At some time in the following year, 1622, she gave birth to Jane.

James now managed two years without a Parliament. William attended the opening of the next, on 19 February 1624, as did his brother, newly elected to the Commons. William kept up a good, though by no means unbroken, record until the dissolution on 29 May. On Good Friday William Laud noted in his diary: 'Viscount Mansfield, running at tilt to practise, with the shock of the meeting, his horse, weaker or resty, tumbled over and over, and brake his own neck in the place; the lord had no great harm. Should not this day have other employment?' Subsequently the great churchman formed a more favourable view, commending William's wise judgement to Charles I and bequeathing 'to my much honoured friend' his 'best diamond ring, worth £140 or near it'.

It was some time in 1624 that Elizabeth's portrait was painted by Daniel Mytens, whom Arundel had brought over from Holland and made the fashionable artist. On 10 August, in the middle of a hot dry summer, James came again as a guest to Welbeck, five years to the day since his first visit. Smythson had in the meantime transferred his main activities from Bolsover and made many improvements at the Abbey. More stables were planned to enclose the west side of the courtyard and were built shortly afterwards.

It was the King's last hunting trip to Sherwood. On 27 March 1625 he died, and for William, as for England, a new chapter opened.

SIX

The New Order

IN JUNE 1625 William attended the new King's opening of his first Parliament. It was a testing time for Charles. Within that same month he welcomed to England Henrietta Maria, whom he had already married by proxy but had never seen.

Facing the assembled Lords and Commons, he presented – small though he was – a figure of conspicuous dignity. He had still a slight stammer, still the unmistakable Scots accent William had heard at Worksop all those years ago. His voice rang through the hall in a high falsetto. He did not, he declared, love to hear himself speak. Those who in the past had endured James's tirades sighed with relief.

William had seen enough of Charles to know that England had now a very different king. Besides being taciturn where his father had been loquacious, Charles was fastidious, not crude, artistically sensitive rather than robust in intellectual disputation, and cold where his father, for all his embarrassing habits, had achieved a bluff warmth and familiarity.

In the palace, too, William found striking changes. The old alcoholic anarchy had given place to a rigid formality worthy of Madrid. When Charles had gone to Spain with Buckingham a few years before on his ill-fated wooing escapade, he had brought something back if not a bride – and that was a new conception of majesty and the protocol required to sustain it. James had eloquently propounded the theory of the divine right of kings, but by absurd antics he had impaired its credibility. Charles took over the theory and deported himself appropriately. The free-and-easy Jacobean Whitehall was transformed into a court of hard-and-fast regulations. Written rules were pinned up in the principal rooms. Woe betide those who presumed on old liberties and strayed from the new punctilio. Debauchery was unacceptable in this new atmosphere. Scandals were driven underground. Charles would, however, have rejected the label of Puritan, understanding it in ecclesiastical terms. His sympathies were with Laud, the sharp-eyed little bachelor bishop, the middle-aged martinet so ambitious for himself and the Anglican Church, who was now with Buckingham's support coming rapidly to the fore. Charles asked him for a list of clergymen marked 'O' for orthodox or 'P' for Puritan. The former should receive preferment, the latter be kept down. Such discrimination did not trouble William. Religion was not among his strongest interests, and he saw the Church mainly as the spiritual arm of the secular power. On balance, he was more at home amid the ordered decencies of this new court, but he was not destined to remain long in London. On 6 July he was appointed Lord-Lieutenant of Nottinghamshire and next day given leave of absence from Parliament. He left at once for Welbeck, applying himself so energetically to his new duties that by 17 July he was sending the Council his first report.

Lords-lieutenant were a Tudor invention, taking over many functions of the medieval sheriff. William was now the King's permanent representative in the shire, responsible for public order and the efficiency of the militia, which, with the end of James's peace policy, required urgent attention throughout the country. The appointment was a clear recognition of William's local pre-eminence.

His task was to hold periodical musters and check the state of training and equipment. The men were supposed to be yeomen and freeholders, but many hired substitutes to serve. William was free to commission his own officers from among the country gentry, but Catholic recusants were barred. As such officers varied greatly in military experience, or had none at all, it was usual to bring in a professional 'Muster Master' from outside, paid out of local funds, who supervised the few days of annual training in each district and picked out suitable non-commissioned officers. William, like other gentlemen with no service behind them, could get plenty of printed drill manuals with which to mask his ignorance.

Even the most zealous lord-lieutenant could not produce quick results from an obstinate inland community so far from foreign threats. 'Powder insufficient,' reported William, but he would 'forbear to levy money on that account'. A year later the 'muscatires' were reasonably well, 'but for pikes and corselets there were not above six in the whole shire right as they should be'. The next day he wrote that he would try to procure a benevolence from the county, but thought they would 'be governed by ill precedents and factions, the dregs of the last Parliament'. He would undertake to supply the deficiencies on his own credit. On 25 September 1626 he requested a warrant authorising Mr Evelyn, the gunpowder-maker, to supply forty-eight barrels 'at the King's price of £4. 3s. 4d. per barrel, for the use of Co. Nottm'. The following August he reported from Bolsover that the trained forces of Nottinghamshire had 'been mustered and found completely furnished every way after the modern fashion'. A levy of a hundred soldiers for the service of Charles's uncle, the King of Denmark, had been delivered to a 'conductor' and were on their way to embark at Hull.

Occasionally William's zeal was over-prompt. On 2 September he had to explain to the Council that a draft of fifty men was already four days' march on the road to Plymouth when he received the further in-struction that twelve should be archers. Sometimes, with the best will, he could not fulfil his obligations. Plague made it unsafe to hold musters and the Council must excuse the lack of the requisite certificates.

While ensuring that arms reached the militia, he had to see that there were none in the wrong hands. Gunpowder Plot was not forgotten. Every rumour had to be investigated. Once William received orders to search the house of Gervase Markham, member of a well-known local family, at Dunham-on-Trent. Some arms were indeed discovered and confiscated, though Mr Markham protested that he was innocent, being 'conformable in religion', and demanded either their return or the pay-ment of compensation. This involved William in a wearisome corres-pondence with the Council, until he satisfied them by enclosing a testimonial from the Archbishop of York: 'Gervase Markham is a bed-ridden gentleman. He has been a constant Protestant from his youth. It is marvelled by what hand any information has been suggested other-wise.'

William had other local tasks of equal delicacy. Buckingham, dominat-ing the new King as completely as the old, expected him to tackle his kinsmen and neighbours about the purchase of honours. His cousin, Robert Pierrepont, was inclined to haggle. James had once offered him, William had to report to Buckingham, a viscountcy for as little as £5000 or a barony for £4000. William himself, he admitted, had 'never heard that a baron was under £9000 or £10,000', but then, he added with dignity, his own peerage had been only 'the quitting of an old debt'. His cousin contended that he was 'not a moneyed man'. William believed him: 'I protest, my Lord, I have done my uttermost, and can get no more out of him but infinite thanks to your Grace for his favour. . . . I think that if your Lordship did speak with him at London, he might be brought to good terms.' Buckingham acted on this advice. Within two months Pierrepont was Viscount Newark, and a year later Earl of Kingston.

Meanwhile, much was happening in the family. Aunt Jane died at Bothal Castle in December 1625. All the Ogle estates now came to William's mother, and she asked him to take over their management. In the following March Uncle William was laid to rest in Bess's great family tomb at Derby. Cousin William became Earl of Devonshire, living so extravagantly that he had to sell land to remain solvent. That would never have done for his grandmother. There were happier events at Welbeck. Elizabeth bore her third, and first surviving, son – another Charles – probably in 1626; and, though precise dates are lacking, a daughter, baptised Elizabeth, followed quickly afterwards. William was excused Parliament in February 1626, but attended in May and June.

That visit to London casts a little doubt on the complete sincerity of a devotional poem which he wrote and inscribed with the unmistakable date of that year, a 'preparatory meditation' on 'the receiving of the Blessed Sacrament on Christmas Day, 1626' and containing the lines:

> My sins I do confess . . .
> By twelve months sickness I have been unable
> To wait for thy crumbs at thy holy table.
> My body's weakness so disturb'd my soul
> Nor eat nor drink I could of thy Son's bowl.

There can scarcely have been a physical disability that kept him from the altar all that time. Were the 'sins' something more grievous than usual? Was his 'body's weakness' not an illness but an inability to resist a temptation? Buried in the mass of his surviving papers, mostly undated, in crabbed handwriting often extremely difficult to decipher, are sufficient indications of his powerfully sensual nature. Elizabeth's successive pregnancies and her poor health must have called for a degree of abstinence he found intolerable, and one which a lordly husband of that epoch was hardly expected to tolerate. Perhaps to this year should be ascribed the manuscript poem, *The Gossip's Hand*, with its all too clear implication of infidelity, delayed only by some scruple on the unknown woman's part:

> With love's hopes long my phansy thou hast fed;
> Now, since my wife is safely brought to bed,
> Thou art my Gossip, honour me to stand . . .
> Think not, though I grow old, I am no other
> But a dull handycraft Mechanique Lover:

> What though my youth's declin'd; I am afraid
> You'll think me a Patriarch with my handmaid.

Whichever year this affair was taking place, the 'Patriarch' could only have been in his thirties, but if the 'handmaid' was literally just that – and there is other evidence in the papers that William, like many another nobleman, had a roving eye for his own household – he may well have been twice her age.

A very different liaison is suggested by several poems addressed to a noblewoman in Derbyshire. One salutes her:

> As Lord of Scarsdale I'll both write and speak
> To thee my sovereign, Queen of the high Peak.

And another:

> Madam, of other wonders let none dare to speak.
> You are the only wonder of the Peak.

This lady is at least easily identified. A punning rhyme of 'Bakewell tanners' with 'thou art too full of Manners' shows that she was the Countess of Rutland, which is confirmed by another passage:

> I wish . . . thy husband Earl . . .
> Judg'd lawful Rutland, and sole Lord of Beaver. . . .

This suggests the date 1632, when the ninth earl, George, succeeded his brother Francis, but presumably could not be confirmed in the title until it was certain that Francis had not left a posthumous heir by his second wife. Whether or not William succeeded in seducing the next countess, he was certainly frank in his invitation. Having praised her charms, he continues:

> As good as handsome too? that makes me grieve.
> No deprav'd Nature? Didst not come of Eve?
> Forbidden fruit, dost thou not long to taste
> The mid-trees knowledge, plucked below thy waist. . . .

We know only that on one occasion Lady Rutland paid a mid-winter visit to Welbeck and in such a hurry that her 'night stuff' was not packed, which was blamed for her catching a severe feverish cold.

But to return to 1626 and William's more public activities. The next year was pleasantly free of Parliaments. When continuing financial difficulties, notably the expensive fiasco of Buckingham's effort to relieve the Huguenots in La Rochelle, forced Charles to summon one in March

1628, William had an agreeable reason for being present. He had just been created – we do not know for what consideration, if any – Earl of Newcastle-upon-Tyne and Baron Cavendish of Bolsover. In this new style he was introduced on 20 March and attended regularly for a month or two afterwards. The Newcastle title was a fitting recognition of his growing prestige in the north. Thereafter, whatever his advancement in the peerage, he remained 'Newcastle', and it will be convenient from this point to refer to him accordingly.

Fresh responsibilities soon crowded upon him. In June Cousin William died, of excessive good living, it was said, and thus after only two years there was a new Earl of Devonshire, a good-looking boy of ten or eleven, inevitably another William. When of age he would follow his father and grandfather as Lord-Lieutenant of Derbyshire. Until then Newcastle, already a commissioner for the supply of lead from that important mining area, must combine the lord-lieutenancy with his own. It was no sinecure. On 24 September 1630 he was writing from Chester-field requesting that some of the Derbyshire landowners be made to answer for failing in their obligations in the matter of the train bands.

He had also to pay visits to Chatsworth, then still the tall Tudor mansion his grandparents had begun to build in Edward VI's reign. He had to keep an eye on the young earl's development. Fortunately the boy had an excellent tutor in Thomas Hobbes, who had taught his father and, with a break of a year or two, had been in the family service since 1608. The ruddy-cheeked, black-haired Wiltshireman – 'Crow' had been his nickname in youth – was a man after Newcastle's heart, full of intellectual curiosity, impatient of academic assumptions, trench-ant in argument and repartee. Sharing scientific interests and political sympathies – not to mention the friendship of Ben Jonson – they got on splendidly. Though Newcastle could not compare with Hobbes in originality and mental power, he held his own well enough to earn the philosopher's respect and friendship. Hobbes was no sycophant. These Chatsworth visits were also brightened by the obviously sincere friend-ship of the boy's mother, that highly intelligent red-headed Christian Cavendish, still in her early thirties, whose 'affability and sweet address', recalled her biographer, 'captivated all who conversed with her'. It was in the first period of mourning, however, that Newcastle wrote home to Elizabeth on 28 July 1629: 'There is great change in Chatsworth since the death of the Lord. For privacy I could be weary, but I will not, out of respect for my lord.'

Another death had touched him more closely. On 18 April his mother died at Bothal. It is hard to accept the further statement in the *Complete Peerage* that she was buried in her husband's tomb at Bolsover on 21 April, which suggests not only indecorous haste but physical impossibility, with something like 150 miles of seventeenth-century roads between the places. Jonson produced no fewer than three poems in tribute to her. One, perhaps excessively exclamatory, ran:

> The best of women! her whole life
> Was the example of a wife!
> Or of a parent! or a friend!
> All circles had their spring and end
> In her! and what could perfect be,
> Or without angles, it was she!

Just before she died her father's barony of Ogle had been revived for her and her heirs. Newcastle could feel now, with some satisfaction, that he was not merely a new-minted Stuart peer but one whose claim to nobility dated from the time of Edward IV.

And still, perhaps a soothing background to all these distractions and activities, the work with John Smythson went quietly forward at Bolsover, at once a tribute to his father's memory and a realisation of a personal dream. The Little Castle was finished at last, with all its imaginative and varied decoration, and was ready for occupation by 1630. But because it was really no more than a house – though a house of exquisite fantasy – it lacked the accommodation for the entertainment of guests on the seventeenth-century scale of hospitality. So the builders were busy now on a completely separate range of grand apartments, the so-called 'Terrace Range', perhaps always envisaged by Sir Charles, running due south, eventually for nearly a hundred yards. Westwards its windows would command the terrace, the precipitously falling hillside and the rolling Derbyshire skyline. On the east it would close one side of the Great Court made from part of the medieval outer bailey. As for the old inner bailey, that too was undergoing transformation. Curving like a great horseshoe from the Little Castle, its ancient ramparts were being restored and refaced to enclose the sort of pleasure garden that was the delight of the early Stuart family. Where towers had once been there would be recessed 'garden rooms' offering shade in hot weather and cosy fire-grates in the cold. The top of the wall would provide an elevated walk from which to look down upon the general design. The centrepiece of that design would be a fountain surmounted by a statue of Venus.

In 1630 came another happy event. On 24 June – for once we have an exact date – Elizabeth bore another son who survived: Henry.

Newcastle had little need to visit London during this period. The 1628 Parliament had been hastily prorogued by Charles to save his unpopular favourite from impeachment. Newcastle sent his proxy to the next Parliament, called in February 1629 – but Buckingham was not there to exercise it, for he was dead by then, knifed by a discontented officer at Portsmouth. There was no further summons to Westminster for eleven years. Charles contrived to govern without Parliament. After Buckingham's assassination he turned for advice to Henrietta Maria. Thenceforth it was to her that he listened more than to anyone else in the world.

SEVEN

The Courtier

ABOUT THIS DATE we see the contradictions in Newcastle's nature emerging.

A hankering for recognition warred with a love of rustic quiet, domesticity and the pursuit of his varied personal interests. He lacked the dynamic drive of the true politician and the feverish self-seeking instinct of the courtier, yet equally he felt aspirations that had never troubled his father. Times were changing. The magnetism of London, growing throughout Elizabeth's reign, became ever more powerful under James and his son. There were five million people in England and Wales, 320,000 packed into the capital, whereas no other town contained more than 25,000. London, men thought, had everything. Many – and their wives no less – thought rural life intolerably boring, and the upper classes thronged into the capital until they had to be discouraged by royal edict, ordering those without their own town houses to withdraw to the country. Newcastle was unusual in finding, as his father had done, great contentment in home life on his estates, but for him it was not wholly satisfying. By now the novelty of his new offices had worn off and he had mastered the problems of administration. He was a big fish in a small pool. He was ready for something more.

There was a new situation at court. No one favourite was dominant. Both the strong men, Laud and Wentworth, were well disposed to him. Charles had known him since childhood and shared his enthusiasm for horsemanship and art. No less important, the vivacious, ringleted little Queen approved of him. This very fine gentleman (a frequent description of Newcastle) had acquired polish abroad and spoke her language well, whereas Henrietta Maria's slowness in acquiring English was notorious. They too had horses as a common interest, for the French girl rode well, to the surprise of the English ladies who at this period seldom did.

More and more of the nobility were acquiring new town houses and Newcastle followed the trend. Today only the name Newcastle Row, in a prosaic commercial area, marks the site of his vanished mansion. Clerkenwell then was agreeably rustic, with numerous titled families settled round its green. When, in 1637, Newcastle had to block a plan to locate a pest-house close by, the Earl of Exeter was only one of the neighbouring noblemen who joined in his protest.

Precise records are lacking as to when, and by whom, Newcastle House was built, but by March 1632 the family chaplain was writing 'from your Lordship's house at Clerkenwell', and drawings made before its demolition in 1793 suggest a date of about 1630. Modern experts detect hints of the artisan or provincial architect, which point to John Smythson or his son Huntingdon. John was now a full-time estate employee, acting also as a bailiff, and if he could be spared from Bolsover it would have been unlike Newcastle to call in anyone else.

It was a two-acre site, formerly a Benedictine nunnery. One hall remained, which Newcastle preserved. The south cloister, six Gothic vaults with keystones carved like flowers, afforded shade in the garden and led through an arch to the convent chapel, which had become the parish church of St James. Through that cloister door, a decade later, young Elizabeth would walk to her wedding on her father's arm.

The new house was of brick, with slender stone pilasters dividing the tall windows of the first floor, and dormer windows peeping over plain parapets above. Like others of this transitional period, it was a country mansion adapted to town conditions. The plan was a half-H. Broad wings came forward to the street, making a small forecourt screened by curtain-walls both sides of the gate. Behind this somewhat reserved façade was ample accommodation for a family of quality. When the Restoration hearth-tax came in the assessment was for thirty-five hearths. But it is unlikely that the family spent much time there. Elizabeth bore in all ten children, of whom five survived. Though plague often reached the Nottinghamshire countryside, Welbeck was on balance healthier than London.

Newcastle, so fortunate in his own parents, was an affectionate father. Extant letters show how, when absent, he wrote to his children and stimulated their responses. Here, in the original spelling, are some of the exchanges:

> Sweet Jane, I knowe you are a rare Inditer –
> Ande hath the pen off a moste redye writer.   W.N.

To which the eldest daughter, who did indeed later compose poems herself, could on this occasion answer only:

> My Lord, I know you doo but Jest with mee
> & so in obdence I right this nothing.   Jane Cavendysshe.

Charles must have started Latin when he received this (undated) injunction:

> Sweet Charles, This letter iff you like itt nott, then
>   race itt.
> Butt Answer itt, for Usus promtus facitt.   W.N.

The young viscount replied respectfully, if briefly:

> My Lord. I can not tel what to wright. Charleles Mansfeild.

Elizabeth, Frances and Henry were saluted in their turn:

> Besse, you muste write to, write butt what you thinke.
> Now you're a Girle, disemble when you Linke.
> Franke prethe write to mee thy runinge hande
> Thatt none can reade, & all less understande.
> Sir, you muste write to, My beloved Harry,
> Thatt asketh blessinge & will never Tarry.

From Clerkenwell it was about a mile and a half to Whitehall. Even when Newcastle had crossed the little River Fleet, by the Holborn Bridge or one of the others, he was still in an area where town and country struggled for supremacy. Lincoln's Inn stood amid real fields, St Martin's Church no longer so. The grazing cattle had vanished from St Martin's Lane, but public outcry had just blocked the Earl of Leicester's scheme to build on the Lammas lands to the west, where even today Leicester Square recalls his defeat. Along the Strand, however, Inigo Jones was laying out the old convent garden like an Italian piazza.

At the Royal Mews (now Trafalgar Square) Newcastle reached the precincts of Whitehall, which, except for the splendid mass of Jones's Banqueting House, was very much the sprawling conglomeration he had explored, wide-eyed, as a boy. Indeed, if he glanced across the tiltyard, he might see his old riding master, St Antoine, still at work.

A man of his rank could bypass the porter's lodge and its fringe of gawping idlers. He could use a side door which led up a flight of stairs to the galleries overlooking the exercise ground. The Yeoman of the Guard on duty knew that, though neither a Privy Councillor nor an officer of state, he was *persona grata*. While humbler gentlemen must approach the great presence chamber by the usual route, Newcastle could walk through the privy gallery, past the council chamber, to the King's privy chamber and withdrawing-room beyond.

In these apartments, looking down into his garden, the royal connoisseur spent many hours in the company he most enjoyed, artists and art-collectors, minor poets and dilettanti of every kind. Laud and Wentworth were busy elsewhere, grappling with problems of church and state. Here, in a florid setting of carved furniture, ponderous velvet and Flemish tapestry, the light gleaming on gilded panels and steel suits of armour, Newcastle was more likely to meet that arbiter of European culture, his cousin's husband Arundel, or Endymion Porter, the King's agent and adviser on picture-buying, or John Suckling, witty, warm-hearted, dissolute and indiscreet, his sandy hair and sanguine complexion ill-suited to his taste for peacock finery. These and many others were, or now became, Newcastle's friends. Less congenial perhaps were such *habitués* as the vain and vindictive Earl of Holland, whom unfortunately the Queen liked so much, and the King's own cousin, the unperceptive and opinionated Marquess of Hamilton, paramount among the grandees of Scotland and Charles's most respected, if not most qualified, adviser on Scottish affairs.

The King loved the cultivated but undemanding conversation of this circle. He himself contributed little. Once, when he favoured Sir Henry Herbert, his Master of the Revels, with a comment of more than a dozen words, Sir Henry considered he had been unusually expansive. Charles fancied himself, however, as a judge of plays. Sir Henry's journal describes him sitting at the window of the withdrawing-room, going through Davenant's comedy *The Wits*, which Sir Henry had drastically censored after complaints by Endymion Porter. The King patiently discussed all the cuts and restored some, and, allowing '*faith* and *slight* to be asseverations only, and no oaths, marked them to stand . . .'.

Newcastle shared the King's interest in the theatre. Their common love of pictures has been noted already. In Whitehall alone Charles had collected some 460 paintings by Titian, Raphael, Holbein, Correggio and other masters. From Rubens he commissioned the ceiling of the Banqueting House, and he quickly established Van Dyck as the portraitist of the English aristocracy. Newcastle soon learned that no gift was more acceptable than a good picture. In 1634 he presented the King with a charming little landscape by Alexander Keirincx, the Antwerp artist who painted the royal castles in Scotland, and on another occasion with a painted panel by Bartholomew Breenbergh. Such gifts were, like complimentary speeches, the inescapable obligation of the ambitious courtier, yet there can be little doubt that Newcastle's regard was real. Deep friendship, difficult for any monarch, was virtually impossible for one as inhibited as Charles; but, in so far as any subject was admitted to his trust, he developed a relationship with Newcastle which no subsequent disaster destroyed. His contemporaries were agreed that Charles possessed remarkable charm. That may explain how the devotion of men like Newcastle survived his more exasperating qualities.

Only in one field, the King's preoccupation with religious issues, was Newcastle unable to pretend any enthusiasm. 'The Earl is too indifferent,' the Queen's papal agent reported to Rome. 'He hates the Puritans, he laughs at the Protestants, and he has little confidence in the Catholics.' Even Henrietta Maria, usually so eager and often so ill-advised in her missionary zeal, seems to have left Newcastle's spiritual welfare alone and accepted him as a dependable, if heretical, friend.

Their Majesties' devotion to their respective faiths in no whit diminished the liveliness of their court. Wotton, who despite his witty sophistication had Calvinist leanings, confessed that at Whitehall he felt like an owl among the gay birds. It was not only Suckling who played the peacock. Fashion for men, as well as women, had taken on a heightened elegance. The age of Van Dyck was at hand, with shoulder-wide collars, plumed hats, and boot-tops brimming with a froth of lace. Every gentleman, Newcastle included, sported a tiny beard and moustache. And Newcastle was, of course, among those who sat for the young Flemish painter whom Arundel had first introduced to England. Van Dyck, returned now from seven years in Italy, was established in some splendour in a riverside house at Blackfriars with his mistress, Margaret Lemon. The artist and his sitter became friends. Newcastle wrote from Welbeck recalling 'the blessing of your company and sweetness of conversation'. He praised the painter's genius, 'for such power hath your hand on the eyes of mankind', and proclaimed himself 'passionately your humble servant'. Not every English earl at that date would have so expressed himself to an artist, however fashionable.

Another London house at which Newcastle was a welcome guest was Endymion Porter's in the Strand. After a youth spent in Spain, Porter had been taken up by Buckingham, and had risen fast thereafter by his own not inconsiderable enterprise. His shrewd judgement was not restricted to the market in art treasures: he collected patents and monopolies with equal financial flair, but sought no office, being content with influence behind the scenes. His wife Olive, a zealous Catholic convert, was a high-spirited hostess who drew a brilliant circle of guests to their panelled parlour. Some of these, if the later allegations of the Parliamentarians were not unfounded, would adjourn to Endymion's study upstairs for more confidential discussions. Newcastle, however, was never given to intrigues. His friendship with the Porters stemmed rather from shared cultural than political interests.

In literary matters he remained staunchly loyal to his old mentor, now sadly out of fashion at court. Jonson's great days as a dramatist – the golden decade of *Volpone* and *The Alchemist* – were far behind him. His collaboration with Inigo Jones in the devising of masques had led inevitably to a tug-of-war between poet and designer, which Jones had won. Jonson's place as a masque-writer had gone to others, notably William Davenant, who claimed to be Shakespeare's godson and did not deny a closer relationship. Charles, while ordering an increase in Jonson's small court pension, did not much care for his work. By this time Jonson was well into his fifties and, though fighting to get back into the theatre, was unable to match the forceful writing of his best period. Two strokes had left him a pale shadow of the rumbustious character who had once lorded it in the London taverns. On 4 February 1632 he was writing to Newcastle at Welbeck, enclosing some verse tributes addressed to himself by Falkland and others:

My Noblest Lord, and my Patron, by excellence. I have here obeyed your commands, and sent you a packet of mine own praises, which I should not have done, if I had any stock of modesty in store. But obedience is better than Sacrifice; and you commanded it. I am now like an old bankrupt in wit, that am driven to pay debts, on my friends credits, and for want of satisfying letters, to subscribe bills of Exchange.

In another, undated letter, having saluted the whole family, 'your Honour, my Honourable Lady, the hopeful issue, and your right Noble Brother', he continued with a lament about publishing delays that will find sympathetic echoes in many an author's heart:

It is the lewd printer's fault, that I can send your Lordship no more of my book done. . . . My printer and I shall afford subject enough for a tragi-comedy. For with his delays and vexation, I am almost become blind, and if Heaven be so just in the metamorphosis, to turn him into that creature he most assimilates, a dog with a bell to lead me between Whitehall and my lodging, I may bid the world good night.

Jonson was in dire straits. In that era the professional writer, whatever his past popularity, was sure of no continuing income. His copyright was unprotected. The lump sum was the custom, whether from book-seller or theatrical management, and it was seldom a large lump. The rich patron was almost indispensable, for there was often more return from the dedication than from the work itself. Newcastle, though he received his share of such dedications, was generous in his help in any case, and was clearly Jonson's dependable supporter. The poet wrote:

I send no borrowing epistle to provoke your Lordship, for I have neither fortune to repay; or security to engage, that will be taken: but I make a most humble petition to your Lordship's bounty, to succour my present necessities this good time of Easter, and it shall conclude all begging requests hereafter, on the behalf of your truest beadsman and most thankful servant   B:I:

Such humility did not come easily to Jonson. Newcastle took the first opportunity to give additional help in a form he could accept without hurt to his pride. An opening soon came.

So far, the Earl's appearances at court had met with cordiality from the King and Queen but no more tangible recognition. At the end of 1631 there had been palace gossip that he might be appointed President of the North, an important office based in York and held by Wentworth, who was to become Lord Deputy in Ireland. Nothing came of this rumour. Wentworth retained his old post along with the new, simply delegating his North of England responsibilities to his vice-president, Sir Edward Osborne. But there was a hint of other possibilities for Newcastle in a letter, dated 13 December 1632, from his friend Lord Cottington, that entertaining straight-faced wit and man of the world whom Charles had made Chancellor of the Exchequer for life:

I must tell you from my Lord Treasurer that you are lively in the memory both of the King and of his lordship . . . my Lord Deputy is precisely sent for, so that you will have one friend more here. You are appointed to attend the King into Scotland which I conceive might be a good motive for your friends to put it to a period.

Pondering the implications of that letter, Newcastle realised that it might also be a good moment, incidentally, to do something for Jonson.

EIGHT

The Quest of Favour

CHARLES was going north for his long-deferred Scottish coronation, but without the Queen, then expecting her fourth child. Newcastle's 'attendance', as it turned out, applied only to the royal passage through Nottinghamshire, which offered a pretext for impressive hospitality. Charles dearly loved a masque. Newcastle, increasingly frustrated in his desire for some conspicuous recognition, resolved that when the court made its overnight stop at Worksop he would put on a lavish entertainment at Welbeck. Characteristically, he did not approach Davenant, Aurelian Townsend, or the other masque-writers then in vogue, but the old friend who was fighting ill-health, age and neglect in Westminster.

Sherwood, when Charles arrived, was in the full green glory of May. He brought a large retinue, including Laud, shortly to be Archbishop of Canterbury, and many more of Newcastle's London friends. 'Both King and Court', wrote Clarendon years afterwards, 'were received and entertained by the Earl of Newcastle, and at his own proper expense, in such a wonderful manner, and in such an excess of feasting, as had scarce ever been known in England.' The Duchess drily records that it 'cost my Lord between four and five thousand pounds'. In the masque, *The King's Entertainment at Welbeck*, performed on 21 May, Jonson had cobbled together a script embodying local references and a contest in riding at the quintain, as an allusion to his patron's sporting prowess. Evidently the King enjoyed himself, but the expenditure did not produce the desired result. On 5 August Newcastle was writing dejectedly to Wentworth, newly arrived in Ireland, and after thanking the Lord Deputy for his past advice – by which he was clearly being guided in his strategy – he reported that the King

seemed to be pleased with me very well, and never used me better or more graciously; the truth is, I have hurt my estate much with the hopes of it, and I have been put in hope long, and so long as I will labour no more of it, but let nature work and expect the issue at Welbeck; for I would be loth to be sick in mind, body, and purse, and when it is too late to repent, and my reward laugh'd at for my labour. It is better to give over in time with some loss than lose all. . . .

He was undecided now whether he even wanted a court appointment. It would be 'a more painful life' and might ruin him. He had hoped to economise that summer by keeping away from court and spending a quiet time in the country. Instead, he was deeply in debt – we may think not surprisingly, since even the fat rent-rolls of the various estates must have been severely over-taxed by the continual building at Bolsover, the recent Welbeck junketings, his expenses in London and the mainten-ance of a growing family. 'Children come on apace, my Lord,' he told Wentworth. He was ready to throw in his hand. 'The truth is, my Lord, for my Court business, your Lordship with your noble friends and mind have spoken so often to the King, and myself refreshed his memory in that particular, so that I mean not to move my friends any more to their so great trouble.'

Normally a man of restrained expression and deliberate judgement, Newcastle betrays by the inconsistency of this letter the tormenting cross-currents that were sweeping him this way and that. Having vowed to seek no more influential support, he gratefully accepts the continued assistance Wentworth has promised and suggests that Lord and Lady Carlisle might be useful. Carlisle had been made a K.B. with him in 1610: Clarendon describes him as 'a very fine gentleman and a most accom-plished courtier', who, 'having spent, in a very jovial life, about four hundred thousand pound . . . left not a house or acre of land to be remembered by'. His wife was a daughter of the Duke of Northumber-land, and most influential – lovely, witty and unprincipled, sung by the poets, close friend to the Queen, and (the gossip ran) even closer to statesmen as far apart as Wentworth and Pym. In the event, however, the Carlisles seem to have done nothing for Newcastle.

The King himself gave no sign. Seldom over-sensitive to other men's financial problems, he did however drop a hint that the Queen, having missed the Welbeck festivities, would enjoy a similar programme on their Midland progress the next summer. Royal hints could not be ignored. Whatever his private dismay, Newcastle decided to double his stake and gamble on the new splendours of Bolsover. The terrace range was still far from finished – there were no state apartments worthy of the royal repose – but if the Cavendishes moved into the Little Castle they could leave Welbeck Abbey vacant for the court. Banquet and masque, however, could be held at Bolsover. By working all hours, the builders could finish the long gallery there in time.

Jonson gratefully accepted the commission for *Love's Welcome at Bolsover*. 'Your Lordship's timely gratuity...fell like the dew of heaven on my necessities, it came so opportunely and in season. I pray to God, my work have deserv'd it, I meant it should in the working of it, and I have hope the performance will conclude it.' He planned the masque in two sections with a break for the banquet. 'His Majesty being set at Dinner,' he wrote, 'Music: the Passions, Doubt and Love, enter with the Affections, Joy, Delight, etc, and sing this song. . . .' After the meal the performance would be continued in the garden round the fountain with its marble Venus rising from her bath.

In allusion to the building operations Jonson provided a dance of Mechanics and characters such as Chesil the carver, Maul the mason, and Fret the plasterer. Turning the pages, Newcastle could not fail to recognise in Coronel Vitruvius, the surveyor, 'a busy man', a mordant caricature of Jonson's erstwhile collaborator and now detested enemy, Inigo Jones. It was a last snarl from the shabby old lion at Westminster. It might divert the court, but it would hardly rehabilitate Ben in the royal favour.

The host had other things on his mind as 30 July drew near. There was a warning from the Secretary of State, Sir John Coke, that a multitude of miners planned to assemble at Welbeck with a mutinous petition. Newcastle must break up this demonstration, 'that their Majesties may peaceably enjoy the honour you intend them without distraction or trouble'. It would seem that, being a popular local figure as well as a competent lord-lieutenant, he dealt with this threat and all went off well.

One would give much for a contemporary description of that great day at Bolsover. It merits more than Clarendon's disapproving reference to 'a more stupendous entertainment, which (God be thanked), though possibly it might too much whet the appetite of others to excess, no man ever after in those days imitated'. The Duchess says that it cost her husband 'in all between fourteen and fifteen thousand pounds', for the locust-like courtiers were at Welbeck for six whole days. Long afterwards, reckoning up what had been looted from the Clerkenwell house during the Civil War, she listed a set of tablecloths, sideboard-cloths and napkins originally bought for the feast at Bolsover. Their cost alone had been £160. Jonson's fee is unfortunately unrecorded.

In default of an eyewitness account one turns gratefully to the

imaginative evocation by a modern poet, Sacheverell Sitwell, writing in
The Thirteenth Caesar in 1924:

> When the sun climbed high enough to see into the garden
> The palaces were down and Charles had ridden far away,
> The towers still were lived in, as the trees are full of doves,
> But the Banquet Hall has never shone with lights again,
> Empty are its windows of the glass that glowed like water
> And long dead the torches that turned the glass to flame. . . .
> But Venus, down the alleys, still stands upon her shell.

Venus still stands.

Charles had indeed 'ridden far away', and Newcastle, on Wentworth's
advice, had ridden with him, 'two or three days journey after his going
from Welbeck', discreetly renewing the suggestion of a court appointment. It is generally assumed that Newcastle was already seeking the
governorship of little Prince Charles, who, though still only four, would
soon have his own separate household. Wentworth, however, refers
repeatedly to some honour involving nearness to the King's person,
and the Venetian ambassador had earlier reported, though mistakenly,
that Newcastle was to be Master of the Horse.

Certainly it was on the governorship that his hopes eventually concentrated, at first sight an odd ambition, but seen on reflection to be quite
in character. Newcastle hungered for honour, but he was no Wentworth.
All he sought was an office of dignity and independence, in which he
would be answerable only to his sovereign. It was not entirely his fate,
but also partly his preference, that both the Civil War and the Commonwealth period found him in isolation, far from the endless intrigues of
the court.

The control of the Prince's household would offer just the right type
of post, important yet congenial. Important, because the personality and
outlook of the next king would be so vital: Newcastle was a realist, he
had heard the hounds baying in Parliament under James and Charles,
and he had no illusions that the future would be easy. Congenial, because
he loved children and believed that, like horses, they needed training.
And training, gentle, discreet, but firm, was something he was good at.
What more splendid assignment, what more eminently worthwhile,
than the training of the future Charles II?

For the moment, though, the King seemed in no hurry to install his
son, at such a tender age, under a separate roof even with the most
conscientious guardian. No monarch cared more for the intimacy of the

family circle, and, like all men with patronage to bestow, he knew the advantages of deferred decision.

The only immediate consequence of the Bolsover masque was to win Newcastle the reputation of a Maecenas. Dedications rained hopefully upon him. First, from the veteran John Ford, came *The Chronicle History of Perkin Warbeck*, one of the best historical plays since Shakespeare's. 'The custom of your lordship's entertainments – even to strangers – is rather an example than a fashion.' A year later, the prolific James Shirley offered *The Traitor*, confessing 'a long ambition, by some service to be known to you', and 'a boldness at last, by this rude attempt to kiss your lordship's hands'. A long and friendly association developed. When Shirley fled from London in the Civil War it was Newcastle who offered him refuge in the north. Inevitably his generosity attracted lesser writers. In 1636 the obscure William Sampson sent him *Virtus post Funera Vivit, or Honour Triumphing over Death*, with flattering references to himself, a verse dedication to his small son Charles, a prose dedication to Christian, Countess of Devonshire, and complimentary couplets about other members of the family, right back to Bess. Sampson's quality was not high. 'Scarce had Aurora shown her crimson face', began an effusive address to Lady Newcastle. The lot of the seventeenth-century author was admittedly hard, but sometimes his patrons were not undeserving of sympathy.

For Jonson Newcastle could do no more, beyond writing a poem himself in tribute when death claimed him in August 1637. He had clearly been in the old man's thoughts until the end. Bedridden though he had long been, Jonson seems to have cherished a wistful dream of travelling once more, perhaps as far as Falkland's Oxfordshire home at Great Tew and even Welbeck. Falkland's own funereal tribute contains the lines:

> Not long before his death, our woods he meant
> To visit, and descend from Thames to Trent.

And among his papers was an unfinished pastoral, *The Sad Shepherd, or A Tale of Robin Hood*, set in the Sherwood Forest where his patron held such sway, and lyrically evoking those woodlands he had seen in times gone by.

During this period Newcastle dashed off a masque to amuse his family, and deprecated their copying it out for preservation. The precise date is unknown, but Jane, the eldest, was twelve in 1634, the year of the Bolsover entertainment. Under the direction, 'to be writ in my book and before the masque book', he good-humouredly admonishes the girls:

Sweet Daughters, know, I was not nice or coy,
But made a country masque, a Christmas toy,
At your desires; but I did not look
You would record my follies in a book.
You'll lose by that. . . . Therefore I'd rather
For your sakes and my own be held a father
Of gravity, formality, precise;
An outside out of fashion is held wise. . . .

He struck a more serious note in several religious poems composed about this time, a good example being *A Divine Meditation upon receiving the Blessed Sacrament on Christmas Day 1637*, beginning:

Thy birth-time's wheel to me turns quickly round,
Christmas again! and find my soul unsound!
I left it well, and thought, at the same rate
To find it so, but 't is in worse estate. . . .

It shows the influence of Donne, who had died six years earlier, but whose collected poems were only just being printed.

Along with these literary interests, and at a similar level of intelligent amateurism, went a scientific curiosity very typical of that age. With his chaplain, Dr Payne, he conducted chemical experiments in a room at Bolsover, and satisfied himself that the sun could be 'nothing else but a very solid body of salt and sulphur, inflamed by his own violent motion upon his own axis'. It was speculation, however, rather than patient research that appealed to him. Here, as in theology, he was sceptical about the conclusive proof of anything. Hobbes, who – secure in his Chatsworth appointment – had no need to curry favour, took him seriously and regretted that their contacts were too often limited to correspondence. Hobbes must have visited him as early as 1630. Sixteen years later, he recalled the occasion when 'I affirmed to your lordship at Welbeck that light is a fancy in the mind, caused by motion in the brain'. Newcastle was particularly fascinated by optics and astronomy. 'My first business in London', wrote Hobbes, 'was to seek for Galileo's *Dialogues*; I thought it a very good bargain, when at taking my leave of your lordship I undertook to buy it for you, but . . . it is not possible to get it for money. There were but few brought over at first and they that buy such books are not such men as to part with them again.' Hobbes was still tutor to the other William Cavendish, then on his way to Oxford but delayed in London by the obligation to appear in a court masque. The philosopher welcomed the delay. 'I shall have the more time for the business I have so long owed to your lordship, whose continual favours make me ashamed of my dull proceedings. . . .'

When he took his pupil on the Grand Tour, Hobbes was a regular correspondent. He warned Newcastle against too generously financing a man who claimed to have invented a burning glass of infinite strength. While thanking him for a present, he emphasised with dignity:' Let me tell your Lordship once for all, that though I honour you as my Lord, yet my love to you is just of the same nature that it is to Mr Payne, bred out of private talk, without respect to your purse.' The subjects of that talk probably included horses, for Hobbes produced a pamphlet, *Considerations touching the facility or Difficulty of the Motions of a Horse on straight lines, and Circular*, which must surely have owed something to his noble friend's specialist knowledge.

Their mutual liking encouraged more personal exchanges. Newcastle confided something of his own disappointed aspirations, and Hobbes answered on 29 July 1636:

I am sorry your Lordship finds not so good dealing in the world as you deserve. But, my Lord, he that will venture to sea must resolve to endure all weather, but for my part I love to keep a' land. And it may be your Lordship now will do so too, whereby I may have the happiness which your Lordship partly promises me in the end of your letter.

This was an allusion to a proposal that Hobbes, when the young Earl of Devonshire came of age, should move over from Chatsworth to Welbeck, where, after tutoring two generations, he would be free at last to follow his own intellectual pursuits. In October he wrote: 'That I cannot conceive I shall do anywhere so well as at Welbeck, and therefore I mean if your Lordship forbid me not, to come thither as soon as I can, and stay as long as I can without inconvenience to your Lordship.' The move, however, was delayed by the pestilence then raging through the countryside, and in the end the proposal came to nothing. When at last the two friends were able to resume their speculative discussions it was in circumstances neither had ever foreseen.

It says much for Newcastle's resilience that he combined so many interests with his unavoidable responsibilities when he was in far from perfect health. That may be deduced from some letters, undated but probably about 1634, from the Dowager Countess at Chatsworth. He had apparently complained of his doctor's dilatory response to a summons. Physicians were few and usually distant, and fashionable ones like Sir Theodore Mayerne (who was certainly his doctor later on, if not at this time) were often content to diagnose and prescribe by letter. Christian clearly had no great opinion of them, preferring her own remedies. She wrote back:

I am sorry your physician is no poster. My hope is you will be past the want of his help ere he arrive to serve you. Let him not cloy you with long courses of physic. Believe me, they are very chargeable to nature and make greater waste than time. The accident I hope will pass as suddenly as it came. If it should have other original than the powder your lordship has taken, I should advise your lordship to come where you may receive the best helps.

Several other letters refer to his health. It looks as though Newcastle suspected that nightmare of the seventeenth century which Pepys survived and so many did not. His friend remained encouraging. She wrote:

I hope you will give me leave to prescribe what my experience has found best to agree with the disease you complain of. Trust me, my lord, it is not months of diet nor strict rule so much as observation of yourself and little ordinary cordials such as require not the physician. The water I sent your lordship you may safely use in such proportion as I write. . . . It's most proper for the stone, very good for obstructions and extremely refreshing.

Whether or not she was correct in her treatment, Newcastle's health improved and there is no record of further trouble.

Still the King made no decision about the Prince's governor. Christian wrote to Elizabeth at Welbeck, commending her 'kind love to my sweet cousins' and adding, 'I believe my lord has weighty occasions that holds him so long in the south'. This may have been in the spring of 1636, when Newcastle was at court and almost in despair. His own letter to his wife, on 8 April, lamented:

There is nothing I either say or do or hear but it is a crime, and I find a great deal of venom against me, but both the King and the Queen have used me very graciously. Now they cry me down more than ever they cried me up, and so now think me a lost man. They say absolutely another shall be for the Prince and that the King wondered at the report and said he knew no such thing and told the Queen so; but I must tell you I think most of these are lies, and nobody knows except the King.

A week later, on Good Friday, he was able to report more optimistically about his rivals:

My Lord Danby certainly did put very far for governor to the Prince but is gone to his government at Guernsey, and they say is denied. My Lord of Leicester has also tried for it but they say he is to go ambassador into France.

Lord Goring also plies it for the same place, but they say he will not get it. The Scots also put in for it but it is not thought they will get it. It is believed absolutely that I must be about the Prince, and some say that I am to have my Lord of Carlisle's place.

Carlisle had been helpful at last, dying in March and leaving a coveted vacancy as Gentleman of the Bedchamber.

The rumours reached Chatsworth. Perhaps it was on this occasion that Christian wrote to him:

Although you have left me to conjecture and that I may err or be misled by common opinion, yet I consent not to report which has bestowed upon you the custody of our prince. I know your expectation will not be fulfilled with little or half favours, and to the highest of your aim my imagination brings you.

Alas, the promise of that spring withered. On 23 May he was writing to Elizabeth, 'I am very weary and mean to come down presently . . . it is a lost business.'

At Welbeck that summer he put on another masque, though less expensively, for Prince Rupert and his elder brother, the Elector Palatine, then on a visit to England. Rupert, a tall, dashing sixteen-year-old, charmed everyone. Besides seeing him at his uncle's court, Newcastle would have met him in the more relaxed atmosphere of Endymion Porter's house, where they were both frequent guests. Rupert left England a few months later. They were not to meet again till Marston Moor.

Even 1637 brought no decision from the palace. But on 21 March 1638 Newcastle broke the seal of a letter dated two days previously from 'the Court of Whitehall', conveying the news he had despaired of ever hearing.

NINE

The Prince's Governor

HIS MAJESTY, wrote Sir Francis Windebank – the 'subtle whirly Windebank' of a contemporary ballad – purposed to 'settle the government' of the Prince, and, 'in his gracious opinion of your Lordship', had chosen Newcastle as 'a chief director in so weighty a business'. He was appointed sole Gentleman of the Bedchamber to the Prince and was to come to court before Sunday, 8 April. The Secretary of State emphasised that the choice was entirely that of the King and Queen. Newcastle was under no obligation to anyone else.

This was an important point. Rejoicing, the recipient at once dispatched an answer in the humble terms appropriate to the occasion. 'This princely employment', he declared, tongue in cheek, 'was beyond a hope of the most partial thoughts I had about me. . . . I have but seldom had the honour to receive letters from you; but such as these you cannot write often.'

Wentworth's congratulations took up the same point. Newcastle was indebted solely to the King. 'My lord, I right well know your own wisdom sufficient to direct your course in the new world you are come into. . . .' Even so, Wentworth took no chances and issued a clear warning against allying himself with any clique at court. It was congenial counsel. Newcastle, doubtless to his own detriment, never departed from it.

Prince Charles was now nearing his eighth birthday, a swarthy child, ugly in babyhood but already developing that charm which was to help him through so many vicissitudes. In an age less rich than ours in embraceable soft toys, he had been particularly devoted to a simple wooden block, which he took to bed with him. Though this was in due course discarded, the disinclination to sleep alone persisted in later life.

The royal children lived in the care of Lady Dorset at the old palace of St James, just across the park from their parents in Whitehall. Henceforth Charles was to divide his time between Richmond and Oatlands, another Tudor palace near Walton-on-Thames, with his own huge establishment headed by his 'governor' and including cupbearers and carvers, grooms, ushers and equerries, a physician, apothecary and two surgeons, and even his attorney and solicitor. To preserve the Anglo-Scottish balance his Master of Horse would be that plausible intriguer, the Marquess of Hamilton. Within a few weeks, however, such a storm was blowing up north of the border, because of the King's religious innovations, that Hamilton had to be appointed Commissioner for Scotland, where he was soon too busy coping with acrimonious Covenanters to have time for his own demarcation disputes with his English colleague at Richmond. Thither Newcastle escorted the boy after his installation as Prince of Wales at Windsor on 12 May. The royal parents returned to Whitehall, and from the official date of his appointment, 4 June, Newcastle was answerable to them alone.

Nine miles upstream from Whitehall, Richmond presented a magnificent silhouette of slender turrets, onion domes and cupolas, riding on the green foam of a great riverside orchard. The ornate royal apartments with their stone façade, the courts and gardens with their fountains and heraldic beasts, combined with the mellow brick quadrangles of the household to cover a full ten acres. Outside the curtain wall spread the elm-lined Richmond Green, and the newly enclosed deer park offered vast spaces in which to ride. That was one part of the Prince's education which Newcastle personally supervised. To him primarily is due the credit for the fine horseman Charles became.

Academic instruction was directed by Dr Brian Duppa, Bishop of Chichester, an agreeable, gentle character whose political soundness and Laudian churchmanship made him a safe choice. He and Newcastle got on well enough, though it is said that the latter, with his *grand seigneur* instincts, disliked having to share the service of the same kitchen. Their little charge, for all his tender years, dined alone with all the pomp of kneeling pages and other obsequious functionaries. Duppa's chief grievance was that he had to teach not only Charles but Buckingham's two orphan boys, whom the King had decreed should be brought up with his own children. George, now Duke, was ten, and Newcastle was one of his legal guardians. Lord Francis was nine, so the Prince was the youngest, and the Villiers boys were not always the best examples. At least, though, they provided youthful company.

The Queen's first letter to Charles is a reminder that not all things can be regulated by protocol.

Charles, I am sorry that I must begin my first letter by chiding you, because I hear that you will not take physic. I hope it was only for this day, and that tomorrow you will do it; for if you will not, I must come to you and make you take it, for it is for your health. I have given order to my Lord of Newcastle to send me word tonight whether you will or not; therefore I hope you will not give me the pains to go; and so I rest, your affectionate mother, Henriette Marie.

The little boy evidently shared the Countess of Devonshire's sceptical view of conventional medicine. Later, when Newcastle was himself away ill, he wrote to him sympathetically: 'My Lord, I would not have you take too much physic, for it doth always make me worse; and I think it will do the like for you. I ride every day, and am ready to follow any directions from you. Make haste back to him that loves you. Charles P.'

On another occasion Newcastle's indisposition was cheered by the boy's company, for he addressed these verses to the Prince:

Sir, I was sick, and you were with me . . .

concluding fondly:

Know your immortal sweetness such a thing,
Though but a prince, makes you a little king.
Your love and judgment, without flatt'ry, can,
Though you're but young, now style you justly man.

The disclaimer of flattery may not convince a modern reader – it was, of course, the natural idiom of a Caroline courtier – but undoubtedly Newcastle formed a genuine affection for his charge which survived some searching tests later on. Charles too, though never given to tangible expressions of gratitude, seems always to have looked back with warmth upon their early association.

Newcastle's educational principles were submitted to the boy himself in a memorandum. It reveals his distrust of the academic approach, his preference for worldly experience. The Prince would need foreign languages, 'though I confess I would rather have you study things than words, matter, than language'. An expert linguist was often 'but a living dictionary'. Newcastle favoured carefully selected history, 'so you might compare the dead with the living' and see where king and subjects had acted wisely or wrongly in the past.

In religious matters the governor had to tread delicately. The Queen was unswerving in her Roman allegiance, the King an equally unyielding High Anglican. The people, whatever theological shade they favoured, were resolved not to have a papist on the throne. The Scottish opposition to the Prayer Book showed that a too devout sovereign could stir up dangerous controversy. Newcastle could only hope secretly that the Prince would grow up with a more flexible faith than his father's. 'Beware of too much devotion for a King,' he counselled, 'for one may be a good man but a bad King.' History showed many who 'in seeming to gain the kingdom of Heaven have lost their own'. The words have a prophetic ring. 'Reverence at prayers', certainly, was a good example, for if the people have no obedience to God 'then they will easily have none to your Highness. . . . No obedience, no subjects.' There was equal peril in excessive fervour. 'If any be Bible mad, over much burn't with fiery zeal, they may think it a service to God to destroy you and say the Spirit moved them. . . .' This could produce 'civil war' or 'private treason'. Again the prophetic ring is unmistakable. But Newcastle had weighed up the Prince and consoled himself: 'But, Sir, you are not in your own disposition religious and not very apt to your book, so you need no great labour to persuade you from the one, or long discourses to dissuade you from the other.'

In his advice on everyday deportment he was obviously mindful of how both James and his son, in very different ways, had made themselved unpopular, the one by boorishness, the other by his frigid hauteur. He wanted the future Charles II to cultivate an ease of manner more acceptable to his subjects. He wrote:

The things that I have discoursed to you most is to be courteous and civil to everybody. . . . Believe it, the putting off of your hat and making a leg pleases more than reward . . . so much doth it take all kind of people. Then to speak well of everybody, and when you hear people speak ill of others reprehend them and seem to dislike it so much, and do not look on 'em so favourably for a few days after.

Civility – or insincerity? Whatever label is given to the lesson, history suggests that it was thoroughly absorbed.

Newcastle was conscientious in his duties and it can only have been for brief periods that he and the Prince were separated. Charles presumably spent Christmas with his parents and Newcastle would be able to join his own family. A letter from the boy seems to herald the end of the holidays: 'My lord . . . I thank you for your New Year's gift. I am very pleased with it, especially with the brass statues. On Monday by 3 of the clock I shall be glad to meet you at Lambeth.'

In 1639, however, a more pressing duty called Newcastle elsewhere. The situation in Scotland was fast deteriorating. Thousands of objectors to the Prayer Book had signed the National Covenant. No earthly ruler should impose an unwanted ritual upon them. They were ready to fight. The numerous Scottish soldiers of fortune abroad began to trickle home. Charles conceived an elaborate invasion plan to re-establish his authority in his northern kingdom. It involved co-ordinated land and sea operations that would have tested a modern military machine and were, in his circumstances, absurdly impracticable. As no regular army existed and he had no money to create one, the expedition was financed like a charitable appeal. The Earl of Worcester subscribed £1500, the Marquess of Winchester £1000, but the affluent Lord Clare regretted that, with seven daughters to marry, he had no money to spare. Men were even scarcer than money. A number of peers excused themselves as being too old or too young or too unwell to take the field, and a surprising proportion of the northern gentry became suddenly attracted to foreign travel. On the other hand, though the King gave much offence by his tactless allocation of commands, traditional loyalty drew men like Newcastle to his standard. Newcastle was outstanding among these volunteers. Besides contributing £10,000, he equipped a troop of 120 knights and gentlemen of quality at his own expense, 'all gallantly mounted and armed', and was allowed to call them the Prince of Wales's troop and lead them himself. Clarendon says they 'consisted of the best gentlemen of the North' and because of their connections 'came together purely on his account'. Newcastle was not unique in this – his friend, the young poet Sir John Suckling, also raised a troop, as did various landowners – but his contribution was conspicuously generous.

The King reached York in late March, welcomed by the local train bands resplendent in silver lace and scarlet breeches, and by Arundel who, being hereditary Earl Marshal, had been made commander-in-chief, irrespective of experience or abilities. Newcastle's own commission was dated, not inappropriately, 1 April. But he was only one of many who had never heard a shot fired in anger. A whole month was spent mobilising the invasion forces, with many a colourful cavalry review in the fields outside the city walls.

In Scotland, meanwhile, the first Scots War, or 'Bishops' War', had made a more effective beginning. The Covenanters had seized without resistance such key positions as Edinburgh Castle, the arsenal at Dalkeith and the port of Dumbarton, where the King had planned to bring in his Irish troops. By the time Charles started for Berwick the news was as heavy as the weather, which, after being unusually wet and chilly, had changed to an oppressive heat-wave.

Newcastle, never one to complain of physical exertion, was enjoying the company of the northern neighbours and tenants he all too seldom met. For more literary conversation he had brother officers like Suckling and Davenant. The main fly in the ointment was his commander, the dark and handsome Earl of Holland, who (says Clarendon) loved neither Wentworth nor Laud 'nor almost anything that was then done in Church or State'. He disliked Newcastle and was jealous of his splendidly accoutred troop. Primarily to please the Queen, Charles had made Holland general of the horse and independent even of Arundel. All the King's military appointments, now and henceforth, were bedevilled by his own weakness, the lack of any accepted system of seniority and his failure to see the danger of divided command.

Pompous farce was the keynote of this campaign. On Whit Sunday, as the army camped outside Berwick, news came that the Covenanters, led by Alexander Leslie, a commander of long experience in the Thirty Years War, had reached Kelso, a day's march away. It was decided that Holland should move out against them at dawn with a thousand cavalry and three thousand infantry. When the order of march was issued, Newcastle found his troop placed in the rear. Touchy on matters of honour, he pointed out that it was the Prince of Wales's troop. It bore His Highness's arms on its colours and could not possibly take such an inferior position. The two men glowered at each other, both earls, neither professional soldiers. Holland refused to move Newcastle's troops to the head of the column, whereupon Newcastle ordered the Prince's colours to be furled and paraded his men, anonymously as it were, in the position allocated.

As it turned out, obedience cost him no glory. The column kept up a steady advance until the late afternoon, or rather the cavalry did, for the sweating pikemen and musketeers dropped farther and farther behind since it had not occurred to Holland that they might have difficulty in keeping up with horsemen. Only as he neared Kelso, and sighted an advancing formation of Scots estimated at eight thousand men, did he notice that he had lost his infantry. He sent a trumpeter forward, asking the Scots to retire. He was answered with a polite but firm suggestion that it would be better if he did. Whereupon Holland, not liking the odds against him, led his cavaliers back to Berwick with their tails between their legs.

After that fiasco the nearest approach to bloodshed was when Newcastle challenged him to a duel. Holland, though no coward personally, delayed until the news leaked to the King, by whose authority, says Clarendon, 'the matter was composed'. By then the gossip had divided the whole court into factions.

The end of the wider conflict is as quickly told. Leslie advanced on Berwick and confronted the English across the Tweed. Charles, sensibly advised by Wentworth from Ireland, saw the impracticability of his invasion scheme. A settlement was agreed on 19 June and within a few weeks Newcastle was back at Richmond.

He found the Prince developing well. 'He hastens apace out of his childhood,' declared Duppa, 'and is likely to be a man betimes.' That winter Suckling twitted Newcastle with preferring the boy's company to that of his friends at court, or even of their Majesties. 'Are the small buds of the white and red rose more delightful', he demanded, 'than the roses themselves? And cannot the King and Queen invite as strongly as the royal issue?' But conscientious as Newcastle was, there were many hours when the boy was with Duppa or his French tutor or Wenceslaus Hollar (who was giving him drawing lessons), and his governor had leisure for his own interests.

About this time he wrote two plays, *The Country Captain*, performed 'by His Majesty's Servants at Blackfriars', probably early in 1640, and *The Variety*, produced there shortly afterwards. *The Country Captain* poked fun at platonic love, then fashionable in palace circles. Sir Francis Courtwell uses it as a pretence to deceive Lady Huntlove, only later disclosing his true intentions. Newcastle's humour is earthy and reflects his lack of sympathy with the sillier affectations of the court. Anthony à Wood says that Shirley 'did much assist his generous patron . . . in the composure of certain plays', and much scholarly detective work has been devoted to identifying his contribution. Playbills did not bear the author's name, and even when this piece was printed nine years later it was attributed only to 'A Person of Honour'. It is quite likely that Shirley helped mainly with professional touches of stage-craft, suggesting cuts and transpositions, the breaking up of long speeches with interjections from other characters, and similar practical changes such as have been proposed to, or imposed upon, the inexperienced playwright down the ages. Certainly Newcastle was always credited at the time with the authorship of both plays. *The Variety* is an inferior effort, which is seized upon by scholars as evidence that it lacked Shirley's improving hand. It repeats the device of a trick marriage, already used in *The Country Captain*, employing it three times to pair off the principal characters – which some feel is going a little too far, but others think permissible in so artificial a play. Even Shakespeare ended some comedies with a wholesale coupling more convenient than convincing.

Newcastle's patronage of other writers continued. Jasper Mayne, later chaplain at Chatsworth, translated Lucian's *Dialogues* for his 'private entertainment'. Robert Davenport addressed a collection of poems to him. Richard Brome, once Jonson's secretary, 'faithful servant and most loving friend', dedicated his play, *The Sparagus Garden*, and wrote a fulsome assessment of *The Variety*:

> I would depose each Scene appear'd to me
> An Act of wit, each Act a Comedy. . . .

A dedication of a more serious kind was that of Hobbes's 'little treatise' on the royal prerogative, which, although not printed, had a wide circulation in manuscript and, by making him a marked man, caused his prudent departure overseas long before the sharpening political conflict turned into the actual Civil War.

On 29 November 1639 Newcastle became a Privy Councillor, a gratifying confirmation of the King's trust. But what he heard at the council table, when he attended, only increased his forebodings for the future. Charles had managed for ten years without a Parliament. He could not carry on much longer; his financial difficulties were too great. Yet what would happen when that Parliament was called and the bottled-up resentment of a decade was at last released?

Parliament was in fact called and opened on 13 April. Newcastle attended and his brother was there in the Commons. Five days later, when a roll was called in the Lords, the Earl was recorded as 'with the Prince and will be present as often as he may'. He came in from Richmond about a dozen times and was in the chamber on 5 May for the dissolution, the Commons having refused to vote supplies unless there was a redress of their grievances. It was well named the Short Parliament. Whether from his governor or from others, the Prince was picking up some gloomy ideas about the way things were tending. Two weeks later, just before his tenth birthday, he startled his father by bursting out: 'My grandfather left you four kingdoms – I am afraid Your Majesty will leave me never a one.' Thunderstruck, the King demanded: 'Who have been your tutors in this?' but the boy refused to say.

Newcastle had an anxious summer. There were whispers of a plot to kidnap, or even kill, the Prince. The guards at Richmond were increased. In September, when the household moved to Oatlands, the Prince's chief cook, a Scotsman, had to be arrested for alleged threats against him.

The household moved again, to Hampton Court for greater security. Newcastle was constantly on the *qui vive*.

These alarms coincided with the brief second Bishops' War. This time the Scots swept triumphantly as far as Yorkshire and had to be bought off, in October, with the humiliating Treaty of Ripon. Two weeks later the King was compelled to summon a Parliament again. This proved to be the Long Parliament, destined to outlive Charles himself. We have no full record of Newcastle's attendances for this opening session. On 6 November he was appointed to the Grand Committee for Privileges and Orders and to the Lords' Committees for Petitions, but this may imply no more than recognition of his status. Ten days later he was absent from the House with his usual excuse, 'attending the Prince'.

The political situation was now looking ugly indeed. The House of Commons was very different from the impotent talking-shop he had known in his youth. It was a formidable weapon, forged and ably wielded by the relentless Pym. There is no need to repeat here the story of the parliamentary struggle that preceded the outbreak of armed strife in 1642. Only its effects on Newcastle must be told.

By the New Year, 1641, both Wentworth (now Earl of Strafford) and Archbishop Laud were prisoners in the Tower on charges of high treason, charges incomprehensible to a mind like Newcastle's, since treason could be committed only against the King who in fact was attempting ineffectively to save them. Unable to secure Strafford's impeachment, Pym set in motion an alternative procedure, a bill of attainder.

Without drastic action it seemed that Strafford was doomed. To the hotter heads at court the best hope seemed a *coup d'état* to restore the King's authority. There was still an army in being, in the north, commanded by the Earl of Northumberland, whose young brother, Harry Percy, was a prime mover in the so-called Army Plot, along with Harry Jermyn, the Queen's Master of Horse, spurred on by his impetuous mistress, and several of Newcastle's friends, Porter, Suckling and Davenant. The idea was for a march on London to seize the Tower and rescue Strafford before he went to the block. This march was to be led by the ambitious and aggressive young George Goring, a most able soldier when not drunk. Northumberland, however, declined to cooperate. It was then suggested that he be replaced by Newcastle, who (his friends thought) would be more amenable and, as a respected figure in the north, would make a credible substitute. There was the additional advantage that, if he suddenly rode north to lead the coup, he could bring the Prince of Wales with him. Whether Newcastle knew the role proposed for him remains uncertain, but if the King himself had given the order he would almost certainly have obeyed. The scheme never came off. Goring leaked it to the Earl of Newport, then Constable of the Tower and Strafford's enemy. The news reached the ears of Pym himself, and early in May became public. Harry Percy, Jermyn and Suckling fled abroad, where Suckling, being destitute, took poison a few months later. Davenant, unable to disguise his famous nose, disfigured by syphilis, was intercepted in flight, but with his usual flair for survival made good his escape overseas at the third attempt.

Nothing now could save Strafford, though on 11 May, on the King's instructions, the ten-year-old Prince had to be taken to the House of Lords to voice his own plea for clemency. The next day, after the anguished King had signed the death warrant of the man he had promised to protect, Strafford was executed. Newcastle had good reason to mourn a man he had admired and one who had befriended him in bygone days. He wrote a tribute:

> Farewell, great soul, the glory of thy fall
> Outweighs the cause. . . .

At Richmond the routine of the Prince's education continued, but within a week or two, as the inquiry into the Army Plot progressed, it became clear that not only Newcastle but even the gentle Duppa was under suspicion. On 29 May the House of Lords resolved:

that the Earls of Newcastle and Carnarvon and the Lord Bishop of Chichester shall be attended with this Order; and that their Lordships be desired to repair unto the Lords Committees appointed by this House, to take Examinations concerning certain late Practices concerning the Army in the North, at Two a clock this Afternoon, in the Lord Keeper's Lodgings, near the Parliament House, to be examined by them.

The interrogation seems to have passed off without trouble, for both Newcastle and Duppa were listed on 7 June as 'absent attending the Prince', and the same excuse is registered after the roll-call on 18 June. Unfortunately, about this time the boy broke his arm while riding in Hyde Park, and his consequent disappearance from public view started a rumour that he had fled north with his governor. When this was quashed, and he joined his mother for his convalescence, there was an outcry because he had quitted the sound Protestant atmosphere of Richmond. In the eyes of Parliament Newcastle could do nothing right.

Though no accusation was brought against him, it was made brutally plain to the King that neither the Earl nor the Bishop could remain in charge of the heir to the throne.

So, after three years' conscientious service, Newcastle lost the appointment he had worked so hard to gain. On 17 July, in a typical gesture, at once defiant and ineffective, the King made him Gentleman of the Robes to the Prince. Newcastle departed, demonstrably without a stain on his character, though with new debts of some forty thousand pounds incurred in the discharge of his duties.

TEN

The Drift to War

ORDINARY life had to go on. During those final troubled weeks, while Newcastle's enemies were pressing for his dismissal, his wife was busy ordering the marriage of their second daughter, Elizabeth. It took place at St James's parish church in Clerkenwell on 22 July. The bride was still only fourteen, and there was probably the usual understanding that the union would not be immediately consummated, for it was not until some years later that she bore a child, a son. The bridegroom, John Egerton, heir to the Earl of Bridgwater, was eighteen. With his brother and sister he had played a leading role in Milton's masque *Comus* when his father became Lord President of Wales. It was a good match, an obvious family arrangement, but one that worked out happily. John remained passionately devoted to Elizabeth.

The wedding over, Newcastle retired to Welbeck where, says the Duchess, he 'settled himself with his lady, children and family, to his great satisfaction, with an intent to have continued there, and managed his own estate'. Jane shared his literary interests. Charles and Henry had a tutor, Mark Anthony Benoist, and Frances no doubt joined in some of their lessons.

Fashionable London had in any case emptied for the summer, as usual. The King went to Scotland, where he laboured deviously, not without success, to repair relations with the Covenanters, a little easier now with their *bête noire*, Laud, impeached and a prisoner in the Tower. Parliament went into recess – Newcastle had been sending his proxy since 4 August – but Pym maintained his dominance by setting up a committee to watch over public affairs until the re-assembly. The Civil War was not twelve months away. It is easy, with hindsight, to see it as inevitable, the nation drifting inexorably towards the weir. In fact, there were powerful cross-currents. That autumn the King's popularity increased in some quarters, while Pym was thought by some former sympathisers to have gone too far.

Newcastle had never been in the King's innermost councils. Diplomatic subtleties were not in his line, and Charles's manoeuvres in Edinburgh, making friends with the insolent Scots, could have been little to his taste. The King, it is now plain, had his plans. He must neutralise the Scots, if he could not win their help, before confronting his enemies at Westminster. He must have an army, and he could raise one only by pretending that it was needed against the Irish rebels and to support the Protestant Elector Palatine in Germany.

Newcastle had no illusions about the need for a dependable army. The Duchess quotes his view 'that, without a well-ordered force, a prince doth but reign upon the courtesy of others'. He felt strongly, however, that 'great princes should be the only paymasters of their soldiers', finding the money themselves. 'For all men follow the purse', and the princes would thus 'have both the civil and martial power in their hands'. His aristocratic instincts were affronted by any claim by subjects to control that power. 'It is a great error in a state', he declared, 'to have all affairs put into gazettes, for it overheats the people's brains, and makes them neglect their private affairs, by over-busying themselves with state business.' Though these remarks were made in later years they owed much to that anxious autumn of 1641.

Parliament re-assembled while Charles was still in Scotland. On 17 November, even as he was adjourning his Scottish Parliament, there was a roll-call in the Lords at Westminster which did notl ist Newcastle among the absentees. Though there are no other clues to his whereabouts at this time, the Queen had been lobbying peers to turn up and defend the King from Pym's machinations behind his back, and it would be very unlike Newcastle to disregard her appeal. But he can hardly have been in London after Christmas, when matters came to a head.

By then Charles had returned and suffered the humiliation of the Grand Remonstrance, in effect a vote of censure, passed by a narrow majority, on his personal rule over the past eleven years. Now he had reason to fear that this overweening House of Commons planned to impeach the Queen herself. So, on his orders, the Attorney-General got up in the House of Lords on 3 January to accuse Pym and his associates of high treason. The next day saw the historic episode of the King's personal entry into the Commons and his unsuccessful attempt to arrest the said 'five members'. From that moment London was in the grip of a revolutionary fever. The Commons, to preserve their independence, removed to the safety of Guildhall. The citizens rose in arms to protect them.

Charles saw the overwhelming odds against him. On 10 January he fled from Whitehall with his family. Soon, from Windsor Castle, he was sending the secret instructions which reached Newcastle at Welbeck on 15 January.

He was, the Duchess records, 'to repair with all possible speed and privacy . . . to Hull, where the greatest part of His Majesty's ammunition and arms then remained . . . it being the most considerable place for strength in the northern parts of the kingdom'. Hull was vital also for communications abroad and the entry of troops and supplies. He was to take control as governor on behalf of the King.

For once Charles had chosen the right man, one of unquestioned loyalty and unhesitating obedience. In all his life Newcastle's courage was never doubted. Sometimes his energy was. But on this occasion he showed the vigorous action of which he was capable.

'All possible speed and privacy. . . .' He said no word even to Elizabeth, less some inadvertent sign betray his intentions. About midnight, says the Duchess, he 'hastened from his own house where his family were all at their rest, save two or three servants which he appointed to attend him'. One was his young equerry, Mazine, whom he had trained himself and considered 'the best horseman that ever I knew'. Together they rode off into the January darkness. They must have ridden hard, for, though the Duchess talks of forty miles, it must have been more like fifty or sixty. Newcastle was forty-eight. It was hardly the behaviour of a lethargic or indecisive man.

When the winter dawn broke they could see the great tower of Trinity church against the eastern sky, and the sullen tawny-yellow waters of the Humber, here three miles wide, tumbling down towards the North Sea. Hull still had its ancient walls. Each entrance was by a pair of gates and a pair of drawbridges over the ditches girdling the town on its landward side. Newcastle deemed it prudent to enter 'in the quality of a private gentleman'. Only when admitted did he reveal himself, and his mission, to the mayor.

At this juncture he needed all his nerve. Indeed, he had little else. His great name and reputation were not an unmixed asset in this Yorkshire town where Parliamentary sympathy was strong. His authorisation was dubious and unbacked by force. Even so, he imposed himself on Hull for the next three days, and might have held the place, if the King had followed up his action more promptly and Parliament less so.

News of the coup leaked. A message from the Commons to the Lords demanded that Newcastle 'show by what warrant' he had acted. On

20 January the peers – who included many frightened men and some who were positively in agreement with Pym – resolved 'that the Earl of Newcastle shall be sent to, to come and attend this House immediately, and the Lord Keeper is to write to his Lordship, to signify so much unto him'.

His Lordship had to think fast. Such a summons was no light matter. After the Army Plot he had no desire to get into trouble again. But if he left Hull now he would be throwing away everything he had gained. So before answering he sent Mazine to Windsor with an urgent report. Would His Majesty come to Hull himself or send official confirmation of his appointment?

The situation was becoming more difficult. Newcastle had hoped, by his personal influence, to attract armed supporters from the mainly loyalist gentry. Parliament meanwhile had named its own governor, Sir John Hotham, M.P. for Beverley near by, a veteran of the Thirty Years War, whose son was energetically recruiting townsmen with Parliamentary sympathies. Sir John had orders to march in and occupy the town. As nobody was anxious to fire the first shot, the mayor sensibly closed the gates against incoming troops of either persuasion. Newcastle remained inside, but virtually alone.

He might still have won the game. There were many loyalists in Hull and, as subsequent episodes indicate, he had a gift for combining an impressive manner with a charm that could win people of very different classes. But this time he was given no chance. The King's nerve broke. He told Newcastle, says the Duchess, 'to observe such directions as he should receive from the Parliament then sitting'. Hotham took over the town, and Newcastle set out for London to face the 'committee chosen to examine the grounds and reasons of his undertaking that design'. He offered no apology. He had obeyed the King's instructions. He was cleared of blame.

There was still lip-service to the King's authority. Parliament asked his permission to transfer the Hull munitions to London. Charles, by then established in York, delayed his answer and went to Hull, as Newcastle had earlier begged him to, to test his opponents' determination. But things had changed vastly between January and April. Hotham could admit no troops into the town without specific instructions from Westminster. Painfully embarrassed, he stood on the ramparts and explained this to the King waiting below, finally kneeling to protest his personal loyalty. Charles kept his temper for a time, though his followers broke into uproar, bidding the garrison throw Hotham over the battlements. When they declined, Charles himself lost control, bade his heralds proclaim the man a traitor, and, impotent to do more, rode furiously away.

Even this drama did not allow Newcastle's earlier attempt to be forgotten. King and Parliament continued to wrangle, by correspondence, over the January incident. Charles described Newcastle as 'a person of unblemished reputation', but in the Remonstrance of the Two Houses on 26 May Parliament complained, says Clarendon, that 'although there was not ground enough for a judicial proceeding, yet there was ground for suspicion; at least his reputation was not left so unblemished thereby as that he should be thought the fittest man in England for that employment'. He had been 'sent down in a private way'. Why did he 'disguise himself under another name'? That, the King answered, 'was because he had not that authority to make a noise by levying and billeting of soldiers, in a peaceable time, upon his good subjects, as it seemed Sir John Hotham carried down with him'. Clarendon, at this date still Edward Hyde, was using his cool lawyer's brain to phrase Charles's letters, but there is a flash of authentic Stuart in the response to the question, why Newcastle as governor of Hull and not Hotham? 'Because', answered the King, 'he had a better opinion of the Earl of Newcastle than of Sir John Hotham; and desired to have such a governor over his towns (if he must have any) as should keep them for, and not against, him.'

With armed conflict looking every day more possible the talk now was all of securing key points, arms supplies and the control of the various county militias. Parliament, with a hitherto obscure member named Oliver Cromwell as active promoter, tried to get this control by passing a bill. When the King refused his assent, it issued the Militia Ordinance with the same object but no need of his signature. The King's riposte was to issue Commissions of Array to his lords-lieutenant. It depended on the political climate in each county which of these two conflicting authorities was obeyed. Newcastle had to leave Nottinghamshire to his deputies, for on 29 June he was appointed governor of the town from which he took his title, together with jurisdiction over the four northernmost counties, Northumberland, Durham, Cumberland and Westmorland. With Hull in unfriendly hands it was vital to hold the other principal port on the east coast and safeguard communications across the North Sea to the Continent, where the Queen had now safely arrived with the Crown Jewels and would be sending over munitions and men, raised on their security.

Again the Earl acted with promptitude. Though he had neither funds nor forces beyond those he could provide for himself, he rose to the urgency of the occasion. Hurrying north to take up his new command, he paused in Durham and ordered the sheriff to mobilise the train bands to serve as a garrison for the town of Newcastle until volunteers could be enlisted. He was breaking the rule that the militia should not be made to serve outside their own county, and there was an outcry, which he ignored. He was able to march into Newcastle at the head of five hundred Durham men and take over the town without opposition, helped by the mayor, Nicholas Cole, and a leading merchant, Sir John Marley, whom he appointed deputy governor. He at once set the drums beating to re-cruit volunteers. It had been a near thing. Had he been a few days later, Parliament would have beaten him for possession.

It was tricky work in those early weeks. It was essential to strengthen the defences of the town itself and of Tynemouth close by. He con-scripted the labour of the local coal-miners, under the direction of some German engineers. The miners, being rather of the Parliamentary per-suasion, rebelled and rioted against the Durham militiamen. Eleven men were killed, but the unrest subsided. There was a mutiny of the train bands left in Durham. The Earl had to ride back with such forces as he could muster and pacify the dissidents. 'I like my Lord very well,' one blunt fellow conceded, 'but not his company.' Somehow men had to be spared at once to garrison the coastal defences at Shields and Tynemouth Castle, for any day might bring an attack from the sea. On 2 July the fleet had declared for Parliament. Robert Rich, that amusing travelling companion in Savoy long ago, now Earl of Warwick, had become its effective and energetic admiral. The blockade of the English Royalists was at hand.

Meanwhile the new governor did all he could to consolidate his position. In the surrounding countryside the Ogle connection was in-valuable; for, more than anywhere else in England, the tough border folk retained their old communal loyalties. From his own and his neighbours' estates the men flocked in, and soon he was reviewing the first companies of his immortal Whitecoats. He had meant to equip them all in scarlet, but only undyed cloth was available. Later on the soldiers preferred to stay as they were, vowing to colour their uniforms with the blood of the enemy. With such fierce followers he was less dependent on the town militia. He had been, in the Duchess's words, 'playing his weak game with much prudence', but every day strengthened his authority. He felt able, 'by the power of his forces', to reappoint the reliable Nicholas Cole mayor of Newcastle for another year. At Durham he instructed an equally reliable Royalist divine, Dr John Cosin, to censor 'all sermons that were to be preached, and suffer nothing in them that in the least reflected against his Majesty's person and government, but to put forth and add whatsoever he thought convenient'.

All this explains why, when the Civil War began on 22 August, with the hoisting of the King's standard on a hilly spur by the ruinous castle at Nottingham, the foremost Cavalier in that county was a conspicuous absentee.

ELEVEN

'The Business of Yorkshire'

To THE NORTHERN Royalists that September the new war must have seemed as unreal as, in another autumn almost three centuries later, a vaster conflict appeared to modern Englishmen.

There was no sudden clash of armies, for there were no armies ready. Far away in the Midlands the King and the Earl of Essex, Parliament's commander-in-chief, were recruiting their respective forces, but many, as in 1939, clung to the hope that after all this terrible thing could not happen. In Yorkshire, for example, the divided gentry were in no mood to plunge into mutual slaughter, and on 29 September a treaty was actually signed, with fourteen formal articles, between the Royalists, headed by the Earl of Cumberland, then Lord-Lieutenant, and the Parliamentarians led by Ferdinando, Lord Fairfax. Whatever happened elsewhere, their shire should not be ravaged by civil war.

This humane agreement was not imitated farther north, where news of it was received with dismay. The Earl of Cumberland, it was felt, was acting weakly if not disloyally. Fairfax was merely playing for time. Would Parliament honour his promise or disown it at the first favourable opportunity?

At Newcastle the new governor pushed on energetically with the recruiting of volunteers and their formation into regiments. Later he was to be criticised for accepting so many Catholics, and his force was dubbed, by hostile propagandists, 'the Popish army'. But the crisis was too grave for doctrinal prejudice and it would have been folly to refuse the profferred help of the Catholic gentlemen so numerous in the region. Indeed, from Shrewsbury on 23 September the King sent an explicit ruling, addressed to 'New Castel' in his own hand:

This is to tell you that this rebellion is grown to that height, that I must not look what opinion men are who at this time are willing and able to serve me. Therefore I do not only permit, but command you, to make use of all my

95

loving subjects' services, without examining their consciences (more than their loyalty to me) as you shall find most to conduce to the upholding of my just regal power. So I rest. Your most assured faithful friend, Charles R.

A month or two later, in a long-distance exchange of arguments with Lord Fairfax, Newcastle robustly defended his action, admitting that he had granted many commissions to Catholics but pointing out that they appeared very loyal to the King, which too many Protestants were not, and might very fitly be used to quell the rebellion.

All these troops, whatever their religious affiliations, had to be paid, clothed, armed and, if possible, given a ration of bread, cheese, meat and beer, though when real campaigning began they often had to be authorised to find 'free quarter', which was apt to degenerate into plundering. Foot soldiers expected six shillings a week, about as much as a farm-hand. Dragoons, fighting as mounted infantry, received roughly twice that, and cavalry troopers nearly three times. Nothing could be expected from the King. The northern Royalists had to finance themselves.

Arms were scarce. Parliament held most of the arsenals and the towns where fresh weapons could be made. Some of Newcastle's volunteers brought their own. Many gentlemen wore their rapiers, far from ideal in the hurly-burly of battle. Sporting guns, however, were not to be despised: a good fowling-piece was more accurate than a musket for picking off an enemy officer. There was a shortage of helmets, breast-plates and back-plates, but in any case less and less armour was now worn, except in aristocratic portraits, for horses were no longer bred to carry the weight. A tough coat of buff leather was the common wear. Newcastle tried to ensure that his army was adequately equipped, the Whitecoats and other infantry with pike or musket, the horsemen with sword and pistols and perhaps a carbine. He was thankful when a ship, having evaded the blockade, sailed into the Tyne with munitions from the King's uncle, Christian IV of Denmark. The arms included 'Danish clubs', and even they were welcome. Down in Warwickshire that October hundreds of Royalist infantry had nothing but cudgels.

Any general tends to put the interests of his own troops first, and in a war particularly fraught with jealousies and misunderstanding he was almost inevitably accused of getting more than his fair share of arms. Sir Marmaduke Langdale assured Sir William Savile in Yorkshire that Newcastle had 'far more than he can tell what to do withal'. Even the King expressed incredulity when his northern general protested his lack. To his own knowledge, said Charles, there had been plenty of weapons in the region. 'Therefore in God's name inquire what is become

Willm Cavendishe 1.stD
of Newcastle married :
1.st Eliz.th Daughter & hei
Willm Basset of Blore....
2.^d Margaret Lucas ...
Daughter to Thos Lucas
COLCHESTER, Es.^q

1. WILLIAM CAVENDISH, when 1st Earl of Newcastle, in the 1630s.

2. BOLSOVER: THE LITTLE CASTLE, begun by Sir Charles Cavendish in 1612, continued by William, and finished in 1630.

3. WELBECK ABBEY: the stables and gatehouse completed by John Smythson in 1625.

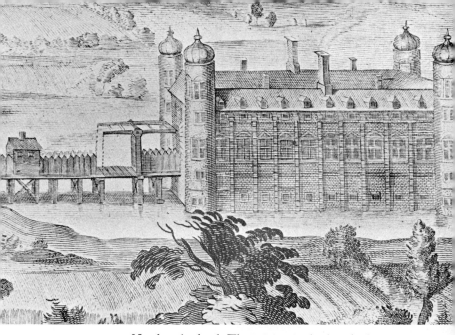

4. OGLE CASTLE, Northumberland. There is some doubt whether the castle ever looked like this, or whether the Flemish artist was working from an unrealised design for reconstruction.

5. NEWCASTLE HOUSE, Clerkenwell Green, a fashionable suburb for the town houses of the Caroline nobility.

6. NEWCASTLE'S FIRST WIFE, born Elizabeth Basset. William Larkin painted this portrait probably about 1618, when she was nineteen and had just lost her first husband, Henry Howard.

8. BOLSOVER: THE PILLAR CHAMBER, or withdrawing room, in the Little Castle. The horse motif of the vault-bosses reflects the young owner's great enthusiasm.

7. NEWCASTLE'S SECOND WIFE, born Margaret Lucas.

9. ANTWERP: the house and garden (today the Rubens Museum) where Newcastle spent his years of exile.

10. THE NEWCASTLES' ANTWERP HOME: the façade of Rubens's studio is on the left.

11. WILLIAM CAVENDISH, a miniature.

12. THE DUKE IN OLD AGE. The artist and date of this miniature are not known.

13. BOLSOVER: THE RIDING SCHOOL, built when the Duke was over seventy.

14 NOTTINGHAM CASTLE: Paul Sandby's west view brings out the dramatic quality of the site which so attracted the Duke

of them . . . for those who are well affected will willingly give, or lend them to you; and those who are not, make no bones to take them from them.' Newcastle may have been justly criticised, and he did not lay himself open again. When another consignment of arms slipped through the blockade, this time sent over by the Queen, he dispatched most of it to the King in the south, with a cavalry escort that should have been returned to him. However, the Duchess relates, 'His Majesty liked the troop so well, that he was pleased to command their stay to recruit his own army.' It was not the last time such an incident occurred. Charles was inclined to confuse an escort with a reinforcement, and to retain any detachment that came into his own theatre of the war.

Meanwhile, in the fields of Northumberland and Durham the new regiments trained without disturbance from the enemy. The musketeers learnt to shoot from beneath the shelter of the slanting pikes, the troopers practised their advance against the porcupine of bristling steel, their pistol volley and their last-minute wheel to the flank. Gentlemen who had served abroad with Gustavus Adolphus and other commanders introduced the new tactics that were coming in. Newcastle leaned heavily on their experience. His own contribution, apart from his wealth and the prestige of his name, lay in his administrative ability. At least those years as lord-lieutenant had taught him something about the creation of an army. At his elbow was his faithful secretary, John Rolleston, who continued with him throughout the war.

So did his brother, whose physical disadvantages did not prevent his taking a full share in all military operations. He 'charged the enemy, in all battles', Clarendon testifies, 'with as keen a courage as could dwell in the heart of man'. In those early months the boys at least, with their tutor, were at Bothal, and could be easily visited since they were only two miles off the highway running north to the border. On 9 November Sir Marmaduke Langdale was writing to Sir William Savile: 'My lord of Newcastle took this day an opportunity to see his children at Bottell Castle. It may be it was to be further in the county and to be near the danger to prevent the rising of the county. . . .' Not all the recruiting went smoothly, and some belligerent opposition was being shown by the wilder folk of Redesdale and upper Tynedale, so Newcastle may well have been combining business with pleasure. When the campaigning started the boys accompanied him, just as the two princes were at Edgehill with the King. The girls stayed with their mother at Welbeck, which was fortified and garrisoned as a Cavalier strong-point.

The quiet in the north was short-lived. Soon Newcastle was receiving urgent appeals for help from Yorkshire. The local agreement there had been broken, first by the younger Hotham, an experienced and forceful soldier, and then by Parliament's formal decision and its appointment of Lord Fairfax as its commander in the county. Nine years older than Newcastle, Fairfax was not a particularly dynamic leader, but he had a great following in the West Riding weaving towns. Also, his son Thomas had seen active service in the Low Countries which, with an aggressive spirit, was to make him, as the legendary 'Rider of the White Horse', the Roundhead answer to Rupert. So, with the Hothams dominating the coast, the Yorkshire Cavaliers found themselves suddenly in a desperate situation. The Earl of Cumberland, they felt, was not the man to lead them. Newcastle was familiar with all the personalities involved – in the small world of Caroline society most of the leaders were acquainted – and he could not disagree. He had to think hard. He had no authority to march into Yorkshire. Even if the emergency justified his acting on his own initiative, would these apprehensive gentlemen give him the support he would need? Would they, in short, dig into their own pockets? No nobleman, however rich, could finance these operations alone. Negotiations continued for some weeks. On 30 October he wrote bluntly:

I am very sorry you pleased to leave out the article for the officers' pay, or coldly referred it to your committee. . . . Last night when I was going to bed, there came colonels and lieutenant-colonels, and said they heard you had left it out, and for their parts that they must think that if you were so cautious not to grant it in paper before we came in, they doubted very much of it in money when they were there, and that the workman was worthy of his hire, and such like discontented words. . . .

If pay was not forthcoming, he foresaw mutinies or 'plundering without distinction', and it would be better not to come at all.

This time the answer must have satisfied him. By 9 November Langdale was writing to the Yorkshire Royalists asking them to have bread and supplies ready for his coming. An order was sent for light-weight cavalry saddles to be manufactured in York: the Earl would pay cash. A manifesto was to be printed in York, explaining his action, and 500 copies were to be sent for distribution in Durham and Northumberland, so that those counties should understand that they were not being deserted. Newcastle, though he would never have made a democrat, was an imaginative propagandist as well as an efficient organiser. In his Declaration in *Answer to Six Groundless Aspersions cast upon him by the Lord Fairfax* he showed himself a hard-hitting controversialist.

Leaving half his forces to protect key positions and communications, he marched south with 8000 men, of whom 2000 were cavalry or dragoons. His waggon-train included pontoon boats, a precaution against the enemy's denying him bridges and fords across the numerous fast and autumn-swollen rivers of the north. Now, for the first time, he found himself a military commander in the field. As his lieutenant-general he had Mountjoy Blount, Earl of Newport, who had been General of Artillery in the inglorious 1639 campaign and whose chief experience of warfare had been to be taken prisoner on Buckingham's disastrous expedition to La Rochelle. Though he was brother-in-law to the charming Olive Porter, his other associations – and the part he had played in the betrayal of the Army Plot – made him a slightly dubious comrade-in-arms. In marked contrast was the tall young Northumbrian William Widdrington, Newcastle's trusted personal friend, who presided over his council of war.

An oft-quoted incident, Newcastle's relaxing with a pipe in his coach before Marston Moor, has created a misleading impression that he campaigned in exceptional comfort. Of course he had a coach. So did Napoleon and Marlborough. No army can be directed without paperwork. Newcastle might have been happier in the saddle, but as a mobile headquarters his lumbering coach and six were indispensable. Letters had to be written, replies preserved, dispatches sent off by his attendant gallopers. He had to collect what maps there were, supplementing them with the services of local guides. It was a war, and a century, in which opposing forces tended to stumble about rather blindly, not always sure of their own whereabouts, let alone the enemy's. Telescopes, or 'perspective glasses', were scarce, but Newcastle, always interested in optical problems, was adequately provided. It may also be assumed that, like his brother, he possessed a pocket watch, but few officers did, so that synchronised action was difficult to ensure; if units were not too far apart it was much safer to rely on signals, a trumpet or a gun.

It was not long before he had his first taste of action. Captain Hotham tried to stop him at Piercebridge, where the Tees came swirling down between steep wooded slopes. There was an old three-arched bridge. Hotham planted an advance party at the northern end. Newcastle sent in two of his Durham regiments, one of infantry, one of dragoons, both incidentally under Catholic officers. They forced the crossing and routed Hotham's men.

Newcastle marched on to York without further opposition. There proudly, under the eyes of his paraded troops, he received the keys of the city from its governor, Sir Thomas Glemham, a distinguished professional soldier. The pacific Earl of Cumberland thankfully resigned as Lord-Lieutenant and retired from the scene.

The fledgling army had completed a gruelling eighty-mile march in November, but Newcastle could allow it only three days' rest. Lord Fairfax was barely ten miles away at Tadcaster on the River Wharfe, while upstream his son held another crossing at Wetherby. Newcastle decided upon a pincer movement. He himself, with the infantry and cavalry, would attack Tadcaster from the east. Newport, taking the cavalry and dragoons, would make a night march against Wetherby, and wheel round upon Tadcaster from the west. Lord Fairfax, expecting an attack, planned to withdraw to more favourable ground outside the town, but Newcastle's arrival on the morning of 6 December was too quick for him, and he could only order his men to their existing defences, covering the bridge.

Newcastle himself was not without problems. There was no sign of Newport's arrival to take the enemy in the rear. Delay meant losing the advantage already gained, so about eleven o'clock he sent his men against the bridge. The Roundhead musketeers waited calmly till the last moment, then poured a devastating volley into the advancing pikemen. For many it was their baptism of fire. They fell back, rallied behind some hedges, and came on again. Some of their own musketeers occupied a house overlooking the bridge, but the Roundheads counter-attacked, drove them out, and took numerous prisoners. A ding-dong battle raged until dusk, when both men and ammunition were exhausted. Fairfax told Parliament that 40,000 bullets, besides cannon-balls, had been exchanged. Newcastle sent urgently to York for more powder and matches, so that with dawn his musketeers could resume firing. But when dawn came, after a long cold night's bivouac in the fields, he found that Fairfax had slipped away. The road to the Puritan weaving towns of the West Riding lay open. As patrols advanced cautiously into Tadcaster a few stragglers surrendered. But for Newport's non-appearance the whole of Fairfax's little army might have been in the net.

What had happened? A local historian, Drake, wrote in 1736: 'Captain Hotham at the beginning of the fight wrote a letter to the Earl of Newport, signed Will. Newcastle, and sent it by a running foot-boy to tell him that . . . he might now spare his pains, and stay till they sent him orders the next morning. This sham letter had the desired effect. . . .' The Duchess does not mention this story, or even Newport by name, referring to him discreetly as the 'then Lieutenant General of the Army', but she does say: '(whether it was out of neglect or treachery that my Lord's orders were not obeyed) that day's work was rendered ineffectual as to the whole design.' In view of Newport's generally ambivalent career it may be wondered whether the sham letter was in fact written, or, if it was, whether Newport was genuinely deceived.

Cheated of a knock-out victory, Newcastle moved south and for the next month or two established his headquarters in the small hilltop town of Pontefract, with its Norman castle where Richard II had been murdered. There was now a wedge driven between the two Parliamentary areas. Lord Fairfax had abandoned the West Riding and withdrawn to Selby, closer to Hull. Seizing this chance, Newcastle sent Sir William Savile to occupy Leeds and Wakefield. Another column went to help the local Cavaliers at Newark, for, with the enemy now holding the Trent Bridge at Nottingham, it was vital to secure the other crossing downstream and preserve north–south communications with the King. He, having failed to force his way back into London, had established his headquarters in Oxford. On 15 December he wrote:

The services I have received from you hath been so eminent, and is likely to have so great an influence upon all my affairs, that I need not tell you that I shall never forget it, but always look upon you as a principal instrument in keeping the crown upon my head. The business of Yorkshire I account almost done. . . .

Newcastle read this optimistic encomium with mixed feelings. The business of Yorkshire was anything but done. He was still building up his army. At times he felt he had more officers than men. He knew he was criticised for granting commissions too freely to zealous gentlemen who then failed to muster their companies at full strength. But was he to reject such volunteers? None knew better than he the prickly pride of the well-connected. And even these under-strength units needed pay and arms. He had tackled the money problem with energy, calling on the gentry to subscribe and heading the list himself. For munitions he must look to supplies from abroad, and with Parliament holding both Hull and Scarborough these would have to be landed in Durham or Northumberland and reach him, riskily, by road. Similarly, an anxiety ever present in his mind was the coming of the Queen herself. Once she had done all she could for the cause, by diplomacy and fund-raising, she was eager to return to England. It had always been one of his main responsibilities to welcome her on landing and to safeguard her journey southwards with the supplies she would bring.

Scarcely had he digested the King's congratulations when bad news arrived from the West Riding. After initial successes Savile had been repulsed at Bradford with heavy casualties and had now lost Leeds again. Thomas Fairfax and John Hotham were roving Yorkshire in a dangerously restless manner, and Sir Hugh Cholmley was always apt to make irritating sallies from the safety of Scarborough Castle.

Fortunately the Parliamentary effort was not co-ordinated. Both Cholmley and the Hothams resented Lord Fairfax's authority and barely acknowledged it. There was even a chance that the younger Hotham might change sides and bring over his father. He was writing ambiguous letters on the pretext of an exchange of prisoners. At that early stage of the war there was still scope for civility, and the leaders on both sides were united by a common class interest. Hotham deplored 'these distractions, that hinder me from attending upon your Lordship'. He wrote:

If the honourable endeavours of such powerful men as yourself do not take place for a happy peace, the necessitous people of the whole Kingdom will presently rise in mighty numbers and whatsoever they pretend for at first, within a while they will set up for themselves, to the utter ruin of all the nobility and gentry of the kingdom.

Such sentiments chimed sweetly with Newcastle's. He gave them discreet encouragement. If the Hothams would turn their coats, or, as he saw it, revert to their proper allegiance, Hull might fall into his hands without a blow. For the moment, however, these tentative negotiations went no farther.

Meantime there was another tricky matter that demanded urgent attention. The annual election day for York's lord mayor was approaching. There was discontent in the city, uncomfortably overcrowded with troops, prisoners of war and refugees. It was vital to have a lord mayor who was politically dependable, so Newcastle wrote a polite 'request' to the Common Council that the outgoing Sir Edward Cooper be re-elected. He signed himself their 'very affectionate friend'. This brought a deferential deputation to Pontefract to say that, much as the Council would like to oblige the Lord General, their charter made it impossible. No man could serve two consecutive years. At this their 'very affectionate friend' nearly lost his temper. 'His Excellency answered that then he must march with his army. . . .' Newcastle's sketchy classical education had taught him more of Julius Caesar than of Athenian democracy. However, he recovered himself, studied the papers the councillors had brought, 'said it was a business of consequence', and promised a considered reply. The upshot was that he simply instructed the Council not to hold an election at all: then they could not be blamed for infringing their charter. Suspecting that this solution might not recommend itself, he took the precaution of telling Glemham, as governor, to ensure that no election took place. The Council did in fact decide to proceed, and the caretaker's wife, Mrs Garbutt, was just setting out the cushions in the hall when Glemham appeared, relieved her of the keys, and filled the place with 200 pikemen and musketeers. That was the end of the argument.

That very same day, 15 January, saw another event with a less satisfactory outcome. A detachment sent north to meet a munition convoy was cut up by Sir Hugh Cholmley at Malton. He defeated another Royalist force the following day and retired in triumph to his Scarborough stronghold. Elsewhere, Sir Thomas Fairfax was becoming more and more aggressive, and there were signs of a general Parliamentarian offensive. Newcastle decided to concentrate his forces, leaving only small garrisons in Pontefract and Tadcaster and shifting his headquarters back to York. There he put in hand the repair and improvement of the fortifications, which paid handsome dividends a year later but did not increase his popularity at the time, since the work involved compulsory labour by 800 townsmen every day and 800 men from the surrounding countryside. The rates went up, in some cases to sixteen times the previous amount, at Newcastle's insistence.

No offensive materialised. Things took a turn for the better. The hoped-for arms convoy was on its way, escorted by a retired Scottish soldier of fortune, James King, recently created Lord Eythin. Cholmley slipped out to intercept the convoy as it crossed the Tees. But Eythin, though elderly, had been a lieutenant-general under Gustavus Adolphus himself. He smashed Cholmley's force at Yarm and captured most of his infantry. He reached York in triumph with 120 waggons, laden with arms, ammunition and coin, sixteen cannon, and a string of packhorses carrying muskets.

He was most welcome also in his own person. Newcastle had discovered the double-dealing of his second-in-command. No certain details are known, but apparently Newport was planning to kidnap the Queen when – as was now expected any day – she arrived from Holland. It was a credible enough story, given Newport's record and connections. It was one of his half-brothers, Warwick, who commanded the navy that was trying to prevent her return, and another, Newcastle's old enemy the Earl of Holland, was constantly changing sides, being at this date with the enemy. Newcastle had had enough. He placed Newport under arrest and appointed Eythin lieutenant-general in his stead. Later, Newport was released and continued his equivocal career throughout the war, but not in the north. We hear of his visiting Warwick's flagship in the Channel and of his being 'present', surely the *mot juste*, at the second Battle of Newbury.

In Parliamentary eyes there was no traitor worse than Newcastle himself. On 2 February he was impeached in the House of Commons for his earlier actions in Northumberland, and it was resolved that he, along with Hyde and nine others, should be expressly excluded from any future amnesty. Endymion Porter was also in this list, grim news for Olive, who had stayed in York when her husband rode south with the King before the outbreak of the war.

For a month past Henrietta had been trying to make the arduous winter crossing of the North Sea. Once she had been driven back by appalling weather. She sailed again, with a Dutch naval escort under Martin Van Tromp to protect her against Warwick's vice-admiral, William Batten, who was watching for her. On 22 February she landed at Bridlington, a small fishing-port perilously situated midway between the Parliamentary strongholds of Hull and Scarborough. The long-awaited news reached Newcastle who, whether by accident or informed calculation, was then at Pocklington, well on the way to the coast. He at once dispatched his cavalry to ensure her safety and followed with his main forces as fast as he could.

TWELVE

'A Sweet General'

THE QUEEN was in high spirits, though shaken by her latest adventures. She had supposed herself safe ashore, lodged in a quayside house with her ladies, who included Endymion Porter's young daughter, Marie. During the night, however, five Parliamentary vessels had moved into Bridlington Bay and opened a bombardment. What happened next the Queen poured out to Newcastle in much the same words, we may imagine, as she put into a letter to her husband:

The balls were whistling upon me in such a style that you may easily believe I loved not such music. Everybody came to force me to go out, the balls beating so on all the houses, that, dressed just as it happened, I went on foot to some distance from the village to the shelter of a ditch . . . but, before we could reach it . . . a sergeant was killed within twenty paces of me.

Her courage was indisputable. Despite the hail of fire, she insisted on rushing back to rescue her dog Mitte, who slept in her bed and had been left behind. When the story of that night and the good news of her safe return reached Oxford, they were treated more grandiloquently by William Cartwright, one of the younger Jonsonian disciples:

> When greater tempests than on sea before
>   Received her on the shore;
> When she was shot at 'for the King's own good'
>   By legions hired to blood;
> How bravely did she do, how bravely bear!
> And show'd, though they durst rage, she durst not fear.

In fact, Batten's squadron 'durst rage' only for a short time, and had withdrawn before Newcastle's arrival. Van Tromp, lying in the offing with his bigger warships, had made it clear that he would blow them out of the water if the bombardment continued. The Queen saw the whole incident as a dastardly personal attack. Newcastle, yielding to none in loyalty and chivalry, could still quite understand Batten's point of view.

The Queen had brought rather more than her seasick ladies-in-waiting, her dog and (probably) her devoted dwarf, Jeffrey Hudson. She had with her more than a thousand Royalist volunteers returning from the Continent, enough arms and ammunition to fill 250 waggons, and £80,000 in cash for the cause.

This money, she soon made clear, she felt unable to touch for her own needs. 'Her Majesty,' writes the Duchess, 'having some present occasion for money, my Lord presented her with £3,000 sterling, which she graciously accepted.' By the end of her stay in Yorkshire even the Queen realised that his purse was not inexhaustible and that the finances of the northern army were precarious. 'And by the road I gave six thousand pieces,' she told Charles, 'for without that, they could not have marched; but this truth should not be known by everybody.'

After the bombardment she moved three miles inland to the greater safety of Boynton Hall. Its owner, Sir William Strickland, being a Parliamentary supporter, was not unnaturally absent, but his family did the honours and set out all their gold and silver plate. When, after the unloading of all her cargoes and a review of Newcastle's troops, she set off on the forty-mile journey to York, she took all this plate with her, nominally on loan, and with a gesture which may or may not have charmed the family left in its place a portrait of herself.

As if the week had not been full enough of romantic drama, there was now the unscripted entrance of that colourful character, the Earl of Montrose. Having long abandoned his early Covenanter sympathies – he had been Alexander Leslie's second-in-command – he was hurrying southwards to urge upon the King the advisability of an armed initiative in Scotland. Hearing of the Queen's arrival, he turned aside to wait upon her at Bridlington, pouring his vehement proposals into ears still ringing with enemy gunfire. She, with commendable forbearance, said she would consider his ideas at leisure when she got to York. This she did, and his enemy, Hamilton, predictably advised against them. Hamilton was sure that Scotland could be kept neutral and that Montrose was talking wildly when he foretold an invasion by the Covenanters. Within the year Newcastle, for one, must have wished they had listened to Montrose.

Another unexpected arrival at Bridlington was Captain Hotham, who rode over from Beverley under safe conduct to discuss the exchange of prisoners. He stayed the night and talked confidentially with Newcastle. He and his father were prepared to change sides. The terms? Sir John to be a viscount and governor of Hull for life; a barony for himself; and £20,000 between them. Whatever Newcastle's private opinion, he said nothing to discourage Hotham. His immediate concern was to get the Queen and her invaluable convoy inside the walls of York. Strung out along the open road, those waggons would be terribly vulnerable to the cavalry and dragoons Hotham had left at Beverley. Perhaps, too, the fellow was justified in arguing that it would serve the King better if he chose the right moment to come over, instead of doing so at once. They parted with the understanding that Hotham would not harass the Queen's journey and Newcastle would not attack Beverley or Hull.

The Queen reached York on 8 March, escorted by Newcastle with eight troops of cavalry and fifteen companies of infantry. The Lord Mayor and aldermen welcomed her on Heworth Moor, outside, the only jarring note being the Recorder's speech, 'full', reported the *Weekly Intelligencer*, 'of disloyalty to His Majesty'. She was conducted to the mansion of Sir Arthur Ingram, the normal lodging of royal visitors. It was a palatial and luxurious residence, its garden walks adorned with statues and topiary, and the whole area, with its fishponds, tennis court and bowling green secluded within high walls, ideal for security. Olive Porter was now all too briefly united with her daughter. The young maid of honour died a few days later, probably from the hardships of the journey from Holland, and was buried in the Minster. Endymion had sent a disguised messenger with a letter to Newcastle which vividly indicates the disturbed state of communications:

I beseech your Lordship not to wonder at this tattered Mercury, as we have had such luck in our cavaliers as we thought this the best way to secure letters. I am extreme glad that the Queen is safe arrived. . . . I have long wished to place my wife in the Queen's Bedchamber. I beseech your Lordship to do in it as you shall think best and oblige me according to your accustomed goodness.

Newcastle never received this letter, or the enclosure from the King to the Queen, for the 'tattered Mercury' was detected *en route*, and the captured papers were read aloud to the House of Commons a few days later.

For an unquestionably affectionate wife, now more than a year separated from her equally devoted husband, Henrietta Maria showed no great impatience to continue her journey to Oxford. She was in many ways enjoying herself. Though deferring to protocol and using a coach for her entry into York, she had otherwise ridden horseback, taken *al fresco* meals at the roadside, and chatted with the soldiers with a freedom that charmed them but would have won her an icy reprimand from the King. Now, installed in Ingram's splendid house, she could take a full part in all the secret conversations that were going on, a personage in her own right, woman and Catholic though she was, no longer obstructed by those suspicious and resentful Protestants surrounding her husband.

Newcastle had always got on well with her. True, her arrival took something away from the almost royal powers which had been delegated to him. He had even the right to bestow knighthoods, a right most rarely accorded to a subject and one which, in the event, he used most sparingly. But if her presence dimmed the personal glory which he transparently enjoyed, he showed only pleasure in her protracted stay, according her all that courtly deference of which he was past-master, while preserving his independence where, as in military dispositions, the responsibility was his own.

Her being in York was useful in winning over Cholmley, that constant thorn in the Cavalier side. Newcastle began the negotiations and sent him a written pass, so that early one morning he entered the city in disguise with a patch over one eye. Henrietta Maria wrote gleefully to Charles: 'Sir Hugh Cholmley is come in with a troop of horse to kiss my hand; the rest of his people he left at Scarborough, with a ship laden with arms, which the ships of the Parliament had brought thither. So she is ours.' Cholmley stayed overnight and returned as secretly as he had come. He was to have three clear weeks before declaring himself, so that his family could escape from London. His plans were betrayed prematurely by the Hothams, who intercepted his messenger at Hull and, since they believed in keeping their options open, tried to retain Scarborough in Parliamentary hands. Cholmley, however, won over most of his garrison and held the place, but now for the King.

Captain Hotham, still carrying on his devious correspondence with Newcastle, strove to minimise the significance of Scarborough. 'You have got . . . but an old castle, which will cost you more keeping than it is worth.' Newcastle tried to tie him down, but he shied away. 'For a letter to the Queen, that I will certainly come in and at such a time, I cannot do it. This enclosed you may show her, if you please, or burn. . . .' The Queen was certainly kept informed of these intrigues, for she wrote to the King: 'Young Hotham hath gone to his father, and 260 [code for Newcastle] waits for your answer.'

Egregious in an era of slippery characters, the captain seems to have been equally prepared, if possible, to win credit with Parliament by subverting Newcastle. Protesting 'my particular affection to your person', he dropped dark hints:

To give you a taste that all is not as you think at Court, I shall freely tell you this, that within this four days some very near her Majesty spoke such words of contempt and disgrace of you as truly for my part I could not hear them repeated with patience, and you will plainly see, if they dare it, you will have a successor.

Newcastle demanded details, and two days after Hotham's first letter – interesting evidence of the speed with which these communications could pass through enemy lines – a second one was on its way.

The words were these: 'that you were a sweet general, lay in bed until eleven o'clock and combed till twelve, then came to the Queen, and so the work was done, and that General King did all the business.' They were spoken by my Lady Cornwallis in the hearing of Mr Portington ... with many other words of undervaluing, which he said were spoken by others .... You can expect nothing at Court: truly the women rule all. ... You have now done great service; that will be forgotten when they think they can shift without you.

Later, on 4 May, came a further innuendo: 'It was said from a good hand that the Queen thought much you did not enough communicate with her and take her directions.' Though some of these slanders were clearly self-contradictory they did not contribute to Newcastle's peace of mind. His loyalty, nevertheless, was unfaltering. In the end Hotham did not come over. Being offered a Parliamentary command in Lincolnshire, he judged it the wrong moment to change sides. Yet it can hardly be said that this long correspondence led to nothing: it was the Hotham letters, falling into Parliamentary hands with Newcastle's coach at Marston Moor, that led both father and son to the block as traitors.

It is certainly true that Newcastle was the object of much criticism. He had many jealous enemies among the courtiers at Oxford and there were others whose comments must be taken more seriously. Clarendon, while terming him 'one of the most valuable men in the kingdom' and 'a man of great courage and signal fidelity to the Crown', has left us the description that has coloured every subsequent estimate:

He liked the pomp and absolute authority of a general well, and preserved the dignity of it to the full; and for the discharge of the outward state, and circumstances of it, in acts of courtesy, affability, bounty and generosity, he abounded, which, in the infancy of war, became him, and made him, for some time, very acceptable to men of all conditions. But the substantial part, and fatigue of a general, he did not in any degree understand (being utterly unacquainted with war), nor could submit to; but referred all matters of that nature to the discretion of his Lieutenant-General King.

Clarendon concedes that when there was any fighting Newcastle was always on the spot, and testifies to his 'invincible courage', well documented by others, but he goes on:

Such actions were no sooner over than he retired to his delightful company, music, or his softer pleasures, to all of which he was so indulgent, and to his ease, that he would not be interrupted upon any occasion soever; insomuch as he sometimes denied admission to the chiefest officers of the army, even to General King himself, for two days together; from whence many inconveniences fell out.

This, if a true picture, would be damning. One can only test it, incident by incident, against the recorded facts, the times and dates and distances, of Newcastle's campaigning. It is hard to reconcile this description with that midnight ride to Hull, the patient reception of his officers, anxious about their pay, who came pressing into his headquarters when he was preparing for bed, or his meticulous attention to details, from the ordering of new saddles to the printing of manifestos, before his advance into Yorkshire. Nor, as one follows the subsequent course of events, does Clarendon's picture become any more convincing.

Clarendon, it must be remembered, was a civilian who detested and distrusted the generals. He found Prince Rupert and Prince Maurice, Sir Charles Lucas and even that stalwart old hero Jacob Astley, all in one way or another unsatisfactory. While, as a prudent lawyer, he liberally documents his main narrative, he cites no specific occasions when Newcastle was lethargic or negligent. That he is writing from hearsay is indicated by his admission that 'the whole transaction of the northern parts, where the writer of this history was never present, nor had any part in those counsels, [was] fit for a relation apart' by a more proper person. Though he adopts a deceptively judicious tone, balancing his criticisms with complimentary phrases, his verdict remains highly suspect.

Only slightly less familiar is the passage from Philip Warwick, Royalist M.P. and one of the King's secretaries at Oxford, who at least visited Newcastle's headquarters in the north. After praising him as 'a gentleman of grandeur, generosity, loyalty, and steady and forward courage', Warwick regrets that:

his edge had too much razor in it; for he had a tincture of a romantic spirit, and had the misfortune to have somewhat of the poet in him. . . . This inclination of his own and such kind of witty society (to be modest in the expression of it) diverted many counsels, and lost many opportunities, which the nature of that affair this great man had now entered into, required.

This is a vaguer criticism – a sincere opinion, though, based on a first-hand impression, if perhaps that of an impatient courier who feels that his own business has not been given its due priority. The Civil War was admittedly full of 'lost opportunities', on both sides and in most theatres. It is easy with hindsight to declare that a wrong decision was made. There was constant disagreement between the King's Oxford head-quarters and the autonomous northern army. Clarendon and Warwick, both with Charles, were naturally inclined to doubt whether Newcastle was taking the right line. Between them, they have created and perpetu-ated the common view of Newcastle as a commander, and too seldom has it been questioned. In one breath he is criticised as an inexperienced amateur and in the next for delegating too much to his professional second-in-command. Both writers seem indignant that he chose to relax in 'delightful company' and 'witty society'. Would they have preferred hard drinking, like Goring's? Or gambling for high stakes? Even the most zealous general has some free time and must occupy it.

In those first months of 1643 Newcastle was building up his staff. Since appointments and disappointments go together, jealousy may have contributed to the whispers against him. Lord Eythin, still com-monly referred to as General King, was four years older than his chief – fifty-three – immensely experienced, but, as Clarendon remarked, with 'the unavoidable prejudice . . . of being a Scotsman'. Young Charles, Viscount Mansfield, was nominally his father's General of the Ordnance, which was about as sensible as his election, two years earlier, as M.P. for East Retford. Both positions have to be seen in their seventeenth-century context. The boy had, as his Lieutenant-General of the Ordnance, the Poet Laureate, William Davenant. The alcoholic Goring was General of the Horse, assisted by another Charles Cavendish, the younger brother of the Earl of Devonshire. Intelligence was in the charge of a Scout-Master-General, the Rev. Michael Hudson, D.D., sometime Fellow of the Queen's College, Oxford.

Here seem to be all the ingredients for a good laugh. As T. Longueville wrote in 1910, 'We find the army of the North, therefore, under a Commander-in-Chief who was utterly inexperienced . . . a drunkard for General of cavalry, a poet for General of Artillery, and a very able divine for "Scout-Master-General".' Yet on close inspection the list appears less risible. Newcastle owed his original appointment to his political import-ance and his organising experience as a lord-lieutenant: when tested under fire, he proved himself more than adequately. Goring, primarily the Queen's choice, not his, indeed 'strangely loved the bottle' (as his secretary, Bulstrode, tells us) and was 'a great debauchee'; but at his best he was a dashing and inspiring leader, a balance to the cautious Eythin. Davenant, true, is now mainly remembered as a writer of masques and plays and an irrepressible theatrical promoter, but he had already served as paymaster of the ordnance in the 1639 campaign. A *protégé* of Endymion Porter's, he had returned to England with one of the Queen's earlier munition consignments. It is most likely that he accompanied her when she went south – his knighthood later in 1643 was conferred by the King himself for gallantry at the siege of Gloucester, so in any case his service with Newcastle must have been very short. As for the apparent incongruity of placing 'a very able divine' in charge of military intelligence, there is no reason to sneer at Hudson, a proto-type of those university scholars who demonstrated their adaptability in the wars of our own century. Hudson fought implacably for the King, whose escape in disguise he helped to contrive after the disaster at Naseby. Despite reprisals against his wife and children, he never gave up the struggle. He was barbarously murdered in 1648, his hands hacked off as he dangled from the battlements of a moated house he had tried to defend. The other Charles Cavendish, from Chatsworth, might appear a glaring case of nepotism, but in fact he was Goring's choice and, though only twenty-two, had already proved himself on active service abroad and at Edgehill. He had a brilliant but tragically brief career, being killed at Gainsborough.

Most of Newcastle's other appointments do not even call for justifica-tion. Besides Eythin, the staff included various officers of impressive experience, such as Glemham, Sir Francis Mackworth as Major-General, and Ralph Errington as Quartermaster-General, a post he had held in 1640.

By late March, his army strengthened in numbers, equipment and morale, Newcastle marched north to concentrate at Malton, so that he could support Cholmley when he defected. The ensuing loss of Scar-borough alarmed Lord Fairfax and, feeling exposed, he began to with-draw towards the West Riding. Newcastle promptly swung round and moved westwards. Fearing interception, the Parliamentary commander ordered his son to create a diversion. Sir Thomas Fairfax exceeded his instructions, retook Tadcaster, and started to demolish its defences. By then Newcastle had reached Wetherby, a few miles up-river. He immedi-ately dispatched Goring with a force of cavalry and dragoons to deal with Sir Thomas. This, on a hot spring day on Seacroft Moor, he accomplished in masterly fashion. The younger Fairfax escaped with a handful of horsemen to join his father at Leeds, but of his infantry 200 were cut down and 800 sent rumbling off in carts to York as prisoners.

That was 30 March. Through April Newcastle was mainly occupied in consolidating his improved position, reoccupying Wakefield with a large garrison under Goring, and coping with other urgent problems, such as his secret negotiations with Hotham. It is unfortunate that his movements cannot be exactly plotted with dates and places. For we know that on 17 April his wife died at Bolsover, but we have no record that he was able to reach her side. He was, it seems, present at her burial in the family tomb there two days later.

THIRTEEN

Divided Councils

How much did Elizabeth's death mean to Newcastle? He was nearly fifty. He had known almost twenty-five years of stable marriage in a period when few people reached old age with their original partners. Even the younger Hotham had been married three times, his father five. Yet, while such bereavements were the common experience, like the appalling infantile mortality, there is no reason to assume that the individual suffered less grief than he would today.

Public duties had imposed frequent separations. What with these, and Elizabeth's health and her husband's passionate nature, there had clearly been infidelities, but nothing approaching open scandal or estrangement. The records of the time are full of known liaisons and of bastards later claiming an illustrious paternity, but nothing like that is alleged against Newcastle. If Clarendon's ambiguous reference to 'his softer pleasures' and Philip Warwick's to 'witty society (to be modest in the expression of it)' have a sexual connotation, they cannot certainly be dated back to the first months of the war while Elizabeth was still alive. It would be even more unwise to take literally the innuendo in a scurrilous Roundhead pamphlet: 'And for Newcastle, he's . . . at best but a playwright; one of Apollo's whirligigs; one that when he should be fighting, would be fornicating with the Nine Muses, or the Dean of York's daughters . . .'. Even the Duchess, while coyly admitting his susceptibility, never suggests that his first marriage was anything but happy.

Now it was ended. Elizabeth was laid to rest. Leaving Welbeck and Bolsover in Jane's competent hands, with garrisons under Colonel Van Peire and Colonel George Muschamp respectively, he hurried back to his headquarters. He had the company of his sons. Frances would be safe with Jane. Young Elizabeth and her husband were far away in Parliamentary territory. John Egerton was not yet twenty and, though Royalist in sympathy, had avoided active involvement. Riding north, Newcastle had no lack of problems to distract his mind, but his personal preoccupations were real enough and should not be forgotten when we turn to his conduct of affairs at this difficult juncture of the war.

Goring's victory at Seacroft Moor had opened up possibilities of a decisive blow against the main Roundhead forces in the West Riding. These, after asking for a parley, had now received reinforcements, taken fresh heart, and broken off negotiations. Newcastle had to decide whether to risk a frontal attack upon them at Leeds. The council of war was divided. Goring, characteristically, was all for storming the town. The Queen supported him. Eythin was cautious, as usual. He argued (she wrote to the King on 24 April) that this might 'cause the ruin of all the army, by too severe a slaughter'. The final decision had to be Newcastle's, and it was a hard one. He had built up this army – he alone knew by what effort – and Eythin's warning could not be ignored. It is arguable that this was one of several opportunities he missed. It is arguable indeed, with hindsight, that his reliance on his veteran chief-of-staff was excessive throughout his command. But equally the affair at Leeds could have turned out disastrously, and he would have been plausibly condemned for disregarding professional advice. He could only ponder the arguments and make the best choice he knew. In a cavalry charge he was as fearless as Goring or Rupert, but as a responsible commander he was closer in age and temperament to Eythin, and inevitably more inclined to accept his view.

If he missed a chance at Leeds, he was energetic enough elsewhere. He put a strong garrison into Wakefield under Goring and Mackworth and cut off vital supplies from the Pennine weaving towns farther west. He sent patrols south to Barnsley and heard that the enemy were recruiting round Rotherham and Sheffield. To counter this threat, he marched thither early in May. At Rotherham the enemy had thrown up hasty defences and, despite the heavy odds against them, they rejected his formal summons to surrender. He accordingly opened up an immediate bombardment and took the town by storm that night, capturing a great stock of arms and a useful £5000 in coin. There was, almost inevitably, a good deal of disorder. Fairfax later complained that Newcastle had broken faith and plundered the place. The contemporary rules of war would in fact have justified his doing so; for, if a defending commander in a hopeless position compelled his opponent to waste the lives of his men in an assault, he sacrificed any right to quarter and any immunity from pillaging. It seems likely, however, that Newcastle did as the Duchess says he did – kept the officers as prisoners of war and encouraged the rank-and-file to enlist in his own forces. But probably there was some looting in the darkness, and unnecessary bloodshed, beyond his control. When he marched on to Sheffield there was no resistance. He was able to walk into the castle, Uncle Gilbert's old home. He was within a couple of hours' ride of his own two houses. What was more important, he held Sheffield's ironworks. Henceforth they would cast cannon for his army.

Now, though, came news of a setback. At Wakefield Goring had been surprised in a night attack by Sir Thomas Fairfax, who had been hardly less surprised himself when he 'found three thousand men in the town, and expected but half the number'. Goring was captured, with many of his troops and much precious ammunition. Fairfax called it 'more a miracle than a victory'. What Newcastle and Eythin called it is not on record.

They displayed remarkable resilience. Not only had the lost troops to be replaced, they had to provide a massive escort for the Queen, about to start her belated journey to Oxford. She left York at the beginning of June. They accompanied her as far as Pontefract, where another crucial council of war was held. The King feared an attack upon Oxford. Should Newcastle continue south with her, taking the whole northern army? Optimists saw a golden chance to unite with the southern Royalists and smash the enemy. Others, like Eythin, saw the peril of leaving an unbeaten opponent behind them: the Wakefield débâcle had just underlined it. There were also the regional feelings so potent in the Civil War. These northerners had little zest for triumphs in the Thames Valley while their own homes lay defenceless to Roundhead reprisals. Newcastle explained to the Queen that he could not ask this sacrifice of them. He detailed his young cousin, now Lieutenant-General Charles Cavendish, to continue as her escort with 7000 men. From Newark, where she released him with 2000 of them, she wrote to Newcastle on 18 June: 'The King is still expecting to be besieged in Oxford. . . . He had sent me a letter to command you absolutely to march to him, but I do not send it to you, since I have taken a resolution with you that you remain.' She signed herself 'your constant and faithful friend'. Such incidents show how difficult it was for the King, as a supreme commander, to achieve any co-ordinated strategy.

Pocketing this cordial communication, Newcastle turned to restore the position in the West Riding. On his road lay Howley House, belonging to Lord Savile, then at Oxford with the King. A stone building, strongly fortified, it had been seized and garrisoned by his Roundhead cousin, Sir John Savile. Newcastle demanded his surrender. Sir John refused, though once the Royalist army had surrounded the house and brought artillery into action, his situation was hopeless. Much as Newcastle disliked useless bloodshed, he had no choice but to order an assault next morning. Though he would have been justified in adding the instruction 'no quarter', he merely proclaimed that Sir John, as the responsible individual, should be shown no mercy. The house was duly stormed, with inevitable casualties, and he was not best pleased to see Sir John marched into his presence without a scratch. He exclaimed angrily, whereupon the apologetic escorting officer offered to have his prisoner shot. No, said Newcastle, it was inhuman to kill any man in cold blood. And he accepted from Sir John the keys denied him the previous day.

It was a week before the advance was resumed. The weather had turned foul, and it was difficult to drag supply-waggons and artillery, especially the big guns, Gog and Magog, over the clogging mire and ruts. They were now in Roundhead country, where information about the enemy's strength and whereabouts was reluctant and unreliable. Nor could the council of war agree whether to move against Leeds or Bradford, or to seek Lord Fairfax wherever he was to be found.

At last they got moving, and by the night of 29 June they pitched camp on the ridge of Adwalton Moor, five miles south-east of Bradford. There, the next morning, they were surprised to see Lord Fairfax and his army approaching. The surprise appears to have been mutual. Fairfax came on. His force looked larger than Newcastle had expected. He did not know till afterwards that his enemy had just been reinforced with twelve infantry companies and three troops of cavalry from Lancashire. Nor, at that distance, could he see that the advancing array included an untrained mass of 'clubmen' who were, as Thomas Stockdale wrote next day to the Speaker of the House of Commons, 'fit to do execution upon a flying enemy, but unfit for other service'. Newcastle was not alarmed by the apparent strength of his adversary, however, for – though the several eyewitness accounts differ widely – there seems no doubt that he had superiority in numbers. He was strong in cavalry, but missed the inspiring Goring to lead them. The ground was not what he would have chosen, for it was broken up with innumerable little coal-workings and traversed with hedges through whose gaps the horsemen could ride only two abreast. Fairfax, on the other hand, had an unusually high proportion of musketeers, for whom such a terrain was ideal. He came on with unwonted determination and battle was joined.

Considerable confusion followed, with charges and counter-charges, in which Sir Thomas Fairfax led his father's small force of cavalry. The Roundhead musketeers lined the hedges and peppered the Cavaliers to good effect. There was hand-to-hand fighting among the mine-shafts. A backward movement by some of the Cavaliers was misinterpreted by their enemies as the start of a retreat. In fact it was probably an outflanking manoeuvre, skilfully executed by Eythin, to throw his cavalry reserve between Lord Fairfax and the town behind him. At a crucial moment Newcastle himself made a characteristic intervention, described in the official preamble to the patent which a few months later created him marquess: 'Our army so pressed upon, that the soldiers now seemed to think of flying; he, their general, with a full career, commanding two troops to follow him, broke into the very rage of the battle, and, with so much violence, fell upon the right wing of those rebels, that those . . . turned their backs.'

Lord Fairfax, fearful of being cut off, now fell back hastily on Bradford, and thence to the greater safety of Leeds. His son, having lost touch with him, fled independently along the Halifax road and reached Bradford by a long detour. Nearly all their recent Lancashire reinforcements made hurriedly for home across the Pennines. Newcastle took 1400 prisoners and 500 Roundheads were left dead on the field. His own casualties had been remarkably light and he had no difficulty in getting his triumphant troops on the road again. By nightfall he was outside Bradford, with his headquarters at Bowling Hall, a mile away. The next morning, having established his batteries on high ground dominating the town, he began a bombardment. Suspecting that the defenders were short of ammunition, he also made sham attacks at intervals to draw their fire.

To offset Bradford's low-lying situation, Sir Thomas placed two drakes, or lightweight cannon, with a strong force of musketeers, on the tower of the parish church below the steeple. As these proved a serious nuisance, Newcastle concentrated fire upon them. The defenders tried to protect the steeple with great bales of wool. The best Royalist marksmen then shot at the cords with remarkable success – if we consider the inaccuracy of seventeenth-century firearms – and 'shouted full loudly when the pack fell down'. The bombardment continued, giving the unprotected steeple 'many a sad shake', and presumably its defenders also, for after a day or two their position became untenable and the Royalist patrols were able to enter the outskirts of the town.

On the Sunday morning, anxious to avoid a bloody house-by-house struggle, Newcastle had a drum beaten for a parley. Sir Thomas sent two officers. He seemed ready to surrender on reasonable terms, but, as he might be merely playing for time, Newcastle continued with preparations to assault if necessary. A message came from his opponent complaining that these were a breach of the understanding. Newcastle's answer did not appear to satisfy Sir Thomas. Some time after midnight, concluding that the negotiations had broken down, Newcastle resumed the bombardment and sent in his troops.

Resistance at first seemed determined and even desperate, but even a local eyewitness and strong Parliamentary supporter, Joseph Lister, admitted that, despite his forebodings of vengeful massacre, 'not more than half a score were slain'. When day broke, most of the Roundhead infantry surrendered. Their cavalry had escaped in the darkness. The order had been *sauve qui peut*, and Sir Thomas had obeyed it as literally as any of his men, for he was last seen as a solitary rider galloping into the dawn. His young wife, riding pillion behind a servant, had been taken and was now ushered into Newcastle's presence as a prisoner of war.

He was, needless to say, equal to the occasion. Lady Fairfax, now best remembered for her fearless protest at the King's trial five years later, was then twenty-five, with a daughter of four at home. Daughter of Sir Horace Vere, Fairfax's old commander in the Low Countries, she was probably a most welcome arrival in the Royalist headquarters. Newcastle entertained her for some days 'with all civility and respect' and then, lending her his own coach and servants, dispatched her to rejoin her husband who had reached the safety of Hull. Sir Thomas himself acknowledged his 'generous act'.

Lord Fairfax had also fled to Hull, abandoning Leeds, where the Royalist prisoners broke free and took over the town even before Newcastle arrived. Now, apart from Hull, he was undisputed master of Yorkshire. There was one setback when Gainsborough was lost to Parliament in a surprise attack and his cousin Charles, attempting to recover it, was defeated by Meldrum and Cromwell. Young Cavendish was stabbed to death, as he lay helpless, by a Roundhead officer. The war grew savager.

Otherwise, Newcastle's military fortunes were at their zenith. He marched to Gainsborough himself. His cannonade set part of the town on fire and after three days it surrendered. Lincoln fell to him without a blow. Cromwell sent out a frantic appeal for reinforcements: 'Haste what you can. Lord Newcastle will advance into your bowels. Better join when others will join ... than stay till all be lost; hasten to our help.'

In this flush of triumph Newcastle sent Major Cartwright to Nottingham to demand its surrender, but Colonel Hutchinson refused 'to yield on any terms, to a papistical army led by an atheistical general', his brother adding that 'if my lord would have that poor castle he must wade to it in blood'. There was less fighting spirit at Westminster. On 7 August the Commons found only a small majority to vote down a proposal to make peace.

Philip Warwick now arrived from the King, crossing the country at some peril, with 'but three or four words under the King's hand, written on a piece of white sarsenet' as his authority, to inquire what Newcastle 'meant to do with his army'. The Royalist strategy, so far as it existed, called for a three-pronged advance upon London by Newcastle, the King's Oxford army, and his West Country supporters. This was the suggestion, scarcely an instruction, conveyed to Newcastle. By way of encouragement he was given the additional appointment, on 19 August, of lieutenant-general in the counties of Lincoln, Rutland, Huntingdon, Cambridge and Norfolk.

Things were not as simple as they looked to the King and his advisers far away. Lord Fairfax had replaced the untrustworthy Sir John Hotham at Hull. He was raising fresh forces, getting arms and equipment by sea. Hull was no beleaguered fortress but a potential sally-port through which a new Roundhead army could pour forth and overrun Yorkshire. The northern Cavaliers looked over their shoulders, thought of their homes, and were reluctant to go farther south. Make sure of Hull, advised Eythin. For once even the Queen supported the cautious policy against the King's wishes. She wrote to Newcastle: 'He had written me to send you word to go into Suffolk, Norfolk or Huntingdonshire. I answered him that you were a better judge than he of that, and that I should not do it. The truth is that they envy your army.' Warwick thought Newcastle was unwilling to subordinate himself to Prince Rupert. If the Royalist manner of running the war seems a tragic farce, it is fair to remember that the Parliamentary command often behaved little better.

Newcastle's decision, again endlessly debatable, was to attack Hull first. He opened the siege on 2 September, bombarding the town with red-hot shot, a tactic that had succeeded at Gainsborough but which this time achieved little. Lord Fairfax countered by breaching the Humber dykes and flooding his entrenchments. Philip Warwick went round the lines and criticised them. Newcastle answered him with a theological witticism, 'You often hear us called the Popish army – but you see we trust not in our good works', which, when repeated to the impatient

Cavaliers in Oxford, did not much amuse them. In fact, Newcastle's men had put a good deal of effort into the construction of forts and earthworks at Sculscoat, Gallow Clowe and other points round Hull. He might have been wiser to control his love of repartee. He remained confident, promising the King that he would come south as soon as he could but that his Yorkshire troops 'utterly refused to march until Hull was taken'. To Prince Rupert he wrote, 'I have no despair in time of Hull'.

The Queen remained his constant, if sometimes embarrassing, supporter. As the siege entered its sixth dispiriting week, his 'faithful and very good friend' wrote for his opinion: 'The Marquis of Hertford desires to be made groom of the stole to the King. If that be, he must cease to be governor to Prince Charles, so that we must place some one else about Prince Charles, which I do not wish to do, without first knowing whether you wish to have it. . . .' Alternatively, she continued, in this extraordinary proposition to a commander so deeply immersed in military operations:

there are two other places and I desire to know which would be most agreeable to you for I have nothing in my thoughts so much as to show you and all the world the esteem in which I hold you, therefore write frankly to me, as to a friend, as I am now doing to you, which you desire: *chamberlain, or gentleman of the bedchamber.*

Newcastle chose to soldier on. October came in, wet and cold. The besiegers shivered in their dank entrenchments. The defenders were in good heart behind their massive ramparts, encouraged by a thousand reinforcements landed from the estuary. Their sorties grew more impudent. At dawn on 11 October Newcastle was brought word at his headquarters at Cottingham of suspicious movements on the ramparts opposite: his sentries had observed the twinkling matches of innumerable musketeers. Fairfax was evidently planning a surprise attack. In fact, the real surprise was more ingenious. As the Royalists mustered to repel a sortie on this northern side of the town it was from the west gates that a powerful attack was launched upon their front-line positions. Royalist reserves charged and won back the lost ground, but the Parliamentary forces rallied, established themselves in some of the Royalist forts, and turned the guns on the besiegers.

While Newcastle was grappling with this problem he received disastrous news from his friend Widdrington, who had been crushingly defeated that same day by Cromwell at Winceby in Lincolnshire. The

Parliamentary cavalry, reported Widdrington, were now 'very good' and extraordinarily well armed. That night Newcastle faced the unpalatable facts. He was not going to take Hull and, with this Lincolnshire reverse exposing his flank, he dared no longer dally in the flooded fields outside. Winter was at hand. He must cut his losses. Without wasting another hour, he gave orders to raise the siege and fall back on York. It was ironic that just two weeks later, on 27 October, he was made Marquess of Newcastle-upon-Tyne with a eulogistic recital of his earlier successes.

Court gossip may have depicted him idling in his headquarters, hearing music, talking books and neglecting his responsibilities, but it becomes increasingly hard to reconcile that picture with the records of the campaign. Within a week of his leaving Hull he had to cope with an invasion of the West Riding from Lancashire and a new threat from Derbyshire, where his persistent adversary, Sir Thomas Fairfax, was busy 'seducing the people'. He dispatched Mackworth and Windham to deal with the Lancashire Roundheads and himself set off for Derbyshire early in November.

Fairfax was at Chesterfield, barely seven miles from Bolsover. At the mere appearance of Newcastle's advance guard, silhouetted on the hills in the sunset, Sir Thomas made a hasty midnight retreat to Nottingham, leaving numerous stragglers to be taken prisoner. Newcastle established his headquarters in Chesterfield for the next few weeks. There were skirmishes in various places, but he had the satisfaction of liberating Chatsworth, without firing a shot, from its garrison of 300 Roundheads. His young cousin, the Earl of Devonshire, was loyal enough in his politics but, after impeachment and expulsion from the House of Lords, he had left England before the outbreak of war and had prudently remained abroad.

By December there was no enemy force nearer than Derby. Sir Thomas had withdrawn to Lincolnshire. The Lancashire incursion had been repelled. Besides restoring the position in Derbyshire, Newcastle had spent an active month recruiting fresh regiments there, obtaining equipment for them from Yorkshire and securing valuable supplies of lead from the mines of the Peak. He now felt he could hand over the local command to Lord Loughborough and march his own forces, by way of Bolsover, to Christmas quarters at Welbeck. It had been a strenuous year and he had just reached his fiftieth birthday.

Though the family was temporarily gathered together again it could hardly be like the old Christmases. The Abbey had become a fortress, permanently garrisoned and now surrounded by a whole army. The war was never far from anyone's thoughts. Dispatches came and went. Newcastle was in regular correspondence with Prince Rupert. 'I am infinitely bound to you', he told the King's nephew on 4 January, 'for giving Sir Charles Lucas leave to come to this army and to come with so many horse.' Lucas, a dashing cavalry commander, was an invaluable addition to the staff, and his appointment as Lieutenant-General of the Horse soon followed. Newcastle was also occupied in making another effort, through one of his officers who was a close friend of George Hutchinson, to achieve the surrender of Nottingham. These conversations came to nothing, and he could hardly have been surprised. The Hutchinson brothers were country gentlemen of the type he understood and respected, wrong-headed, of course, but men of honour, not to be bought.

That January brought one message which altered everything: the Scots had come over the border, and as allies of Parliament.

FOURTEEN

'If York be lost. . . .'

How far did the invasion come as a surprise? The Scots had long been negotiating with the English Parliament. For obvious reasons they feared a victory by the King who had so recently tried to impose an unwanted ritual upon their church. On the other hand, 1643 had ended with the North of England, except for Hull, firmly in Royalist control, and they were not so fanatical as to hurl themselves unnecessarily against a formidable enemy. Recent heavy snowfalls also seemed to rule out immediate danger.

Ideally, of course, a commander prepares for every contingency. No one would have been happier than Newcastle to maintain an adequate deterrent force on the border, but it could not be done. In this odd, amateurish war he lived from hand to mouth, having not only to command his troops but to recruit them, raise funds for their equipment and pay, and then somehow keep them together and induce them to serve where he wanted them. His dispositions cannot always be judged by modern professional standards. On this occasion he had already sent one of his most experienced officers, Glemham, to inspect the defences in Northumberland. Probably he inclined, as usual, to the advice of Eythin, who had been so long abroad that he may not have been the most reliable forecaster of what his fellow Scots would do.

In fact, the long-discussed alliance had been confirmed in Edinburgh while Newcastle was occupied in Derbyshire. Almost within hours the Scots had received the first instalment of the money promised by the English Parliament to finance their invasion. Faithful to their contract, they appeared at Berwick on 18 January, led as in 1639 by old Alexander Leslie, Earl of Leven.

The Marquess hurried back from Welbeck. Despite his recent recruiting efforts his main army was much depleted since the summer, when he had deployed 15,000 men round Hull. On 28 January, the day he left York for Newcastle, he wrote to Rupert: 'I know they tell you, sir, that

I have great force; truly I cannot march five thousand foot, and the horse not well armed. . . . Since I must have no help, I shall do the best I can with these.' The Scots numbered 'fourteen thousand as the report goes'. He might have blenched had he known that this was an underestimate. They had actually 18,000 infantry, 3000 cavalry, 500 dragoons and 120 guns.

It would be a desperate race for the town from which he took his title. Glemham was falling back from Alnwick, demolishing bridges and delaying Leven as best he could. Newcastle sent Eythin ahead with the first troops. In the end, the old soldier of fortune, so often criticised for caution, left his men to follow as fast as possible and rode hell-for-leather to encourage the town's small garrison by his own arrival. The Marquess was close behind. He left the new governor of York, Sir John Bellasis, to muster all the further troops available.

It was foul weather for forced marches – first snow, then thaw and floods. Luckily it slowed the Scottish columns more than the hard-riding Cavalier generals. For men of their years both the Marquess and his lieutenant made excellent time. He himself reached Newcastle on 2 February, 'the night', he was able to inform the King, 'before the Scots assaulted the town'. Leven was astounded to learn he was there. His summons to surrender had been addressed to the mayor and corporation, a breach of etiquette which, to the Royalist commander, was as glaring as a breach in the walls.

The Scots had expected no opposition. They now had to await the arrival of their heavy artillery by sea. Even when it was hauled into position, on 7 February, Leven was slow to start serious operations. The 'sweet general' was more aggressive. He burnt the northern suburbs to deprive the besiegers of cover, a painful and unpopular act, and he ordered the sinking of ships in the Tyne to prevent a naval attack on his rear. He also managed to inflict so many casualties on the Scots that, rather belatedly, they had to fetch surgeons from Edinburgh.

So far, so good. Nevertheless, on 13 February a realistic appreciation of the position warned the King that his northern supporters were 'beset' by a 'great Scotch army before us' and were now threatened also in Yorkshire by the Fairfaxes, father and son, and another 'great army about Newark'. The Marquess's own force amounted only to 5000 infantry and 3000 cavalry. The latter, always a mixed blessing in a beleaguered town, he sent back across the bridge into Gateshead, whence they made some useful raids upon outlying Scots units, notably at Corbridge.

Late in February Leven made a move. Leaving enough men to maintain the somewhat apathetic siege, he marched his main army inland, as if intending to cross the Tyne and bypass the town. The weather was grim. A blizzard was followed by high winds and more snow. For nearly a week the Scots camped in the open, strung out for miles along the river bank. They made no attempt to cross by any of the numerous fords and the Marquess concluded that they would not until the weather improved. Unwisely, he relaxed his own cavalry patrols – this was one of his least pardonable errors of judgement as a general – and Leven seized his chance. His men waded through the icy river at three different places. By 4 March his army was in Sunderland, having traversed the Durham countryside.

It was not in fact quite the catastrophe it should have been. The Scottish army, though large, well paid and well equipped, was deficient in training and fighting spirit. Leven did not exploit his success with any triumphant sweep southward. The Marquess was able, if not fully to retrieve the situation, at least to contain it. He left a sufficient garrison to hold the town of Newcastle and marched after the invaders, trying to bring them to battle. Whenever they came within striking distance the canny Leven took up a position where the Royalist cavalry could not charge him. These chess-like manoeuvres went on for a month, Leven using Sunderland as a base while Durham city became the Cavalier headquarters. Here Montrose made another of his characteristic appearances, requesting troops for a guerrilla campaign in Scotland – not in itself a bad idea but one which Newcastle had not the men to support. He received Montrose courteously but could provide only a small detachment.

It was grim campaigning weather, that March. Food must have been short, for the Queen wrote banteringly from the comfort of her Merton College rooms at Oxford: 'My cousin, I have received your letter . . . and am very glad you have not yet eaten rats. So that the Scots have not yet eaten Yorkshire oatcakes all will go well, I hope, as you are there to order about it. Your faithful and very good friend, Henriette Marie R.' Newcastle was constantly in the field but not until 24 March was he able to engage the enemy. That Sunday afternoon there was a fierce infantry clash near Sunderland, renewed next day when he threw in his cavalry, now usefully strengthened by Sir Charles Lucas and his men from Yorkshire. The Scots were driven back into Sunderland, where the weight of their artillery prevented the Royalists from pressing their advantage. Newcastle was far too weak to attempt a siege – his one hope was to beat Leven in the open field – so he withdrew to Durham, thirteen miles away. That same day he wrote ominously to Prince Rupert: 'If your Highness do not please to come hither, and that very soon too, the great game of your uncle's will be endangered, if not lost.' He was clearly in low spirits, feeling not only that 'fatigue' he was supposed to avoid so skilfully – he had in fact been campaigning almost continuously for eighteen months – but also the criticisms that filtered through to him from court. These provoked him to offer his resignation. On 5 April the King seized pen and wrote back in his own hand:

By your last dispatch I perceive that the Scots are not the only, or (it may be said) the least enemies you contest withal at this time; wherefore I must tell you in a word (for I have not time to make long discourses) you must as much contemn the impertinent or malicious tongues and pens of those that are or profess to be your friends, as well as you despise the sword of an equal enemy. The truth is, if either you, or my L. Eythin leave my service, I am sure (at least) all the North (I speak not all I think) is lost. Remember all courage is not in fighting; constancy in a good cause being the chief, and the despising of slanderous tongues and pens being not the least ingredient. I'll say no more, but, let nothing dishearten you from doing that which is most for your own honour, and good of (the thought of leaving your charge being against book) Your most assured real constant friend, Charles R.

This encouraged Newcastle to renew his plea for help, but another personal letter from the King brought little comfort: 'you must consider that we, like you, cannot do always what we would; besides our task is not little that we struggle with. . . . You may be assured of all assistance from hence that may be, without laying ourselves open to imminent danger. . . .'

By the time he broke the seal of this missive Newcastle was facing 'imminent danger' of his own. It was not just that Leven was on the move at last and established near Durham on Quarrington Hill. It was the staggering news from Yorkshire. Bellasis had been defeated and captured by the Fairfaxes at Selby. Most of his infantry and guns were lost. York itself was threatened. Just as, three months earlier, he had had to leave post-haste for the north, now he must rush back with equal urgency to save the situation in his rear. It was 12 April. He can have wasted no time, for on 16 April he was marching his army in good order through the gates of York. Leven was following at a cautious distance and had made no attempt to harry his retreat.

Newcastle needed all his fortitude as he took stock. Only the city garrison of 500 men remained to supplement his weary army, now re-

duced to 4000 infantry and 3300 cavalry. The latter he dared not keep
for lack of fodder if he was to be cooped up inside the fortifications.
These were strong enough, since all the recent work, and long enough
in all conscience – over three miles of ramparts to be manned – and some
outlying gun-posts might allow the townsmen still to graze their stock
in the westward meadows, but such pasture would not keep cavalry
chargers fighting fit. So regretfully, and just in time, as the armies of
Leven and Fairfax took up their allotted positions encircling the city,
he sent Sir Charles Lucas and all but a few hundred of the cavalry to
escape under cover of darkness to the north Midlands, where they would
be of more use to the cause.

He was now, he reckoned, outnumbered roughly four to one. The
odds would worsen if the Earl of Manchester came up from East Anglia,
as he might, with the army of the Eastern Association. The Scots, having
shed some stragglers, were down to less than 17,000. Fairfax had only
5000, but they were better soldiers, and as Newcastle paced the battlements he saw that they covered a sector on the east almost as long as that
held by the Scots to the west. For all their numbers the besiegers could
not complete the encirclement, and on the northern part of the perimeter
their two armies were linked only by a tenuous line of outposts. The
Ouse divided them, and, since Newcastle controlled the permanent
crossings, they had to build a pontoon bridge downstream before they
could move troops quickly from one side to the other. In those first
weeks they seemed content to consolidate their hold on the country
round about, but who could tell when they might attempt an assault,
perhaps at several points simultaneously?

He had told the King he could hold out for six weeks, perhaps eight,
but hoped for relief earlier. His most likely deliverer was Rupert, whom
Charles had sent in January to deal with the Parliamentary forces in
Cheshire and Lancashire, fearing lest 'they may lose me all those
counties, not without hazard to my Lord Newcastle's armies, whose
assistance and advice I hope you will not want in this business. In all this,
I show you but my wish and opinion yet in no ways to prescribe you,
but freely to leave you to your own judgment, as being upon the place.'
These phrases are significant when Rupert's later strategy is considered.

While the Prince was busy in the north-west, Newcastle made preparations for a long siege. He ordered a search of food stocks throughout the
city. They were plentiful, but he fixed a basic daily ration. The unpopular
burden of billeting his soldiers was fairly apportioned. Army funds were
low, and those who shirked paying their dues were firmly dealt with.

One fugitive Northumbrian had arrived in York with £800: when he refused to make a contribution Newcastle seized the cash and two of his horses, valued at another £60. All 'the Gentry and Inhabitants' had to swear an oath of loyalty, nearly forty lines long. A special prayer was prescribed before the sermon in the Minster, when, after remembering the royal family, the archbishops and clergy, Oxford and Cambridge, the congregation were pointedly invited to 'beseech God to be near unto him . . . whose affairs have a nearer and more immediate influence upon us here, his Excellency, William, Marquess of Newcastle, Lord General of his Majesty's Forces in these northern parts . . .'. The near and immediate influence of his lordship was not in doubt.

Gratifying though it was to hear these sonorous phrases unrolling over his bowed head, Newcastle would have welcomed some definite answer. Rupert had taken Stockport and Bolton, with great slaughter of Roundheads. Lucas had joined him. So had Goring, released in an exchange of prisoners. Now the Prince was marching on Liverpool. When would he remember York?

Meanwhile, the Earl of Manchester was approaching, with Cromwell as his lieutenant-general and 9000 men. The city would now be closely encircled. On 31 May Newcastle asked leave for ladies to pass through the lines. It was refused. Four days later Manchester's army of the Eastern Association took over the northern sector. Communications with the outside world became increasingly difficult. Finally they were reduced to signal fires on the Minster roof, which it was hoped might be interpreted in Pontefract.

The allied generals had now some 30,000 men against 4800 or less, and there was no excuse for inaction. Batteries were planted closer to the walls and on 6 June Manchester's troops penetrated the suburbs. Two nights later the Scots attacked the three outlying forts in the western meadows and took two: Newcastle held the third by a vigorous sortie, using some of his few mounted men. The next day Fairfax tried to mine the Walmgate Bar. To deprive the enemy of cover, Newcastle set fire to some of the suburbs, but the wind helped the besiegers to put out the flames. 'We are now', wrote one Scotsman, Robert Baillie, 'within pistol-shot of the walls, and are ready to storm it . . . it cannot but be a bloody business.' Newcastle still had no notion when, if ever, help would arrive. Playing for time, he wrote to Leven in courteous indignation: 'I cannot but admire that your Lordship has so far beleaguered this city on all sides, made batteries against it, and so near approached to it, without signifying what your intentions are, and what you desire or expect, which is contrary to the rules of all military discipline and customs of war.'

With no less courtesy Leven answered, preserving the fiction that he was not in rebellion against Charles, that he wished to reduce the city 'to the obedience of King and Parliament'. Negotiations, in which Manchester and Fairfax joined, went on for a week, a truce being maintained. Newcastle's representatives insisted that his whole army should be allowed to 'depart with colours flying, drums beating, match lighted, with their arms, etc', while the other side put forward quite different conditions. These the Royalist commissioners refused even to submit to their commander, and Leven had to send a copy himself the next morning. Newcastle rejected the terms with the same air of pained surprise as he had adopted at the start of the discussions. It was 15 June. He had gained a precious week. It is probable that he had never seriously considered surrender.

On the previous day the hard-pressed Charles wrote to Rupert:

If York be lost, I shall esteem my crown little less . . . but if York be relieved, and you beat the rebel armies of both kingdoms, which are before it, then but otherwise not, I may possibly make a shift (upon the defensive) to spin out time, until you come to assist me: wherefore I command and conjure you, by the duty and affection which I know you bear me, that (all new enterprises laid aside) you immediately march (according to your first intention) with all your force to the relief of York. . . .

It was a doom-laden letter. When the King told Lord Culpepper the courtier exclaimed: 'Why, then, before God you are undone! For upon this peremptory order he will fight, whatever comes of it.'

At York the besiegers had not been idle during the talks. The next morning, Trinity Sunday, there was a shattering explosion at the north-west corner of the city, where a mine was set off under St Mary's Tower, which collapsed outwards, leaving a convenient slope of rubble by which Lord Manchester's assault troops could clamber up. Inside stretched the gardens, bowling green and orchard of the Manor, normally the official residence of the Lord President of the Council of the North. Here there now raged a sanguinary struggle with Newcastle's White-coats, whom, according to the Duchess's account, he energetically rallied and led in person. Five hundred Roundheads had got in, but in a short time fifty lay dead, 250 were taken prisoner, and the remainder went slithering down the bank of rubble in ignominious retreat. To Newcastle's relief there was no attempt to follow up the assault and no attack elsewhere. The mine had been an individual effort by one of Manchester's divisional commanders, informing nobody, and the chance of synchronised action by the other armies had been thrown away.

Nor did the next few days produce more than the usual exchange of shots. The besieging armies were dispirited. There was sickness in their ranks and near-mutiny in Fairfax's regiments. That general was writing to the Committee of Both Kingdoms on 18 June that 'many run away, who I cannot in justice punish having nothing to pay them withal'. Newcastle's men were also behind with their pay, but at least they were unable to desert. Though Manchester's men were well paid, and the Scots adequately, the latter were, like Fairfax's men, very short of ammunition.

On the day Fairfax wrote his letter, Rupert at Liverpool was opening the King's. Stung by its tone, he made swift preparations to obey. Newcastle, now completely isolated, knew nothing. In a desperate bid to make contact with Rupert wherever he was, he sent out nine separate messengers. Only one got through the enemy lines.

The besieging generals were better informed of the Prince's movements. He was sweeping over the Pennines with 8000 infantry and 6500 cavalry. By 26 June he was at Skipton, on 30 June at Knaresborough, only fourteen miles away. That night Newcastle's sentries, accustomed to whiling away the hours of darkness in conversational exchanges with the enemy outside the walls, found that they were getting no response. The summer dawn revealed that the besiegers had vanished, leaving their baggage and siege artillery. About noon a certain Captain Legg rode in with the news that Rupert was near. Newcastle dashed off a dispatch of emotional gratitude:

You are welcome, Sir, so many several ways, as it is beyond my arithmetic to number, but this I know you are the redeemer of the North and the saviour of the Crown. Your name, Sir, hath terrified the great generals and they fly before it. It seems their design is not to meet your Highness for I believe they have got a river between you and them, but they are so newly gone as there is no certainty at all of them or their intentions, neither can I resolve anything since I am made of nothing but thankfulness and obedience to your Highness' commands.

FIFTEEN

Marston Moor

ALTHOUGH numerous dispatches had passed between them, Newcastle had not set eyes on the Prince since his English visit in 1637, when he had stayed at Welbeck. Rupert had spent three years as a prisoner of war in Austria. Since rushing to his uncle's aid in 1642, he had been wholly occupied in operations elsewhere. He was General of the Horse and was subordinate to no one but the King. The Marquess's own commission made him equally autonomous in the north, but he had tried to counter malicious gossip by emphasising to Charles that he 'would never make the least scruple to obey the grandchild of King James'. Now, though fully prepared to defer to the Prince, he not unnaturally looked forward to being consulted, and it is clear from the King's earlier letter to his nephew, hoping he would have Newcastle's 'assistance and advice', that Charles expected the same. Rupert could know nothing about the state of the garrison, and he would presumably want to hear all that Newcastle could tell him about the strength and morale of the allied armies and the likely reactions of their three different commanders.

Newcastle knew that his own men, though still full of fight, were as tired as he was. He had promised to hold out for six, perhaps eight, weeks. The flag was still defiantly flying after ten. Before that there had been a similar period of campaigning in bitter winter weather, including desperate forced marches, first to the Tyne and then back to York. It had been a rough time. And though, ironically, tomorrow should have been pay-day, his weary troops had not received a penny for weeks past. Who could blame them if, at this moment, they were scouring the deserted enemy lines for anything they could pick up?

Even the impetuous Rupert, after his cyclonic sweep across the Pennines, would be glad of a breathing space. Their combined forces would still be outnumbered, but the very size of the enemy armies would make it hard for Leven, Manchester and Fairfax to keep together in the field, away from organised camps and supplies. After a few days they would be forced to draw off in different directions. Shortage of food and fodder, added to differences of opinion between the generals, would break down the uneasy alliance. There was another argument against too hasty action: Rupert would be glad to know that any day now would see the return of Sir Robert Clavering, lent by Newcastle to Montrose but now coming south with 2000 men, perhaps more. Such reinforcements were worth waiting for.

So, as the Duchess records, 'my Lord immediately sent some persons of quality to attend His Highness, and to invite him into the city to consult with him'. He was piqued when, in place of Rupert, Goring arrived as his messenger, not to consult but to convey his orders. Goring's position was ambiguous. After the prisoner exchange three months before, he had claimed his old post as Newcastle's General of the Horse, with Lucas demoted to second-in-command. The cavalry were by then operating independently in the Midlands, but were distinguished from other formations as 'the Northern Horse'. Since May the Prince, never a man to argue with, had virtually taken them over. So that night Goring faced Newcastle, who was still nominally his general but who had not seen him since his disastrous defeat at Wakefield, and delivered Rupert's instructions. Newcastle and Eythin were to join him on the road at four o'clock in the morning, with all their forces. He had out-manoeuvred the enemy by approaching York from an unexpected direction, and they were now falling back southwards by a route that took them west of the city.

There were to be no consultations, no courtesies. Newcastle mastered his resentment and ordered the garrison to parade at two o'clock in the morning. He kept back only a small force under Glemham to hold the city. Eythin was more rebellious. He had served with the Prince on the Continent in 1638 and blamed his rashness for their defeat at Vlotho, when Rupert was captured. His latest notion, to take on 30,000 men with 20,000, seemed utter madness.

The responsibility for what happened in the next twenty-four hours is as warmly debated by modern historians as it was by the participants. There are good arguments for Rupert's bold gamble, though no excuse for his inadequate liaison with Newcastle. The Marquess may have been over-cautious and unimaginative. He may have stood too tetchily upon his dignity, though to be strictly accurate he did not stand, but moved, albeit not as rapidly as the Prince expected. Unaccustomed though he was to peremptory orders, he did not disobey. Nor did Eythin –

flagrantly – though there seems little doubt that he dragged his feet to the point of sabotage.

Two hours after midnight the garrison duly paraded. Inevitably there had been some slackening of discipline, some excessive celebrations of the city's deliverance, but subsequent events show that there was nothing seriously wrong with Newcastle's army. As they mustered in the July darkness the word went round that they would be paid before they marched off, and that Eythin had given orders accordingly. Whether he had will never be known. He denied it afterwards. There may have been a genuine misunderstanding or an unfounded rumour which, because it really was pay-day, the men were eager to believe. At all events, they broke ranks, some slipping away to forage for loot in the empty quarters of their late besiegers. It was not easy to round them up again. Arthur Trevor, not an eyewitness but a Cavalier who arrived with dispatches later that day, recorded that 'the Prince [an obvious error] and the Marquess of Newcastle were playing the orators to the soldiers in York (being in a raging mutiny in the town for their pay) to draw them forth ... which was at last effected, but with much unwillingness'. Rupert, of course, was miles away, unaware of Newcastle's problems, but it is entirely in character that Newcastle should indeed be rushing from place to place in the dawn light, haranguing his men. And that finally, aware that he was already late and trusting Eythin to bring up the main body of infantry as fast as he could, he set off with his small mounted column to the rendezvous.

He left the city by Micklegate, taking an old paved track, now vanished, which led to the village of Hessay. The enemy, in their retreat towards Leeds, had spent the night round the next village, Long Marston, and Rupert was eager to catch them before they got away.

There is no need to recount in detail the oft-told story of Marston Moor or to discuss the all-too-plentiful evidence, mostly honest but much of it wildly contradictory, afforded by numerous eyewitnesses and contemporary reporters. It was, more than most battles, a muddle, heroic tragedy mingling with black comedy. It is, however, possible to disentangle a reasonably coherent record of Newcastle's personal experiences.

Some time that morning – nine o'clock, noon, there is no certainty – he caught up with Rupert, by then fuming with impatience. The Prince was still only twenty-four and even in later years never learnt to be tactful. He cut short Newcastle's apologies, observing coldly, 'My lord, I wish you had come sooner with your forces, but I hope we shall yet have a glorious day.'

Newcastle now had a chance to survey the position. The old track through Hessay had brought him to a great expanse of moor, boggy in patches, dotted with gorse and furze. To the south, at the foot of the gentle slope, there was a road. Beyond that there was a hedge and then a steeper hillside covered with ripening corn. On that hill opposite – there were actually two ridges, one above the other, with a dip between – the enemy were busy taking up their positions. Rupert had been in time to overtake their rearguard, which was commanded by their best fighting generals, Leven's son, David Leslie, Sir Thomas Fairfax and Cromwell. Unlike their elders, these men were quite ready to try conclusions with the Prince. They had stood their ground and sent an urgent appeal to the main armies, which had marched as far as Tadcaster but were now hurrying back.

Rupert was positive (again the documentary evidence is debatable) that he had the King's absolute instruction to force a battle. Newcastle could only beg him to delay, at least until Eythin came up with the infantry. He had, he insisted, 'four thousand as good foot as were in the world'. Rupert saw the sense of that, but his temper was not improved as the hours passed. Eythin did not appear until mid-afternoon, possibly with the deliberate intention of making it impossible to attack that day.

The Prince now made amends for his previous discourtesy. He produced a draft of his battle dispositions and invited their opinions. The elderly Scotsman spoke his mind: 'By God, sir, it is very fine in the paper, but there is no such thing in the field.' He thought the line had been drawn up too close to the enemy and on unfavourable ground. When Rupert offered to make changes, he said it was too late. The Prince was still determined to attack. The old antipathy flared up between them. 'Sir,' said Eythin, 'your forwardness lost us the day in Germany, where yourself was taken prisoner.' Newcastle, with no part in that old quarrel, could only stand there, infinitely embarrassed. When an opportunity offered, he inquired what service the Prince desired of him.

Rupert seems never to have given a plain answer, for when the battle took place the 'Lord General' of the northern army was assigned no specific responsibilities and fought as little more than an individual gentleman volunteer. Probably Rupert meant only to postpone his decision, for he remarked that, as it was now so late, he would not after all fight until next morning. Was he sure, Newcastle inquired, that the enemy would not? The Prince was confident that the initiative lay, as usual, with himself, and, observing that Newcastle had left his coach standing on the trackway in the rear, suggested that he 'repose himself till then'. This may have been genuine thoughtfulness for a man more than twice his age, or there may have been a flick of sarcasm. Pointedly he himself went off to supper and did not honour the Marquess with an invitation to join him.

Newcastle accordingly retired to his coach and sought consolation with his pipe. He had scarcely lit up when he was startled by 'a great noise and thunder of shooting'. The Prince, by now 'set upon the earth at meat a pretty distance from his troops', had misjudged the enemy. Leaping from his coach, Newcastle saw their whole line moving down from the ridge opposite, a human wave about to break upon the Royalists. With only two or three hundred yards between the armies, there was little time to think. He could only arm and swing himself into the saddle. At that moment the sombre evening sky sent lances of rain hissing across the battlefield. The Royalist musketeers, crouched behind the hedgerow along the roadside, could scarcely keep their matches alight as the enemy came plunging through the corn.

Newcastle meant to join his own infantry, but they were some distance away and he 'was no sooner got on horseback', says the Duchess, 'but he beheld a dismal sight of the horse of His Majesty's right wing, which out of a panic fear had left the field, and run away with all the speed they could'. Cromwell, in fact, had charged and broken them. For a few moments Newcastle managed to rally them, but 'they immediately betook themselves to their heels again, and killed even those of their own party that endeavoured to stop them'. Cholmley provides corroboration of her account, describing how Rupert came up and cried, ''Swounds, do you run? Follow me!' but was equally ineffectual in staying their panic.

Seeing the Prince there, Newcastle wheeled and galloped towards the centre of the Royalist line. His brother followed, and his page, with Mazine and another officer. His sons may have been in some safer place at the rear, with their tutor, but they could not have been far away. Sir Charles Lucas had urged him to send them off before the battle, but, said Newcastle, 'his sons should show their loyalty and duty to His Majesty, in venturing their lives, as well as himself'.

Now, in the confusion of the battle, the Marquess and his companions must have been thankful to encounter Sir Thomas Metham and a troop of gentlemen volunteers who, continues the Duchess, 'formerly had chosen him their captain, notwithstanding he was general of an army'. It is unlikely that, in all the smoke and clamour, his phrases were quite as well turned as she reports them: 'Gentlemen, said he, You have done me the honour to choose me your captain, and now is the fittest time that I may do you service; wherefore if you'll follow me, I shall lead you on the best I can, and show you the way to your honour.'

Reaching the centre, they found that a great mass of allied infantry had crossed the road, broken through the line of Rupert's foot regiments and were being held by Newcastle's, formed up in their rear. A counter-attack was urgently needed to relieve the pressure. Sir William Blakiston's brigade of cavalry was drawn up close by. Whether or not Newcastle himself ordered them to advance, he certainly joined them with his own troop, riding on the left wing as they hurled themselves upon the horde of pikemen. A ferocious struggle followed. He lost his sword, refused to deprive any of his gentlemen, and continued the fight with his page's half-leaden and primarily ornamental weapon. With this he somehow cut down three of the enemy. One pikeman defied him, 'though my Lord charged him twice or thrice', but this hapless hero went down before the other Cavaliers. Newcastle remained unscratched, though Metham and several others were killed around him. The charge cut a broad swathe through the allied centre. Leven, seeing so many of his men routed, concluded that the day was lost.

Meanwhile, on the left Goring and Lucas began well with what had once been Newcastle's cavalry. Though their line was broken by Sir Thomas Fairfax's first charge, they hit back with such fury that the Roundhead troopers were soon fleeing in as wild a panic as Rupert's men on the other flank. Sir Thomas was cut off, and escaped only by plucking the distinguishing white favour from his hat. Some of Goring's men, assuming the battle won, fell to the congenial task of looting the enemy baggage. Many Parliamentary soldiers made the converse assumption and stayed no longer on the field. A simplified bird's-eye view would have shown the armies locked in ding-dong struggle in the centre while on one flank the Royalists had been routed and on the other their opponents.

No one, of course, had that all-embracing view. The action had begun about seven, and though it was 2 July the sky was so overcast that the light waned early. The moor was flatter than the cornfield opposite and the scattered bushes obstructed vision, as did the copious smoke of seventeenth-century gunpowder. Arthur Trevor, arriving with a dispatch from Ormonde for the Prince, found so much 'fire, smoke and confusion', with 'runaways so breathless, so speechless', that no one could tell him where Rupert was.

At one point indeed, isolated in the rout as Fairfax had been, Rupert had evaded capture only by crouching in a beanfield. Less fortunate than these two generals, Lucas had been unhorsed and taken prisoner. Goring, his initial success reversed by Cromwell's Ironsides, had galloped away with the fugitive remnants of his cavalry. On both sides most of the principal commanders jumped to the pessimistic conclusion that their enemies had won. Lord Leven had long ago fled along the road to Leeds. Lord Fairfax hastened away in the gathering gloom to Cawood, ten miles off, and, it is alleged, retired to bed. Premature reports of a Royalist victory reached both Oxford and London.

Newcastle and Eythin seem to have been the senior Cavalier generals now remaining on the twilit field. Rupert, certainly no coward, had been swept along the road to York by the rout of his own cavalry. Of the enemy commanders the younger generation, Cromwell and Sir Thomas Fairfax, were doggedly turning chaos into triumph. Cromwell had kept his cavalry under control after their first success, had wheeled across the moor to defeat Goring on the other wing and was now cutting up the centre of the Royalist line.

When the outlook was obviously hopeless, Eythin, professional to the last, seems to have extricated some of the infantry and retired in good order to York. The Whitecoats – Newcastle's 'Lambs' – so called most likely from their colonel, Sir William Lambton – either got no order to retire or could not act on it. They stood their ground, first peppering the Parliamentary cavalry with their shot, and, runs the admiring testimony of their enemies, 'when they came to charge stoutly bore them up with their pikes, that they could not enter to break them'. They held out thus for an hour, till their own musketeers had exhausted their ammunition and they were being picked off by the carbines of Fraser's dragoons. 'When the Horse did enter,' said a Parliamentary captain, 'they would have no quarter, but fought it out till there was not thirty of them living.' Such was the spirit of the army Newcastle had raised, after all it had gone through. 'Every man', we are told, 'fell in the same order and rank wherein he had fought.' Though the Duchess's highly partisan biography must always be read with the utmost caution, it is interesting to see how closely it accords with the eyewitness enemy descriptions. The Whitecoats, she says, showed 'such an extraordinary valour and courage in that action, that they were killed in rank and file'.

We may imagine with what anguish Newcastle saw the annihilation. There was no more he could so. Of the Royalist generals he was, if we accept the Duchess's account – and there seems no evidence to contradict it – 'the last in the field'. He rode off towards York with his brother, and near the city encountered Rupert, in what must have been the distinctly uncongenial company of Eythin. 'His Highness asked My Lord how the business went? To whom he answered, That all was lost and gone on their side.'

SIXTEEN

A Ship from Scarborough

IF NEWCASTLE slept that night it can only have been through utter exhaustion, for, since his army had paraded at two o'clock in the morning, he could have had little rest the night before. His thoughts must have been bitter enough to hinder sleep. In two hours he had seen his forces destroyed in a battle which, in his view, need never have been fought. He had seen the men who had trusted him go down – old friends, neighbours, tenants, humble labourers, men of all sorts who had taken up arms in loyalty as much to him as to their remote sovereign. Others were missing and might well be dead. He could not know yet that the gallant Lucas was among the 1500 prisoners, along with George Porter, Endymion's son (a less serious military loss, since even his own brother-in-law, Goring, conceded that he was 'the best company but the worst officer that ever served the King'). Newcastle could not guess at the awful total of Royalist killed. The modern estimate is about 4000, with a high preponderance of officers and country gentry.

With the morning came consultations and recriminations. The enemy had not yet followed up their victory, so that there was no immediate attack on York which might temporarily have united the survivors. Rupert felt, not without some reason, that his gamble would have come off if only Newcastle's troops had been in time. The Marquess and such of his staff as remained – Eythin naturally the most vehement – defended their actions and deplored that such a risk had ever been taken. Eythin declared gloomily that this disaster had destroyed the Royalist cause. What, he asked the Prince, would he do now?

'I will rally my men,' said Rupert.

Eythin put the same question to Newcastle, though he may by then have known the answer. 'I will go into Holland,' said the Marquess.

Rupert urged him to stay and recruit fresh forces. He could scarcely have realised what he was asking. Newcastle could not do all that again.

He had already bled the north white in the King's service. Only two choices remained: to retire gracefully, as he had wanted to do three months earlier, or to join Charles as an individual volunteer, a general who had lost his army. He could imagine the delight of his detractors. 'No,' he said, 'I will not endure the laughter of the court.'

It is a pity that this dramatic scene has been given such prominence by writers lacking space to fill in the background. The contrast between the resilient determination of the Prince and the apparently childish pique of the Marquess is too tempting to miss, but the impression left is unfair. Newcastle is immortalised as the Cavalier who deserted the cause in a huff, 'the princely nobleman', in Virginia Woolf's neat but inaccurate phrase, 'who had led the King's forces to disaster with indomitable courage but little skill'. Few realise that he was never blamed by Charles, who had most right to complain. Few recall that within a year or two it was Rupert who, with poetic irony, was himself overruled when he advised against fighting the battle of Naseby, Rupert who was court-martialled for (quite properly) surrendering Bristol, and Rupert who, seeing the cause lost in the south as well, left England with a safe-conduct from Parliament. That was something Newcastle never had. He was on the select list of the unforgivable, who, if captured, would have received no mercy.

He was not alone in his decision to lay down his commission and quit the country. Besides Eythin there were Mackworth, who had commanded the northern infantry regiments in the battle, Sir William Carnaby, who as Treasurer of the Army knew better than most how impossible it would be to create another, Lord Widdrington, several colonels, including Sir Arthur Basset of Newcastle's own regiment, and numerous other officers. Some, in the end, did not go. Others returned to resume the struggle elsewhere. Glemham remained, to hold York as long as he could. Rupert saw no point in staying to be bottled up in the city he had just relieved. He retreated into Lancashire, meeting Clavering and the promised reinforcements as he went, and picking up Goring with the fugitive Northern Horse, so that eventually he was able to rejoin his uncle with a sizeable force.

Newcastle and his party, their decision once made, wasted no time. That same day they rode to Scarborough, where Sir Hugh Cholmley and his beautiful wife received them as hospitably as possible in the limited accommodation of the dilapidated castle. Besides those already mentioned, there were Lord Carnwath and Lord Falconbridge, Dr Bramhall, Bishop of Londonderry, the two Cavendish boys and their tutor,

Benoist, Sir Charles Cavendish, Newcastle's steward and personal servants, and his indispensable master of horse, Mazine. They were about seventy altogether.

Newcastle wondered whether Cholmley would obstruct their departure. On the third day, the governor having found two vessels to take them to Hamburg, he confessed this fear. 'I wish you could stay,' Cholmley admitted, 'but if you have committed an error, I know my duty. It is not for me to call you to account, but obey, you being my general.' He himself would hold Scarborough as long as possible for the King. He kept his word. After withstanding a year-long siege he surrendered on terms and, following Newcastle's example, crossed to the Continent.

It is significant that Newcastle and Eythin embarked in different vessels. Was there a coolness between them? Did Newcastle, so long reliant on his lieutenant's judgement, feel that he had gone too far on this last occasion? In her biography the Duchess seldom mentions Eythin, or, as so many still called him, General King. She says her husband forbade her 'to mention any thing or passage to the prejudice of any family or particular person'. We can only speculate about what she would have told us, if uninhibited, about the end of this military association.

Newcastle had fresh problems to occupy his mind as the two ships stood out into the North Sea. Would they be intercepted by the enemy? If they got safely abroad, how would they live? He asked his steward what money he had left. 'Ninety pounds,' was the discouraging reply. For the first time in his life he would have to consider his personal expenditure. Soon these worries were forgotten in a more immediate alarm: his elder son went down with smallpox, and then young Henry also became very ill. In his case it proved to be only measles, but as the anxious father paced the deck he must have wondered how many more misfortunes were about to fall upon the family.

They reached Hamburg without further incident on 8 July, and both boys made a good recovery. The party broke up. Newcastle was forced to reduce his expenses by sending home some of his personal servants. It was not easy. It was not merely that he had been accustomed all his life to keeping up a certain state, but material display was essential if a man was to receive respect – and credit. Economy could easily be self-defeating. Little is known of those first weeks in the great German trading city, but they can hardly have been cheerful. 'The Marquess of Newcastle is still at Hamburg in a poor condition,' wrote John Constable from Rotterdam. 'I believe he now repents his folly, but General King is in great pomp.' It must have been a relief when the Scotsman moved on to Sweden, where he was so highly thought of. Queen Christina gave him a Swedish peerage and a pension, and he died at Stockholm eight years later.

The news from England was depressing and came all too regularly, Hamburg being a key city in the network of foreign posts. On 2 August Welbeck, though 'very regularly fortified' with a sizeable garrison and 'eleven pieces of cannon', yielded on terms to the overwhelming forces of the Earl of Manchester, who was there in person. It was some comfort to know that there had been neither bombardment nor looting, though the Cavendishes had taken the wise precaution of burying their plate under the brewhouse. The inventory survives, a long narrow piece of paper listing '1 great salt, 3 flagons' and many other items. Manchester behaved well to Jane and Frances. 'I have engaged myself for their quiet abode there,' ran his official report, 'and to intercede to the Parliament for a complete maintenance for them.' The young ladies seem to have had close contact with their married sister during this period, for Jane and Elizabeth collaborated in writing a comedy, *The Concealed Fancies*, and *A Pastoral*, neither publicly performed, composed at some time between 1644 and 1646.

Bolsover surrendered ten days after Welbeck. York had yielded two weeks after Marston Moor. The Royalist effort in the north was dwindling to a few pockets of resistance such as Scarborough and Carlisle. Newcastle was well aware of the malicious talk against him at court. Nor did the Roundhead journalists miss their opportunity. 'A great pretender to wit,' jeered the news-sheet, *Mercurius Britanicus*: 'First, Enter *Newcastle*; one that in time of peace tired the stage in *Black-Friars* with his *Comedies*; and afterwards, one that trod the stage in the *North* with the first *Tragedies*.' Another pamphleteer, similarly deriding his theatrical efforts, wrote: 'But the Earl of *Newcastle*, the brave Marquess of *Newcastle*, which made the fine plays, he danced so quaintly, played his part a while in the North, was soundly beaten, shew'd a pair of heels, and exit *Newcastle*.'

At least he still enjoyed the confidence of the King and Queen. Henrietta Maria and Newcastle had been almost simultaneous fugitives. The worsening of the King's situation had driven her to the supposed safety of Exeter, where in June she had given birth to another daughter, the future 'Minette'. Endangered by Parliamentary successes in the west, she was forced to leave her baby temporarily with Lady Dalkeith and make a hazardous crossing to Brittany. From Paris, on 20 November, she wrote to Newcastle:

I shall assure you of the continuance of my esteem for you, not being so unjust as to forget past services upon a present misfortune. And therefore believe that I shall always continue to give proofs of what I tell you, and you will see how I shall behave, and with what truth I am, Your very good, and affectionate friend, Henrietta Maria R.

More formal, but no less gratifying, was the King's letter from Oxford, dated 28 November:

Right trusty and entirely beloved cousin and councillor we greet you well. The misfortune of our forces in the North we know is resented as sadly by you as the present hazard of the loss of so considerable a portion of this our kingdom deserves: which also affects us the more, because in that loss so great a proportion falls upon yourself, whose loyalty and eminent merit we have ever held, and shall still, in a very high degree of our royal esteem. And albeit the distracted condition of our affairs and kingdom will not afford us means at this present to comfort you in your sufferings, yet we shall ever retain so gracious a memory of your merit, as when it shall please God in mercy to restore us to peace, it shall be one of our principal endeavours to consider how to recompense those that have with so great an affection and courage as yourself assisted us in the time of our greatest necessity and troubles. And in the mean time if there be any thing wherein we may express the reality of our good intentions to you, or the value we have of your person, we shall most readily do it upon any occasion that shall be ministred. . . .

The most acceptable token of this esteem would have been the repayment of a fraction, even, of the money Newcastle had advanced to the King, but it would have been useless to hope for that. Fortunately his credit was good in Hamburg, a city with many English connections. He kept up appearances by buying nine horses of the local Holstein breed and a coach to replace the one lost at Marston Moor. But he was still in low spirits when, on 4 February, he wrote to the Prince of Wales, now fourteen, congratulating him on his appointment as a royal figurehead in the West Country:

After the great misfortunes and miseries I have suffered, the first joy and only comfort I received was to hear of your Highness's health and your being a general . . . it is no small comfort to me and mine that we have lived to see you a man; and could I but see peace in our Israel, truly then I care not how soon death closes my eyes. But whilst I crawl here in this uneven world your Highness must be troubled with me. . . .

For all his show of pious resignation, Newcastle was planning a move to Paris, where Henrietta Maria's court was a rallying place for the *émigrés*. On 16 February he put to sea again with his sons, his brother and the rest of his party, and sailed along the coast to Rotterdam, where he sent a servant to present his compliments to Rupert's mother, the exiled Queen of Bohemia, whom he had known at the court of her father, James I. From Rotterdam he proceeded in his new coach, with a chariot and two waggons behind. This careful maintenance of appearances was rewarded when he reached Brussels and received calls from the Marquis of Castel Rodrigo, the governor, and other notables. He was welcomed with similar honours at Cambrai and the French frontier town of Peronne, both governors inviting him to choose the password for the night. It was all faintly reminiscent of that stately progress to Savoy more than thirty years before.

They reached Paris on 20 April. Henrietta Maria had a suite in the Louvre, assigned to her by her sister-in-law, Anne of Austria, who was acting as regent for her seven-year-old son, Louis XIV. Newcastle hurried to pay his respects to his exiled queen and, with a prodigal gesture he could ill afford, presented her with seven of his nine new horses.

The change in her must have shocked him. The radiant young woman he had last seen at Pontefract had aged noticeably in the two years between. A difficult confinement had been followed by the hardships of her escape and by continuing poor health. Now she was harassed by financial troubles, a beggar in her native country; and, observed her friend, Madame de Motteville, 'No one could look at her without an emotion of compassion.'

It was on this occasion that the Duchess, so often quoted already, began to gather her own eyewitness impressions for Newcastle's eventual biography. 'It was my fortune to see him the first time, I being then one of the Maids of Honour to Her Majesty.'

SEVENTEEN

Maid of Honour

MARGARET LUCAS was probably about twenty-one. Her year of birth is not absolutely certain. But beyond question she was young for her age, bashful and tongue-tied in sophisticated company, especially now, since she knew no language but her own. She was the baby of a large Essex family of brothers and sisters, including the Charles Lucas taken at Marston Moor. Through him she must have heard something of his general. Whether Newcastle had heard, or remembered hearing, anything of his sister is more doubtful. Now, however, he saw her, a demure attractive girl with a good figure, full lips, and brown ringlets framing a pleasant face. His acquaintance with her brother afforded an obvious excuse to engage her in conversation. Though Sir Charles had by now been exchanged and was governor of Berkeley Castle, Margaret had not seen him nearly as recently as Newcastle had. The Lucases were a united, almost clannish, family, and this chance to hear of his adventures in the war helped her to conquer her shyness.

She had not been without her own share of adventures in the preceding twelve months. After a sheltered upbringing at Colchester she had escaped to become a maid of honour to the Queen at Oxford. The family had at first opposed this, knowing her and fearing she would be out of her element in that worldly atmosphere, but, as she had married sisters at Oxford, her widowed mother overcame her misgivings. The family's anxiety had been justified. Margaret had come to no harm but she had not been happy. She had few conventional accomplishments, no small talk, no taste for cards or dancing. 'I durst neither look up with my eyes, nor speak, nor be any way sociable,' she confessed afterwards. 'I was thought a natural fool.'

This uncongenial existence in the Queen's apartments at Merton had not lasted long. When Henrietta Maria quitted the college and fled westwards, Margaret went with her. She had shared in the general concern for the Queen's condition. This was the time when the anguished King wrote to the physician, Mayerne, 'For the love of me, go to my wife!' There had soon been fear too of the enemy, as the Parliamentary forces threatened Exeter. There was a real risk of the Queen's capture. Then, after the birth of the child, there had been the flight into Cornwall and a terrifying voyage from Falmouth, with a Parliamentary warship in hot pursuit with guns blazing, and the Queen, some of her old fighting spirit restored, bidding her captain blow up his vessel rather than strike his flag. Margaret was never to forget the horrors of that crossing, increased by a frightful tempest and seasickness. They had landed on the rocky coast of Brittany, clambering up dizzy cliffs to shelter in a thatched hovel. Crowning irony, the apprehensive inhabitants had taken them for pirates. Looked back upon, it was a marvellous story. And Margaret, once she conquered her diffidence, was a fluent enough narrator.

Despite the hampering protocol of court, a mutual attraction quickly developed. A naturally sensuous man, Newcastle was coming to life again after a long preoccupation with acute problems and demanding duties. He had been two years a widower. His sons could so easily have died during that escape to Hamburg, leaving no one to carry on his name. The idea of re-marriage and a second family was not only appealing but almost a duty. That he was old enough to be Margaret's father was no disadvantage. She had scarcely known her own father, and she clearly had a strong capacity for hero-worship, hitherto lavished mainly on by-gone characters like Julius Caesar. She was flattered by Newcastle's attention. His easy manner was less alarming to her than the ambiguous banter of courtiers closer to her own age.

One thing, besides etiquette, hindered the growth of their friendship: with the advent of summer the Queen moved to the old château of St Germain-en-Laye, ten miles from Paris. The Cavendishes, like most of the other impecunious exiles, remained in such lodgings as they could find in the city. Though Newcastle was *persona grata* at St Germain, the Queen's past protestations of friendship did not, as he might have hoped, give him a privileged place in her councils. Her confidant was Harry Jermyn, on whom she leaned as the French Queen-Regent leaned on Mazarin, though there could have been no greater contrast than that between the suave, rouge-cheeked Italian cardinal and the coarse-grained humorous Englishman, portly and broad-shouldered as a dray-man, whose subsequent astuteness as a London property-developer is recalled by the street that bears his name. A court dominated by a man like Jermyn had no place for Newcastle. At the end of July Sir Charles Cavendish told a friend that their stay in Paris was 'not likely to be long'.

But Newcastle lingered, riding out to St Germain from time to time, and maintaining a busy exchange of letters.

June had seen the King's defeat at Naseby. A fresh wave of Cavalier fugitives reached Paris, among them Endymion Porter. He had been with Charles on that disastrous day and brought letters from him to the Queen. Her welcome was chilly. She seldom liked the men who had most influence with her husband. 'The Queen', Porter lamented to Mr Secretary Nicholas, 'thinks I lost my estate for want of wit, rather than my loyalty to the King my master.' Newcastle, assuming that Margaret would have known him at Oxford, must have expressed regret that she had not shown him more cordiality. She defended herself rather primly: 'As for Mr Porter, he was a stranger to me, for before I came to France I never saw him or at least knew him to be Mr Porter or my Lord Newcastle's friend. I never speak to any man, before they address themselves to me, nor look so much in their face as to invite their discourse.'

No one foresaw what a lengthy exile stretched ahead. The war continued, the King was still a free man. In August he passed a few days at Welbeck, which had been briefly reoccupied by the Royalists. It was tantalising for Newcastle, far away in Paris, remembering those very different royal visits of long ago.

Soon the reports from England absorbed him less than the news – or lack of news – from St Germain. He was wooing Margaret assiduously and, as convention demanded, professed himself distracted:

> Thus I do think, 't is strange I never heard
> From my dear love so long; is the way barr'd? . . .
> It is so long, so long ago, since met,
> I doubt you will me utterly forget.
> It is now how long? it is, let me see,
> Since I had letter, or did hear from thee.
> I vow it is, protesting, here I may,
> 'T is since I heard from you, 't is one whole day.

His sense of humour did not desert him. Another poem begins:

> When one doth ask, what news, I pray you Sir?
> I answer yet I did not hear from her.
> S'ounds, I mean Bristol, says he, can you tell?
> I answer, I do hope that she is well.
> The peace is made in Ireland they say?
> I tell him, I do think she'll send today.
> . . . Says he, your answers mad do make me.
> I swear I love her, else the Devil take me.

He depicted himself in his lonely lodging:

> I now sit down with pen and ink and paper,
> Invoke my Muse by my dim single taper . . . ,

to which she replied, gently rebuking him:

I think you have a plot against my health in sending so early, for I was forced to read your letter by a candle light, for there was not day enough, but I had rather read your letter than sleep, and it doth me more good. . . . If you cannot read this letter blame me not, for it was so early I was half asleep.

Their almost daily exchanges were carried by his servants and her maid, Elizabeth Chaplain. He sent her his portrait as a love-token. She treasured it as a good likeness, but said his poems conveyed an even truer impression of him. The verses are, in fact, technically rough and amateurish. It was not done for an aristocrat to polish his literary effusions, and Newcastle, so conscientious and painstaking in other matters, was content to dash off his rhymes with dilettante negligence. He would show endless patience in the schooling of a horse. Only Pegasus, the Muses' favourite steed, would he allow to run lame and ungainly. His poems are full of affected conceits and hyperbole, but occasionally achieve a simple tenderness. While he could write:

> The fresher flowers, Spanish scents, they stink,
> To your balm's dew, like privy or our sink.
> The handsom'st of your sex to me appears,
> Compar'd to you, like men of four score years,
> Not women . . . ,

he could also tell her:

> Dear, you nor none else know
> Why you should love me so;
> There's nothing that can be
> Worthy of you in me . . . ,

or, eulogising her physical attractions:

> And your each curled hair those locks doth grace,
> Like pencill'd shadows for your lovely face.

Margaret's letters were more circumspect. She invariably addressed him as 'my lord' and signed herself – her spelling was idiosyncratic even for that century – 'your most umbell sarvant, Margreat Lucas', sometimes expanding this under the stress of her emotion to 'your admiring, loving, honouring, humbell and obedient sarvant'. Another sample of her original spelling, 'I am infinnightly obleged to you whos afectshoins are above so powerful a parswashon', is perhaps sufficient argument for modernising further passages.

Like all courts, St Germain was a hotbed for gossip. The sheer impotence of the exiles to influence important events increased their capacity for petty malice. She continually reminded her suitor of the widespread hostility to their relationship and the care with which she must guard her reputation. 'St Germain's is a place of much censure, and think I send too often.' And again:

I fear others foresee we shall be unfortunate, though we see it not ourselves, or else there would not be such pains taken to untie the knot of our affection. I must confess, as you have had good friends to counsel you, I have had the like to counsel me and tell me they hear of your professions of affection to me, which they bid me take heed of, for you had assured yourself to many and was constant to none. . . .

She had answered them that Lord Newcastle was too wise and honest to do so. People warned her that the Queen would be angry at not being taken into her confidence. She had been stung to ask them 'if I should acquaint the Queen with every compliment that was bestowed on me'.

Some of the advice pressed on them was kindly meant. Newcastle's close friend, Lord Widdrington, feared that he was making a mistake. Those who knew him best, like those who had seen most of Margaret, had good reason to think them an ill-matched couple, not only in the thirty-year age gap between them, but in their true natures. Was Newcastle blind – or was he strangely perceptive, seeing in this odd girl what no one else did? His friends thought he might have looked higher for a second wife. Margaret's friends – or perhaps more accurately Newcastle's enemies – pointed out that he was penniless and, unless the war took a better turn, might never enjoy his vast estates again. As for Henrietta Maria, she had a moral responsibility for the unmarried ladies serving her.

The lovers were honest with each other. 'My lord,' she wrote, 'I have not had much experience of the world.' And again: 'I must tell you I am not easily drawn to be in love, for I did never see any man but yourself that I could have married.' He in turn good-humouredly admitted his age, but pleaded:

I know I'm old, it is too true,
Yet love, nay, am in love with you . . .

> No man can love more, or loves higher;
> Old and dry wood makes the best fire.

True, he had no money, and Margaret's mother wrote from England that in present circumstances it was impossible to transmit a marriage portion. He merely broke into cheerful song:

> Sweet heart, we are beggars; our comfort's, 't is seen,
> That we are undone for the King and the Queen;
> Which doth make us rejoice, with royal brags,
> That now we do foot it with royal rags.
> We cannot borrow, nor take up of trust,
> So water we'll drink, and bite a hard crust:
> Let care go kill cats, what comfort's in sorrow?
> Therefore let tomorrow care for tomorrow.

With the coming of autumn he inquired constantly when the court would return to the Louvre and make their meetings easier. 'I hear the Queen comes to Paris this next week,' she wrote, 'to the solemnities of Princess Mary's marriage.' This was to be only a brief visit, celebrating the union of a foreign princess with Wladislaw of Poland, and Margaret wondered whether to ask leave of absence, as a means of damping down the gossip about their relationship. It is unlikely that Newcastle agreed to missing any chance to see her. He was growing impatient, as is darkly hinted in her postscript, 'My lord, let your eye limit your poetry', and other phrases, both in her letters and in his verses, suggest that he was becoming more ardent than was proper. By early November, when the royal wedding took place in the Palais Royal, their own was secretly agreed.

> The Princess Mary married King of Poland,
> And you, my dear, do marry Prince of Noland.

It would have to be a quiet affair. For the Anglican members of the Queen's entourage Charles had appointed a chaplain, that same Dr Cosin who had been with Newcastle earlier in the north and had censored sermons by unreliable clergymen. The Queen disliked Cosin and grudgingly allowed him only a room in the Louvre for prayers. For a full service he had to use a private chapel at the home of the English Resident, Sir Richard Browne. Thither went the faithful Elizabeth Chaplain to consult with Lady Browne, a kindly woman who, as we know from John Evelyn who married her daughter, made her house a sanctuary for all the English *émigrés* in their distress.

Even in these final weeks Margaret, still troubled by the opposition of Newcastle's friends, was offering to release him from the engagement. He would have none of it. He was not a man to tolerate interference from anyone in his own affairs. He would brave even the Queen's displeasure. So the arrangements went forward. 'I will bring none to our wedding but those you please,' she wrote.

The date of the ceremony is not known, but by 20 December Lady Lucas had received the news in Colchester and was writing to thank her new son-in-law for so honouring her daughter and making Margaret 'extremely happy . . . for oftentimes these come not together, but by yourself she hath attained to both'.

EIGHTEEN

What news from England?

IT WAS PERHAPS before the wedding that Newcastle, in optimistic antici-
pation, began one poem:

> There is no happy life,
> But in a wife . . . ,

but another, entitled *Love's New Year's Gift*, shows that he went on
writing verses to Margaret for some time after they were married. They
seem to have settled into a happy relationship from the start, although
Margaret, on her own admission, was not strongly sexed. 'It was not
amorous love,' she wrote, 'I never was infected therewith, it is a disease,
or a passion, or both; I know only by relation, not by experience.' His
own nature, we know, was quite the reverse. She did her best to please
him in this as in other matters, but it is unlikely that her sexual feelings
were ever fully awakened. Yet, whatever his disappointments, there was
no doubt of his devotion.

After the ceremony she moved into the Cavendishes' lodgings, bringing her maid. So, from December 1645 we have in Margaret a continuing
first-hand source for Newcastle's life. But the Duchess (as she had become by the time she wrote his biography) is tantalising in her disregard
of dates and details, so that we have no idea of what the lodgings were
like or where in Paris they were located. Nor, less surprisingly – since
her husband was to approve her manuscript – does she tell us what his
sons thought of their new stepmother, so little older than themselves.
They were probably not enthusiastic about the match. In later years,
certainly, he was distressed by the coolness shown her by the children
of his first marriage.

His brother behaved with the utmost kindness. Considering that Sir
Charles was an intellectual and she, even by the standards of female
education at that time, conspicuously ignorant, and that he was a
notable mathematician, whereas she was impatient of logical reason-

ing, we can only marvel that they developed a friendship as close as it was certainly innocent. This is illustrated by a poem she wrote some years later. She had been a prolific and fanciful scribbler in childhood and, stimulated no doubt by her husband's literary interests, began to write again. After a time she turned to verse, fairyland being a favourite theme. This poem opens:

> Sir Charles into my chamber coming in,
> When I was writing of my Fairy Queen:
> 'I pray,' said he, 'when Queen Mab you do see,
> Present my service to her Majesty;
> And tell her I have heard fame's loud report,
> Both of her beauty and her stately court.'

The impression given is that the good-natured little man, far from teasing her about her childish fantasies, entered into the spirit of them and, by taking her seriously, helped to build up the confidence she so badly needed.

Newcastle himself, after his lyrical outpourings, turned back to his old interest, the drama. There was in Paris that year a struggling English company providing entertainment for the *émigrés*, but before the end of 1646 a Parliamentary news-sheet gloatingly reported that they were 'for want of pay dissolved. . . . The English audience being there so poor and few, that they were not able to maintain the charges of the stage. It is wonder sufficient to me, how they can maintain themselves.'

Newcastle, said another, *The Kingdom's Weekly Intelligencer*, 'has writ several things for the English Company that did lately act in Paris which showeth in him either an admirable temper and settledness of mind . . . or else an infinite and vain affection unto Poetry, that in the ruins of his country and himself he can be at the leisure to make Prologues and Epilogues for players.'

He was indeed adjusting himself to exile with conspicuous 'settledness of mind'. Margaret relates how they lived on credit. The tradesmen 'shew'd themselves very civil to My Lord, yet they grew weary at length', and once his steward had to warn him that there would be no dinner that day.

My Lord being always a great master of his passions, was, at least shew'd himself not in any manner troubled at it, but in a pleasant humour told me, that I must of necessity pawn my clothes to make so much money as would procure a dinner. I answer'd, that my clothes would be but of small value, and therefore desired my waiting-maid to pawn some small toys, which I had formerly given her, which she willingly did.

The meal duly consumed, Newcastle graciously received his assembled creditors and, 'by his civil deportment and persuasive arguments', secured not only an extension of credit but a cash loan, so that Elizabeth Chaplain was able at once to redeem her trinkets. Subsequently the faithful maid was sent to England to see Margaret's brother John, now Lord Lucas, and ask for the small marriage portion due to her. The boys' tutor was similarly dispatched to find out whether any money could be got out of the country to Newcastle. Benoist had no success. Though the Marquess was no longer in arms against Parliament, no one in England dared to assist him.

It requires some imaginative effort to appreciate the conditions at this date. The intrigues, the ideological conflict, the political animosities, match those of our own century. Then, however, there were no instantaneous communications, no complete control of frontiers and passports. Europe had not yet invented an all-powerful bureaucracy or a police state. True, letters *could* be intercepted. The King and Queen corresponded with increasing difficulty. The French and Portuguese diplomats helped to some extent. More often they relied on intrepid couriers flitting to and fro across the narrow seas. In the Louvre the English poet, Abraham Cowley, assigned to cipher-work by Jermyn, toiled far into the night. For notables such as Newcastle correspondence with England had its risks and uncertainties. Lesser folk, if they behaved discreetly, might escape harassment. The simple-minded zealots of the seventeenth century had not learnt the refinements of psychological blackmail. It did not occur to them in their innocence to use the relatives of an *émigré* as hostages for his good behaviour.

By this date the King was beaten. We know that: he did not. Nor did the exiles. For in Britain there were three distinct forces on the other side, out of whose dissensions victory still seemed possible. They were Scotland, the English Parliament, and the New Model Army under Cromwell and the younger Fairfax. Charles, never happier than when most devious, sought to play them off against each other. On 5 May 1646 he surrendered himself to the Scottish army at Newark, and stepped out upon the tightrope of manoeuvre and intrigue which was to be cut by the axe more than two and a half years later.

The organised military effort of the Royalists now ceased. Prince Charles was safe in Jersey. The Queen wanted him with her, away from the influence of his chief adviser, Hyde. She sent an impressive deputation to persuade him. Newcastle was not included, although, as the Prince's former governor, he had a strong claim to be considered.

Leaving an angry and disapproving Hyde in the Channel Islands, young Charles appeared at St Germain in July. Rupert turned up three weeks later. More and more Cavaliers arrived. Newcastle saw many familiar faces. The atmosphere was sultry, not only with the unusually hot summer but with reunions and recriminations. Goring had been in France for some months already – he had craved leave of the Prince on health grounds but had quit England without waiting for permission. Now, his gout remarkably improved, he had become a general in the Spanish forces. Rupert took service with the French, and soon the old comrades were facing each other in battle. To Newcastle, who regarded war as a regrettable evil, not a congenial profession, there was a certain wry humour in all this. Paris was very gay that winter. The English colony staged their own masque on New Year's Eve. It was like old times.

In January came the news that the Scots were handing over the King to the Parliamentary commissioners. From their custody he was snatched in June by a military detachment under Cornet Joyce. He became the Army's hostage, a bargaining counter that its leaders, now effectively Cromwell and his grim son-in-law, Ireton, could use against Parliament. Charles was kept in honourable captivity at Hampton Court. He was allowed to confer regularly with Scottish envoys and to see his children, James, Henry and Elizabeth. The Queen had only Prince Charles and young Henrietta, brought over to her by the faithful Lady Dalkeith. For the exiles 1647 was a year of impotence. The King must play this hand alone.

They had their own troubles, poverty the commonest. Porter moved to Brussels, where his life-long Spanish connections ensured him better credit. Newcastle sought another means to repair his fortunes: if his sons could be matched with affluent brides, there might be some discreet arrangement to relieve his own indigence. The seriousness of his difficulties, and the good humour with which he faced them, can be illustrated by one of his letters, intercepted and derisively published in a contemporary news-sheet:

None will lend me two shillings here, but fly me . . . as if I was the arrantest knave and rogue in the world. I vow to God the ridiculousness of it makes me laugh heartily. . . . Again to pass the time away withal, my Lord Bishop of Derry, my Lady O'Neill and myself gravely set in council, as wise and provident parents to provide the best we could for our children, agreed upon a match between my son Harry and her daughter, and gravely articled, bought 18 pennyworth of riband for the wooing, the old lady a lean chicken in a pipkin for the dinner, with 3 preserved cherries and 5 drops of syrup by them for the banquet. One wiser than the rest asked how it should be performed, which our wisdoms never thought of before, so when my estate was examined, besides the Parliament's selling of it, that my debts were so great with what was entailed upon my son Charles as I could estate nothing. The old lady was very angry at that, but I had more reason than modesty, I examined her, having examined old ladies in my time, and found she had as little. So the times have broke that grave intention – yet the jointure and portion being alike one might think it might go on. And so Harry is a lusty bachelor begging homeward for England.

Charles went too. There was talk of good matches for them both, but once back in England the youths declared their unreadiness to marry and remained lusty bachelors for several years.

There was, however, a temporary alleviation of their father's difficulties. The Queen gave him nearly £2000, some return at least for the £3000 he had given her in Yorkshire. He was able to take a house and furnish it on credit, which his new show of prosperity encouraged the Parisian tradesmen to extend. Now he could entertain in some style. Hobbes, who had been in Paris for years and was tutoring Prince Charles in mathematics, was a frequent guest at his table. So was Descartes, who corresponded regularly with Sir Charles Cavendish and dedicated several books to him. So was another of Sir Charles's correspondents, the Provençal Pierre Gassendi, professor of mathematics at the Collège Royal, a friend of Galileo and a forward-looking scientist. The peasant-born Marin Mersenne came too, his intellectual interests ranging from the theory of music to the possibility of flying. If such men were drawn to the house primarily by their connection with Sir Charles there is no doubt that Newcastle was a fully accepted participant in their discussions, but the talk rolled over Margaret's head. She never mastered French, but it would have been all one if they had spoken English. She was not uninterested in scientific speculation, and loved to use terms she picked up, but she preferred to weave fancies from what she overheard, rather than attempt to follow a coherent explanation or line of reasoning.

Newcastle was now able to indulge his old love of horsemanship. Paris was still the great equestrian centre. Evelyn, three years earlier, had described the academies of de Plessis and de Veau, 'whose schools of that art are frequented by the nobility; and here also young gentlemen are taught to fence, dance, play on music, and something in fortification and the mathematics. The design is admirable, some keeping near a hundred brave horses, all managed to the great saddle.' Here Newcastle must have found much congenial society. He bought himself a Barbary horse for about £180, and another mount from a fellow exile, young 'Madcap' Crofts, for £100 to be paid on their return to England. No one doubted they would one day return, but few realised how distant was that day. Hope fed on news of dissension between Parliament and its generals. In November the King slipped out of Hampton Court and reached the Isle of Wight. He remained at Carisbrooke Castle, still not free, unable to escape overseas, yet feeling that in some degree he had outwitted his enemies. In Paris the English kept Christmas more merrily, and the Queen had two plays performed for their diversion.

In the spring Newcastle was bidden to a conference at St Germain. The Queen and Prince Charles were there, Rupert, Ormonde, and the inevitable Jermyn. They discussed the chances of resuming the military struggle. Newcastle faced realities: they could do nothing without the help of the Scots. 'You are too quick,' said the Queen sharply, hating the idea of any religious concessions. Had she but known, her husband had just made a secret deal, which was to lead in July to another Scottish invasion of England, this time on his side.

Before that, the war flared up again in many places. A mutiny of Parliamentary troops at Pembroke set South Wales alight. In the north, Carlisle and Berwick were seized by Cavaliers. Pontefract was surprised, Scarborough declared for the King. There were risings in Kent and Cornwall and many other places. Best of all, late in May there was a naval mutiny and a number of warships crossed to Holland. Soon they were joined by the young Duke of York, who, while pretending to play hide-and-seek with his brother and sister, had escaped from St James's Palace in disguise.

Things were moving fast. At St Germain the atmosphere was heady with optimism. Various schemes were tossed about. Rupert wanted to rescue the King by a surprise landing on the Isle of Wight and then sail up the Thames to take London. By the end of June he was off to The Hague with Prince Charles to take over the repentant fleet. The Queen watched their departure with misgivings. Was Rupert leading her eighteen-year-old son to disaster? Seeing Newcastle as a steadying influence, she begged him to go after them.

The willing and obedient Marquess had to confess to one prosaic obstacle: he could not stir from Paris until he had satisfied his creditors. The Queen pledged herself for his debts and for his immediate needs there was a whip-round among his friends, raising a few hundred pounds. Hobbes lent him about ninety. So he got off at last in a little chariot holding only Margaret and himself. His brother and Lord Widdrington packed into a brand-new coach he had just acquired, along with Elizabeth Chaplain and other senior servants. Others followed on horseback or in the three baggage waggons. All the creditors turned out to see them off, Margaret recalls, with 'many hearty prayers and wishes' (understandably) for their safe return.

En route, they were accorded all due deference. At Cambrai they were welcomed with a torchlight procession. What was even more appreciated, the governor, 'a right noble Spaniard', sent all kinds of provisions to their lodgings and told their host to accept no payment for anything he supplied. In this style they reached Antwerp, crossed into Dutch territory and found accommodation with an English merchant's widow, Mrs Beynham, at Rotterdam.

Now came a setback: the Princes and their eleven ships had sailed, no one knew whither. With customary zeal, Newcastle chartered a boat. He would do his best to find them. Margaret for once put her foot down. He might as well look for a needle in a haystack. He submitted meekly. How right she had been was proved when his friends Widdrington and Throckmorton insisted on setting forth but returned crestfallen, after being blown halfway to Scotland by a storm, without a glimpse of the Royalist fleet.

Before long that armada itself was back, having accomplished nothing, and by the end of the summer all the high hopes of 1648 were in the dust. The ill-co-ordinated risings were crushed. Cromwell smashed the Scottish invaders in Lancashire and on 25 August they surrendered. Three days later Charles Lucas, who had defended Colchester in a heroic siege, capitulated to Fairfax – and the same evening faced a firing squad. The struggle was becoming ever more savage. For Margaret her brother's execution was yet another grievous blow, closely following the deaths of her eldest sister and her mother.

What now? There seemed no point in returning to Paris. Prince Charles for the time being remained at The Hague. Newcastle found life in Rotterdam expensive. There were so many friends and acquaintances passing through, and he could never quite rid himself of the Welbeck tradition of open house to all. He borrowed in all some £3000 from his kinsman, the Earl of Devonshire, and other sources, but it was soon spent. He decided to pay off some of his servants and move to Antwerp, where it might be easier to economise. He went to The Hague, assured the Prince of his readiness for any service required, and then recrossed into the Spanish Netherlands.

Margaret, who seldom checked anything, says he had spent nearly six months in Rotterdam, but it can hardly have been three, for late October saw him in Antwerp. Perhaps he left her in Rotterdam while he looked round. At Antwerp he lodged at an inn until he encountered Endymion Porter, who, 'being not willing that a person of such quality . . . should lie in a public house, profer'd him lodgings at the house where he was, and would not let my lord be at quiet until he had accepted of them'. From this base Newcastle went house-hunting and 'lighted on one that belonged to the widow of a famous picture-drawer, Van Ruben, which he took'. Here, in what modern art-lovers know as the Rubens Museum, he was to make his home for much longer than he could have anticipated.

NINETEEN

The House in Antwerp

RUBENS had died in this house eight years before. Newcastle may have met him on his visit to England in 1629. He must certainly have been familiar with his work, especially the Banqueting House ceiling at Whitehall, and he might have heard of his Antwerp home from Van Dyck, one of many artists who had worked there. It was not Welbeck, but even in this opulent Flemish city it evoked, declared the humanist, Van de Wouver, 'the astonishment and admiration of visitors'. It would do very well. Rubens's young widow, now remarried, was glad to let it to so distinguished a tenant.

The place has now been restored with such loving scholarship that it can be seen much as it was in Rubens's day, and consequently in Newcastle's. Then, as now, a narrow lane, giving no promise of the magnificence to come, brought one to the entrance of a cobbled court-yard. Within, to the left, lay the house proper, a discreet Flemish build-ing of limestone and brick. To the right, taller and ornately Italian, rose the studio in which Rubens's vast conceptions had been realised. Busts, statues and frescoes, marshalled on its façade in a sort of hierarchy – Olympians above, pagan philosophers below, and the less reputable mythological personalities, such as Silenus, in the lowest tier – presented a useful recapitulation of classical lore.

Linking residence and studio stretched a grandly baroque portico, crowned with statues of Minerva and Mercury, its three arches framing a garden with formal walks and flowerbeds, bordering poplars and a honeysuckle arbour, as depicted in *The Walk in the Garden*, now in the Munich Pinakothek. The vista ended in a pavilion, adorned with Hercules, Bacchus and other antique celebrities for whom space had not been found elsewhere. Rubens had done much of this building in the full flush of enthusiasm after eight years in Italy. Also, says Roger de Piles, who knew his nephew, 'between the courtyard and the garden he

F
161

built a circular room, like the Pantheon in Rome, lit only by a single opening above'. He used this as a second studio and a setting for the works of art he had collected in Italy. Newcastle decided it would serve him as a riding-house. Here, and in the garden, he would school his horses in all their intricate evolutions.

The mansion itself was an echoing emptiness, cheerless on a Flemish winter's day. Expanses of cold floor, paved in black and white patterns, cried out for the furniture that had once stood upon them. Filling such spaces was a daunting prospect. Luckily, says Margaret, a Mr William Aylesbury, 'a very worthy gentleman, and great friend to my lord', was in Antwerp as agent for the Duke of Buckingham, and he lent £200 of what, strictly, was the Duke's money. This enabled Newcastle to establish his credit with the tradesmen and to order meat, drink and provisions of every kind, 'which certainly was a special blessing of God, he being not only a stranger in that nation, but to all appearances a ruined man'. The civic authorities were so delighted to have a man of his rank settling in their bourgeois community that they waived all local taxes and excise duties for the duration of his stay.

Now, surely, his luck was turning? At last he had a house not inppropriate to his dignity. He and Margaret, after three difficult years, could create a real home. Perhaps Margaret, having found a haven of tranquillity, would give him the second family he craved. She had always known that this was expected of her. There seems no doubt that she co-operated dutifully, if not with natural enthusiasm, but so far she had not become pregnant. Her maternal, like her other instincts, were not powerful. A woman, she wrote later, 'hazards her life' bearing children 'and hath the greatest share of trouble in bringing them up'. But Newcastle's continued devotion to her argues that he was not dissatisfied with her responses, and when, in the preceding spring, he had written to consult Sir Theodore Mayerne, the question he posed was about sterility and its possible connection with Margaret's low spirits. From his book-lined study in Chelsea the eminent physician replied: 'Touching conception, I know not if in the estate she's in, you ought earnestly to desire it. It is hard to get children with good courage when one is melancholy.... Be in good health and then you may till your ground, otherwise it will be time lost if you enter that race frowningly.'

Since then there had been plenty to deepen her depression – her brother's execution and the bestial desecration of her mother's and sister's graves at Colchester. Now Newcastle wrote again to Mayerne. Margaret had been attended by Antwerp doctors without perceptible benefit. She was apt either to overdo their treatment, by bleeding herself or taking extra purgatives, or to disregard their advice completely in favour of her own remedies. Mayerne answered frankly that 'the nature of the disease' was less of a problem than 'the disposition of the patient'. She must follow medical advice. His own was to abandon the blood-letting – she had lost far too much already – and take only the gentlest laxatives, for 'by too much scouring a kettle it is at last worn out to holes'. She should take more exercise. A sedentary life was bad for her. Unfortunately it was Margaret's chosen way, and even Newcastle could not budge her from it. She was against energetic exercise for anyone. She wrote: 'Tennis is too violent a motion for wholesome exercise, for those that play much at tennis impair their health and strength and wast-ing their vital spirits through much sweating . . . weaken their nerves by overstraining them.' Even gentlemen should not go in for swimming. Its sole value was to save them from drowning and there was more risk in learning the art than advantage in possessing it. She herself had thank-fully given up dancing, which was too frivolous for married people. She did not much care for going out. She was happiest writing – she had little interest even in household activities – or 'only walking a slow pace in my chamber, whilest my thoughts run apace in my brain, so that the motion of my mind hinders the active exercises of my body: for should I dance or run, or walk apace, I should dance my thoughts out of measure, run my fancies out of breath, and tread out the feet of my numbers.' Struck by one of these fancies she would exclaim aloud, 'I conceive! I conceive!' To Newcastle's disappointment all these concep-tions were purely literary.

He did not discourage them. They helped to dispel her melancholy, and it could not have been uncongenial to share his wider reading and experience with so avid a listener. She was that, for she pays open tributes to the superior wisdom of 'my lord', and her writings show her frequently regurgitating his views, especially on topics such as war and statecraft, with which she had little acquaintance. In later years she was to read more, but at this stage she relied heavily on whatever she had picked up in conversation, first from her brothers, now from her husband and his circle. Her literary influences are often second-hand, clearly derived from Newcastle's tastes. They read plays together, and it was largely through him that she developed her enthusiasm for Shakespeare, on whom she was the first woman to write. In her *Sociable Letters* she declares: 'So well he hath expressed in his plays all sorts of persons, as one would think he had been transformed into every one of those persons he hath described.'

In general she was much less interested in other people's writings than in her own. Originality and spontaneity were what she esteemed. Unfortunately, 'originality' meant whatever suddenly came into her head, without any realisation that she had heard it from someone else, and without any attempt to check whether it had been expressed before. Her sketchy background laid her open to the criticism of *naïveté* and unwitting plagiarism. As 'spontaneity' meant refusing to plan, verify or revise, what she thought her greatest assets tended rather to be liabilities.

Newcastle felt no call to play the heavy critic. She was not writing for publication, nor in those early Antwerp years was she attempting any unified work in which her faults would have been conspicuous. She was dashing off little essays of varied lengths on whatever occurred to her. Some might have done very well for women's magazines, had such publications then existed. She wrote sensibly on cosmetics, warning against the dangers of mercury-based preparations but approving powder, hair-styling and the careful choice of dress and accessories. 'Dressing is the poetry of women,' she wrote, adding realistically, 'and is the cause of employing the greater part of a commonwealth.' Childless herself, she remembered her mother's precepts: treat a child generously, and you will encourage in it a generous spirit; corporal punishment breaks the understanding and destroys all ingenuity, and the mere threat of it 'confuses the brain' and 'disquiets the mind'. Conscious of her own educational shortcomings, she wrote defensively 'Of Gentlewomen that are sent to board Schools', though elsewhere she maintained inconsistently that only lack of education made women unequal to men. Often she would venture into fields of which she had little experience or comprehension, writing 'Of Tyrannical Government' or 'Memory is Atoms in the Brain set on Fire'. In other essays the autobiographical basis is all too obvious, as when she wrote of second marriages: 'It is to be observed that when a second wife comes into a family, all the former children, or old servants, are apt to be factious, and do foment suspicions against her, making ill constructions of all her actions.'

That first year in Antwerp saw the publication of Newcastle's plays *The Country Captain* and *The Variety*, which had been performed at Blackfriars before the war. They were published at The Hague by Samuel Brown, 'English bookseller at the Sign of the English Printing

House', and also in London by Humphrey Robinson at the Three Pigeons and Humphrey Moseley at the Prince's Arms in St Paul's Churchyard. It would, of course, have been illegal to act them in Puritan England, and their author would have been arrested had he set foot in the country.

TWENTY

The Years of Exile

THOSE FIRST months in Antwerp were darkened by more than wintry skies. News from England came quickly and was bad. Besides having excellent postal connections, Antwerp received all the news-sheets and pamphlets published by the Dutch, who followed English affairs closely. The exiles could read day-by-day reports of the King's trial and see artists' graphic impressions of the drama. Early in February Newcastle may well have been shattered by the Dutch print depicting his master's decapitation outside the Whitehall 'Bancket Haus' on 30 January. The subsequent news that on 14 March he himself had been sentenced to death in absence must have seemed no more than a vindictive postscript.

His former pupil, now lodged in the Binnenhof Palace at The Hague, became thus in the eyes of all loyalists King Charles II. To Newcastle this brought no change. Hyde was firmly entrenched as the new monarch's adviser and was determined to keep Newcastle out of the inner circle. Their relations were outwardly friendly enough – Hyde had a really warm regard for his brother, but he had no opinion of Newcastle as a serious statesman. When Charles paused for two days in Antwerp on 21 June, *en route* to visit his mother in France, the Marquess could scarcely be kept out of the festivities, but it was no more than the renewal of an old, if genuinely affectionate, association. The King continued on his journey and Newcastle relapsed into his private life in the Vaart straat.

He was not forgotten, however. The next year, on 12 January, he was made a Knight of the Garter and a Privy Councillor. He travelled thirty miles to take the oath at Breda when Charles returned to Holland. He found a sharply divided Council. The younger men, Buckingham, Lord Percy and the King's secretary, Robert Long, favoured the view he himself had urged two years earlier at St Germain, that a deal with the Scots offered the only hope of a restoration. Hyde, Mr Secretary Nicholas and old Lord Cottington were against such a policy, and, being barely on speaking terms with its supporters, did not welcome another. 'You will find the Marquess of Newcastle a very lamentable man,' Hyde warned Nicholas, 'and as fit to be a general as a bishop.' Nicholas accepted this estimate. 'God help us,' he declared, 'when Mr Long, Newcastle and Buckingham rule in Council!'

A delegation of Scottish Covenanters had just arrived, headed by the Earls of Cassilis and Lothian, with three ministers of the kirk to keep them on the right lines. The two sides crowded into the King's bedroom, with his brother-in-law, the Prince of Orange, as a kind of arbitrator. His good offices were soon required. Cassilis opened truculently: 'It is not our purpose to flatter, but to be faithful and free.' One of the ministers delivered a hectoring tirade against the whole house of Stuart. Charles and his councillors controlled themselves, but when the Scots went on to demand that he disown Montrose and Ormonde, his most vigorous supporters in Scotland and Ireland, Newcastle exploded. Mindful of the ministers, Cassilis sanctimoniously reproved him for bad language.

Charles was more diplomatic. He swallowed the insults and pretended a disarming docility. He flattered the ministers by according them private audiences, listened meekly to their dogmatic harangues, and then played off one against another. Even he, though, could not wriggle out of paying a heavy price for Scottish aid.

His father had steadfastly refused to accept the Solemn League and Covenant on the religious affairs of his two kingdoms. The new king was forced to do so. Newcastle agreed with Buckingham and other councillors in the cynical view that he was justified in signing anything before he had bound himself with the coronation oath. Charles did secure some minor concessions. He need not sacrifice Ormonde. He could keep Montrose if he transferred him to Ireland. But on the very day, 27 April, that the terms were agreed, Montrose was defeated by the Covenanters at Corbiesdale, and on 21 May, before Charles had embarked for Scotland, his finest champion in that country was barbarously executed in Edinburgh.

Newcastle wanted to accompany the King, but the Scots meant Charles to be their puppet and refused to have so awkward an opponent in his party. He had to content himself with a mission as ambassador extraordinary to the King of Denmark, seeking foreign help for the cause, after which he could only return to Antwerp and await events. As time passed, he must have seen that he was well out of the Scottish expedition. Nearly all the Englishmen in the King's entourage were being replaced by Scots. They came streaming back to the Low Countries with disquieting reports. Buckingham was one of the few allowed to remain. Newcastle, his boyhood governor in the old Richmond days, had optimistically asked him to jog the King's memory about some money he had promised. Buckingham now wrote apologetically, acknowledging Newcastle's great kindness in the past but explaining that there would be no remittance:

The best counsel that I am able to give you, considering your own condition, and the present state of our affairs, is to make your peace, if it be possible, in England, for certainly your Lordship's suffering for the King has been great enough to excuse you if you look a little after yourself now, when neither he is able to assist you, nor you in a possibility of doing him service.

More and more Royalists were now 'making their peace'. In London the Committee for Compounding sat regularly at Goldsmiths Hall. The delinquent had to file a sworn statement of all his possessions, acknowledge his political error, and submit to the regime. He was then fined in proportion to his assets and the enormity of his offences. Many a Cavalier, seeing no hope, humiliated himself for the sake of his family. Even Newcastle might have been allowed to do so, the government being desperate for ready cash. Endymion Porter, broken in health and spirit, went back just before he died and compounded. But Newcastle would not consider it.

The Scottish venture dragged on for more than a year. The promised invasion of England, when at last it came, ended with disastrous defeat by Cromwell at Worcester. Charles became a hunted fugitive with a price on his head. Newcastle's intense personal affection for him was never more vividly revealed than in those weeks of uncertainty. His emotion was so violent, Margaret recorded, 'that I verily believed it would have endangered his life'. It was about six weeks before news came that Charles was safe in France with his mother at St Germain. If Newcastle had an impulse to hasten there it was checked by the King's announcement that he did not wish any of his 'servants in those parts' to travel to Paris 'since His Majesty could not yet resolve how long he should stay there'. Only Hyde, who had settled with his family in Antwerp after a diplomatic mission to Madrid, disregarded this instruction, hurried to Paris and resumed his old ascendancy over the King.

Before departing, Hyde (says Margaret) 'proved himself a noble and true friend'. There was no hope of a restoration in the foreseeable future. Even Newcastle, obstinate in his loyalty, had to consider if anything could be saved from the wreck of his personal fortunes. His brother, who had played so much less conspicuous a part in the war, had been allowed to compound already, but since he had not returned to England his estates had been sequestrated again. The only chance of protecting the Cavendish interests was for Sir Charles to go back now, before the estates were sold and became irrecoverable. Sir Charles hesitated. Newcastle begged Hyde to add his persuasion. Sir Charles not only agreed to return, but took Margaret with him, so that she could claim a wife's allowance from Newcastle's confiscated assets. They sailed early in November 1651, with just enough money to get them to London. Arrived at Southwark, Sir Charles had to pawn his watch to pay for their lodgings.

In Antwerp Newcastle waited anxiously to hear the progress of their mission. His brother's former steward was proving helpful, had got them credit and established them in Covent Garden. On 10 December Margaret appeared before the Committee for Compounding, but met with no sympathy, 'by reason my Lord and husband had been the greatest traitor of England (that is to say, the honestest man, because he had been most against them)'. Having married him after his offences, she had forfeited consideration.

Margaret stayed on in London. Probably there was no money for the return journey, and she was enjoying the reunion with her surviving brothers and sisters. Everything now depended on how Sir Charles fared with the Committee. Newcastle sent her word 'that if his brother did not presently relieve him, he was forced to starve'. He was driven to call a meeting of his creditors, whom he addressed with all his usual charm and persuasiveness, and with the usual result: they suspended their demands and promised to supply all his needs. No sooner had the wolves left his door than he received £200, which Charles had scraped together with much difficulty – he and Margaret were often at their wits' ends to pay for their Covent Garden lodgings.

Then things took a better turn. Charles's case was settled. He was fined £5000. He was able to pay this and his personal debts by selling some of his land below its true value. He was left with a comfortable, if reduced, estate, but putting the family interest before his own he at once applied himself to saving Welbeck and Bolsover.

The immediate danger was to Bolsover, that beloved creation of his father's and his brother's fancy. At first the victors had behaved with consideration. The Council of State had instructed the Derbyshire Committee:

To avoid the charge of a garrison in Bolsover Castle, and yet to prevent danger if it should be surprised and kept by an enemy, we refer it to your care to do it so as the house itself, as it relates to private habitation, may be as little prejudiced as may be; but let the outworks abroad, and garden walls of the frontier court that are of strength be demolished, and all the doors of the house be taken away and slight ones set in their place; as also the iron bars of the windows.

But the next year, 1650, complete demolition was ordered. The castle was sold for the value of its materials, and when Charles managed to buy it back in 1652 the lead had already been stripped from the gallery roof and some of the domestic offices round the courtyard pulled down.

Glad though he was to know that Bolsover was saved, Newcastle, now about to enter his sixtieth year, must have wondered if he would ever see the place again – or, for that matter, his children. Jane and Frances were still unmarried: how would he ever find portions for them? Elizabeth was now Countess of Bridgwater. He had an eight-year-old grandson he had never seen. Margaret, on reaching England, had reported that his sons 'were no less in want and necessity' than themselves, but they had now found wives. Henry had married Frances Pierrepont, of that old Nottinghamshire family with which they were already connected, and Charles had taken a Dorset bride, Elizabeth Rogers of Bryanston.

Charles, like his uncle, had compounded for his own estates, and the wording of his 'Discharge of Delinquency' indicates how the petitioners had to humble themselves before the Committee. Having 'examined the papers in the case of the Lord Mansfield', it found:

that the said Lord Mansfield and his mother did about April, 1642, solicit of the said Earl that the said Viscount might return back to the Parliament, which was denied, and that he did endeavour by all means to procure his father's leave to travel beyond the seas, which was also denied, and that although he was constrained during the first two years of the war to wait sometimes on his father, and when he rode did wear a sword, yet he never acted any thing in the war by way of assistance. . . .

This sounds rather unlike the young man who was, at least in name, General of the Ordnance. Probably the truth lay between the two.

How, it may be asked, was Margaret spending this long period of separation? Innocently, beyond doubt. She drove with her sisters in Hyde Park, attended a musical evening at Henry Lawes's house, ran into Hobbes and asked him to dinner. Perhaps remembering those dinner-parties in Paris when she had scarcely said a word, the philosopher excused himself. Perhaps too he was put off by the flamboyant eccentricity of her dress which she began to develop at this time.

Increasingly her time was spent in writing, which offered escape from society and conventional womanly occupations. She poured out verse. She wrote of fairyland. She ventured into scientific and philosophical fields, weaving fancies round terms such as 'atoms' and 'vacuum', which she had picked up without fully understanding. Her happiest efforts sprang from her own countryside observation, birds or a hunted hare that excited her compassion. Prose or verse, her work was confused, sometimes chaotic, in thought and construction. It was not form that concerned her but 'fancy'. Care she equated with pedantry. 'Every one', she declared, 'may be his own grammarian.' It was 'against nature for a woman to spell right.' It would have made no difference if Newcastle had been there. Hardly a painstaking craftsman himself, he never tried to correct her. At least her naïve claim to originality was in one way substantiated, for now – before Lucy Hutchinson, Aphra Behn and others – she became the first Englishwoman to write not only for her own pleasure but for publication. While in London she arranged for the printing of her *Poems and Fancies*, and before the volume could appear had a second, *Philosophical Fancies*, in the press.

It was then, early in 1653, that Newcastle fell ill. Margaret dutifully hurried home after a fortnight's argument over a passport – she steadfastly refusing to make any political commitment. Newcastle, much recovered, welcomed her back, as did a hasty assemblage of his optimistic creditors, 'supposing I had brought back a great store of money . . .'. Newcastle smoothed over this little misunderstanding and the Antwerp tradesmen bowed themselves out empty-handed, renewing their offers of continued credit.

Copies of her first book arrived a few weeks later, quickly followed by the second. What did Newcastle think of them? We can only surmise. His own writing was marked by a bluff common sense, laced with humour, with elaborate conceits admitted only because they were the courtly vogue. He hated ridicule, and even in Antwerp he could not have failed to hear that the books had had a mixed reception, fulsome flattery from some, derision from others. The astringent young Dorothy Osborne heard that her writing was 'ten times more extravagant than her dress', and after reading it was 'satisfied that there are many soberer people in Bedlam'. Margaret's verse is certainly curious, and, except for Virginia Woolf, has seldom met with the appreciation of posterity. But not for nothing does Newcastle's tomb describe him as 'the loyall Duke'.

Whatever private reservations he had about her work, he always supported and encouraged her efforts, contributing prefatory verses to her later volumes. One line at least will strike a sympathetic echo in most authors' hearts:

Censure your worst, so you the book will buy. . . .

On 4 February 1654 Sir Charles died, a sad blow to both of them. Prudently he had willed his estates to his nephew, but with the tacit understanding that he would hold them for his exiled father. There was some spare money, however, that could be discreetly transmitted to Antwerp, and henceforth Newcastle had a certain assured income, though never enough for the standard of life he maintained. That same year Jane married the Charles Cheyne whose name survives in Chelsea, and later, on 24 November, Frances married Oliver St John, who was to become Earl of Bolingbroke. On both these happy occasions the bride's father was a wistful absentee.

So he entered his seventh year in Antwerp. The marriage remained childless but happy. Margaret continued hopelessly undomesticated. Once, upset by gossip that her maids had nothing to do but sun themselves in the garden, she made a pathetic attempt to assume control, but was soon thankful to relinquish it to the housekeeper and retire to her study, a room conspicuously devoid of books since she feared the distraction of other writers' knowledge and ideas.

He tried to get her out, taking her to fairs and carnivals where the mountebanks and masqued revellers amused her. When winter gripped the city he persuaded her to wrap up warmly and venture into the white Brueghelesque world outside. She was charmed by the people sliding on the frozen Scheldt. He almost tempted her to join in. The only regular excursion she really enjoyed was the daily 'tour' when, at the fashionable hour, all the best people drove round the city in their coaches. Now, with the increasing number of English exiles, it was like Hyde Park. Happy to indulge her, Newcastle ordered another expensive coach. She seldom paid visits, but she enjoyed a musical evening with a Portuguese merchant's family, the Duartes, where the girls sang and the son, Gaspar, set some of Newcastle's songs. Margaret sang the simple old English ballads that suited her best.

Newcastle's old friends passed frequently through Antwerp. Margaret relates that one, in crossing the North Sea, had been 'set upon by picaroons'. The pirates discovered that he knew the Marquess: 'Whereupon they did not only take nothing from him, but used him with all civility, and desired him to remember their humble duty to their Lord General, for they were some of his Whitecoats that had escaped death; and if my Lord had any service for them, they were ready to assist him upon what designs soever. . . .'

Newcastle was engaged in no 'designs', though he would 'gently reprove' Margaret when she despaired of an eventual restoration. The King came to Bruges, then settled at Brussels. Newcastle maintained contact, asking Nicholas to get him confirmed in the offices he had held under Charles I, and seeking from Sir Edward Walker, Garter King of Arms, authority to use the style of 'Prince'. This was granted, and probably pleased Margaret as much as the tradesmen. On the title-page of her next book, *Nature's Pictures drawn by Fancies Pencil to the Life*, she blossomed forth as 'the thrice Noble, Illustrious, and Excellent Princess, the Lady Marchioness of Newcastle'. She described the contents as: 'Comical, Tragical, and Tragi-Comical, Poetical, Romantical, Philosophical, and Historical, both in Prose and Verse, some all Verse, some all Prose, some mixed, partly Prose, and partly Verse. . . .' She was determined for once to make everything quite clear.

Margaret's attempts at drama were extraordinary. She had no stage sense. *The Matrimonial Trouble*, in which a jilted heroine takes revenge on her lover, is a ravel of six sub-plots. The pursuing female recurs often in her plays. In *Love's Adventures* Lady Orphan has been intended from childhood to marry Lord Singularity, whom she has never seen save in a portrait revealing 'his noble soul . . . thro' his lovely, and lively, countenance'. To escape her, Singularity flees to Venice and becomes a *condottiere*. She follows and enters his service as a page. Like Shakespeare's Viola, she is ready even to woo another woman on his behalf. She also fights in battle, rescues him from the enemy, and is promoted lieutenant-general by the oddly unobservant Venetians. In Rome she disputes with the College of Cardinals and the admiring Pope offers her the choice of a cardinal's hat or a saint's halo. Declining both, she discloses her true sex to Singularity, whose former reluctance is instantly abandoned.

There is not much sign here of the Jonsonian theories which Newcastle admired, but he sensibly refrained from fruitless criticism or discouragement, and even helped her by contributing songs and occasional scenes, which she scrupulously acknowledged. In *The Lady Contemplation* three suitors, rejected by the virtuous heroine, all attempt to seduce Moll Meanbred, a country wench well able to look after herself. Margaret asked her husband to write these scenes as they demanded a coarseness of which she felt incapable. Newcastle found no difficulty. His dialogue is natural and earthily humorous, theatrically effective and immediately distinguishable from the stiff speeches Margaret gives the same gentlemen in their scenes with the heroine.

Much of his own time was spent with his beloved horses. The two brought from Paris had unhappily died, but, he recalled later: 'Poor as I was in those days, I made shift to buy at different times five Barbs, five Spanish horses, and many Dutch horses, all the most excellent horses that could be, and among them a grey leaping horse, the most beautiful that ever I saw.' The Duc de Guise offered him 600 gold pieces for this animal, but, whatever his financial worries, Newcastle would seldom part with a horse, protesting that he 'never was a good horse-coper, selling being none of my professions'. The economics of his famous 'riding school' are obscure. It was the animals that were schooled, rather than the riders, but it may be that in some discreet and gentlemanly fashion his hospitality was recognised by some of those who flocked to admire, and learn from, his outstanding equestrian skill.

This was now famous throughout Europe. Besides his English visitors, people came from France and Spain, Germany, Poland, Sweden and elsewhere. Charles II came, as did the Duke of Oldenburg and the Prince of East Friesland, who both presented horses to their host. Christina came too, fresh from her abdication. She was staying with an Antwerp merchant and had presumably discarded the male attire in which she travelled. So enthusiastic a horsewoman could not have missed a meeting with Newcastle. He recalled it in carefully chosen phrases: 'I had the honour to wait on the Queen of Sweden when she was at Antwerp, and she used me very graciously, and civilly; and an extraordinary lady, I assure you, she is in all things.' One morning Margaret gleefully counted seventeen coaches disgorging 'persons of quality', when the Marquess of Ormonde and the Earl of Bristol brought the entire entourage of the Spanish viceroy. A subsequent viceroy, the Marquis of Caracena, came and begged Newcastle to give a personal display, which he could hardly refuse, though he had been unwell for the previous two months.

I rid first a Spanish horse called Le Superbe, of a light bay, a beautiful horse ... He went in curvets, forward, backward, sideways, on both hands; made the cross perfectly upon his voltoes; and did change ... without breaking time, that no musician could keep time better.

A musician himself, he emphasised elsewhere: 'There is no man, that hath not a musical head, that can be a good horseman, because all horses ought to go in a just and musical time.'

That particular morning he rode two other mounts for the viceroy. Le Gentry, 'a brown bay with a white star in his forehead', pirouetted so rapidly 'that the standers-by could hardly see the rider's face when he went'. The Spaniards crossed themselves and cried: '*Miracolo!*' Newcastle confessed afterwards, 'I was so dizzy that I could hardly sit in the saddle.'

He had tested all the traditional French and Italian methods, modifying them as he thought fit. He was critical of the revered Pluvinal, whose 'method of the Three Pillars, of which his book pretends to be an absolute method, is no more than an absolute routine; and hath spoil'd more horses than ever anything did'. He had read every other writer on the subject.

But all that while I thought still, all was labour in vain; and that there was something, not found out, which they and their books missed. Whereupon I began to consider so seriously, and study so earnestly, all the particulars that concern the manage; that at last I found this method, which is as true as it is new, and is the quintessence of horsemanship.

His innovation was his method of using the cavesson, the stiff noseband employed in training. Pluvinal tied the loose ends of the reins to pillars. Newcastle fastened them to the pommel of the saddle or kept them in his hand. He was a gentle teacher – 'I would neither hurt his mouth, nor his nose, nor anything else about him if I could help it' – and he made little use of the switch, but, while showing the highest respect for a horse's intelligence, he 'followed not the horse's disposition as most do' but uncompromisingly imposed his will upon it. 'The horse must know you are his master.' Those inclined to dismiss Newcastle as a dilettante should read him on his favourite theme:

They think it is a disgrace for a gentleman to do anything well. What! Be a rider. Why not? Many kings and princes think themselves graced with being good horsemen. . . . He that will take pains for nothing shall never do anything well; for arts, sciences and good qualities come not by instinct, but are got by great labour, study, and practice, wherefore these men will none (I thank you) till they be as easily learnt as the Seven Deadly Sins.

It was during the Antwerp years that he decided to condense a lifetime of thought and experience into a book of his own. He handed his draft to a French translator, for it seemed best, when addressing an international public, to adopt that language. It was to be printed in Antwerp as an elegant folio volume, with forty-three copperplate engravings designed by Abraham van Diepenbeke, who had already contributed frontispieces to Margaret's books. The horsemanship illustrations embodied views of Welbeck, Bolsover and Ogle, and a Cavendish family group, including all the sons-in-law and daughters-in-law, an imaginative concentration impossible to achieve in real life. All this, together with the best of bindings, paper and typography, proved formidably expensive. Newcastle wrote to Secretary Nicholas:

I am so tormented about my book of horsemanship as you cannot believe, with a hundred several trades, I think, and the printing will cost above £1,300, which I could never have done but for my good friends Sir H. Cartwright and Mr Loving; and I hope they shall lose nothing by it, and I am sure they hope the like.

For once the munificent patron needed backers himself. The book duly came out in 1658, entitled *La Méthode Nouvelle et Invention Extraordinaire de Dresser Les Chevaux.*

This pecuniary embarrassment did not, however, deter him from giving a magnificent banquet and ball when Charles II visited the city late in February that year. It was a proud moment with so many Stuarts gathered under his roof, not only the King but his brothers, the future James II and Henry, Duke of Gloucester, and his sister Mary, Princess of Orange. Michael Mohun, later a leading actor in the Restoration theatre, appeared robed and garlanded to deliver welcoming verses composed by Newcastle, and Lady Moore sang one of his songs, set by the Master of the King's Music, Nicholas Lanier. No expense was spared. It took sixteen gentlemen to carry in the dishes, with others to bring in the wine. Dancing went on till midnight, when Mohun recited an epilogue prophesying His Majesty's happy return to England.

That night, even allowing for the elation of the hour, the wine and the candlelight, many must have thought it mere flattering optimism. Cromwell looked immovable. He had smashed the Scots and Irish, he had overwhelmed the opposition in England. Yet six months later, on 3 September, he was dead. At last the political horizon was flushed with the dawn of hope.

TWENTY-ONE

Restoration

AT OXFORD, preserved among the Clarendon Manuscripts in the Bodleian, bound in white parchment with handsome gold tooling and blue silken strings, is the memorandum Newcastle submitted to Charles II as his restoration became a practicable possibility. It is a thoughtful, if reactionary, document, coloured by harsh experience and the inbred class prejudice of a lifetime; but it reflects also the intellectual influence of Hobbes and, in its appreciation of commercial factors, the effect of long residence in Antwerp. Newcastle was an archetypal Tory before that label was current. But he was neither stupid nor incapable of learning.

He had witnessed the tragedy of a king who claimed God-given authority but lacked the earthly means, financial and military, to back it. Charles II must not find himself in that position. He must control the army, 'for without an army in your own hands you are but a king upon the courtesy of others'. He must control London, 'for so you master all England'. Other ports must have dependable garrisons, and the counties their train bands, but those of London, so important to the Parliamentary victory, must not recover their old preponderancy, for, 'as one said, what should they be armed for but in time of peace to play the fools in Finsbury Fields in training there – and in time of war to play the rebels against their king, so still I conclude, Master London and you have done your work'. The sovereign must never again be chronically short of money and dependent on Parliament to vote supplies. Revenue would be better raised from customs duties, fairly and efficiently levied on a prosperous and expanding commerce, with low interest rates, new industries introduced from abroad, and a favourable export balance.

Newcastle's religious prejudices had been reinforced by the wranglings of the past two decades. Only the Church of England should be permitted, for Roman Catholicism and Presbyterianism carried 'the same firebrands of covetousness and ambition, to put all into a combustion'.

There should be uniformity and a strict press censorship, preachers confining themselves to printed sermons. Theological argument should be conducted in Latin, to be read only by the educated, for 'controversy is a civil war with the pen which pulls out the sword soon afterwards' and 'the Bible in English under every weaver's and chambermaid's arm hath done us much hurt'. The bishops must supervise the schools and see that no weavers could disseminate subversive heresies. Newcastle's Yorkshire campaigns seem to have left him with a permanent distrust of the textile worker.

In pleasing contrast to these grim authoritarian recommendations was his plea that the King, while bringing back all the court ceremonies and festivities, would ensure that the common people were freed to enjoy their former sports and pleasures, with hearty feasting, traditional holidays and all the fun of the fair. It was an eloquent appeal for the revival of Merrie England.

As he penned it, there was no guarantee that Charles would ever have the chance to follow his counsel. Richard Cromwell had succeeded his father as Lord Protector. Anything might happen. One could say no more than that public sentiment was veering back towards a monarchy.

Newcastle had still to be cautious in writing to his family. An undated letter, signed with the appropriate pseudonym 'John Forreste', went to Viscount Mansfield:

Most Noble Sir, My wife says she doth condole with you for the loss of the little lady, but congratulates very much with you for the safety of your sweet and worthy Lady, and hopes this will be a warning to her after, to take heed of too much violent exercise. In that case she makes no doubt but God will bless you with many sons. . . .

This may well have been addressed to Henry, for on 31 May 1659 Charles died at Bolsover, 'of a dead palsy', as Brian Duppa told Sir Justinian Isham. The young widow 'not being with child', it was soon possible to establish beyond question that his younger brother was the new viscount. On 11 October Newcastle was writing to Henry:

Now for what is in our power, I pray you to live at your own houses, We. and Bo., which will much conduce to your health. The next is for your goods, which troubles me much, that so long gathering by your ancestors should be destroyed in a moment. This is my earnest advice to you. First they are appraised, and goods are never appraised at a third part of their value; and then you may buy them and no ill bargain if you took the money at interest or your father-in-law laid out the money and had all the goods in his hands for his security. My intention is but to save the goods for you, that is all the design my wife and I have in the business, for she is as kind to you as she was to your brother and so good a wife as that she is all for my family, which she expresses is only you.

Two weeks later he was emphasising that he and Margaret resigned their interest in the house contents 'wholly and totally' to Henry. 'There are many good pictures, besides Vandykes and Steenwijcks. Pray leave your dovecot where you are now and live at We., which will conduce much to your health and your lady's and the little ladies.' Henry so far had only daughters. Two successive boys, both christened William, had died soon after they were born.

As often happens, there were some recriminations about missing items. On 15 November Newcastle wrote again:

I believe your sister [-in-law]'s servants have made great spoil of the goods, for the painter told me the cases of crimson velvet for the chairs in the parlour at Bolsover were there a little while before your brother Charles died. But we must part fair with her, and repair it as well as we can. The gold lace and embroidery of the purple velvet bed was worth £300 at least, and five chambers at Bolsover were furnished with very fine hangings at £4 a stick. The pictures there were most rare, and if you think they are a little spoiled, I will send over the painter to you again. If ever I see you I will make We. a very fine place for you. I am not in despair of it, though I believe you and I are not such good architects as your worthy grandfather. If I am blessed with the happiness of seeing you, it will be a thousand pounds a year better for you than if I should die before.

In these last years of exile his interest in dramatic writing revived. There has been much scholarly discussion and a tendency to credit anything of merit to the professional playwrights with whom he sometimes collaborated. Clearly his talents were modest, but he had an authentic impulse to create. In Antwerp, isolated from helpers, he composed *A Pleasant and Merry Humour of a Rogue*, a thirty-eight-page play in eleven short scenes, which has been preserved in his own handwriting. Later, it is true, Shadwell had a major hand in its development into a longer piece, *The Triumphant Widow, or The Medley of Humours*, but this first version was unaided, if not strikingly original. It has Shakespearean echoes, the rogue Footpad deriving from Autolycus, and the comic constable, with billman and watch, from Dogberry. But Newcastle has his own moments, if only in odd lines of lyrics, such as 'White as the singing swan I go', though he is unable, or too casual, to sustain the quality.

Meanwhile, in England farsighted men prepared to abandon the sinking ship. By January 1659 Newcastle was writing to Nicholas:

There are many noblemen, or at least lords, that are comed over to Paris . . . but those lords that can take such sudden apprehensions of fears so far off, I doubt will hardly have the courage to help our gracious Master to his throne – woeful people – and the next generation of lords they tell me are fools. It will be a brave Upper House!

By 9 March 1660 matters had moved far but were still uncertain, as he emphasised to the Secretary of State:

I cannot conclude what will be the issue of the great distractions and cross interests in England. That the King will be called in is probable, but on what conditions the Lord knows. I am not of the opinion to come in on any terms, and be trammelled and made a Duke of Venice of, which is but Lord Mayor during his life.

April saw the election of a new Parliament, predisposed to a restoration on any reasonable terms. Charles issued his famous Declaration of Breda, which was read in Parliament on 1 May and accepted. A week later he was proclaimed King. Within four more days the waiting fleet sailed for Holland to bring him home.

It was characteristic of Newcastle – but unwise if he hoped for much influence under the new regime – that he hastened to The Hague only when the restoration was assured. He had never been an effective schemer, never grasped the elementary truth that an ambitious politician must stay close to the centre of things. He too naïvely assumed automatic recognition of his past loyalty and services. He had hopes of high office, perhaps Master of the Horse. He was quickly disillusioned when he waited upon Charles at the Mauritshuis. His old pupil received him with the usual suave charm but soon indicated that Monck wished to be Master of the Horse. Monck had served Cromwell and fought at Dunbar, but that was now irrelevant – it was Monck who had just marched his army on London, dissolved the old Parliament and made the King's return possible. Charles was less interested in old faithfuls than in new turncoats. The mood of the moment was expressed by another, Edward Mountagu, who had just handed him the navy on a plate. 'We must have a little patience,' Mountagu told his kinsman, Pepys, 'and we will rise together. In the meantime I will do you all the good jobs I can.'

Newcastle was not the man to hang about the court, hoping for scraps. When the Duke of York, newly appointed Lord High Admiral, invited him to sail to Dover with the royal flotilla, he excused himself and chartered a vessel for his own party. Once again he was cutting himself off. But, what with Hyde's continuing dominance as the King's adviser and the need to cultivate the new supporters, it probably made little difference.

Despite this grandly independent gesture, Newcastle could afford only 'an old rotten frigate', which, Margaret records, 'was lost the next voyage'. Most of the party 'turned back, and would not endanger their lives in it'. She herself escaped the dilemma, for she had had to stay in Antwerp as a 'pawn for his debts' and to make his apologies to the civic authorities for his inability to take leave of them in person. His one staunch companion was young Lord Widdrington, son of his old comrade-in-arms. Newcastle himself, 'transported with the joy of returning into his native country', was quite heedless of risk.

Luckily no tempest blew. Indeed, after sailing from Rotterdam they were becalmed six days and nights, during which, the vessel being well stocked with food and drink, 'he pleased himself with mirth, and passed his time away as well as he could'. At long last, creeping up the Thames estuary, they saw the smoke-pall over London. 'Jog me,' he begged, 'and wake me out of my dream! For surely I have been sixteen years asleep, and am not thoroughly awake yet.'

They landed at Greenwich, where he pronounced the supper the most savoury he had ever tasted and the 'scraping fiddlers' at the inn 'the pleasantest harmony' he had ever heard. There was, too, a happy re-union with his son. Henry, full of anxiety, had tracked him down after a fruitless journey to Dover where he had expected to find him in the royal party. Told of his father's much earlier departure, and in such an unseaworthy vessel, he had almost given him up for lost.

Within a day or two Newcastle was back in his old place in the House of Lords when the King briefly addressed the combined Houses and then commanded the Lord Chancellor 'to deliver his mind further', which Hyde did at some length. It was almost a week before Newcastle attended again. Although there were daily sittings, Parliament was not debating, much less deciding, major policy, only local or specialised matters, and he did not reappear until 7 June when Sherwood Forest was on the agenda and he was appointed head of the commission to arrest the destruction of the woodlands. He attended again on 13 June, when he was put on the Committees of Privileges and Petitions, the first of which held its opening meeting the next day. He was in his seat on 15, 19 (Sherwood again) and 21 June, when the peers accepted the

Lord Mayor's invitation to a banquet for the King on 5 July. He was absent on 22 June when an order was made to stop the devastation of his own woods. During the next month he was in the House on several occasions, but not on 31 July when he was listed among those absent without excuse and liable to a five-shilling fine.

On 7 August a bill was introduced 'for restoring unto William Marquess of Newcastle all his Honours, Manors, Lands and Tenements, in England, whereof he was in possession on the 23 October, 1642, or at any time since'. He not unnaturally attended this and half a dozen subsequent days that month. The Earl of Bristol spoke warmly in his praise, so warmly that Buckingham leapt up to complain of an implied slight to himself. Buckingham had made his peace with Cromwell three years before and had ingeniously, if shamelessly, repaired his fortunes by marrying Fairfax's daughter on the eve of her marriage to the Earl of Chesterfield. Bristol said, with restraint, that he thought Newcastle 'a man of more merit'. There was nearly a duel. Some time later, during the coronation preparations, Sir Edward Walker, Garter King of Arms, expressed the following view on comparative loyalties to the King:

And although multitudes of his loyal subjects of all degrees had not, until this time, openly owned his Majesty but had lived at home with the hazard of their lives and fortunes, under the oppression of barbarous tyrants, expecting and contributing to this happy change, whose merit was no less than that of others, whose more immediate service required their attendance on his Majesty in his low and wandering condition in France, Spain, Germany and the Netherlands, yet because they were but few in number that did so, it will not be impertinent to name them for the honour of themselves and their posterities, viz: Their Royal Highnesses James Duke of York and Henry Duke of Gloucester, Sir Edward Hyde, James Marquess of Ormonde, William Marquess of Newcastle, returned from Antwerp. . . .

Whatever enemies or critics Newcastle had, they did not oppose the bill restoring his former honours, and it passed quickly through all its stages, receiving the royal assent on 13 September. He was not present that day.

He could see by now that there was no future for him at court. The King preferred the society of younger, more frivolous men. He had better, quite literally, mind his own business – raise money quickly so that he could settle his Antwerp debts and bring Margaret home, and face the formidable practical problems of restoring his estates. His kinsman, Devonshire, lent him £1000. With the help of Joseph Ash, an

English merchant in Antwerp, he was able to let Margaret have £5000, which, with £400 she borrowed from another Englishman there, John Shaw, enabled her to make a dignified departure.

Arriving in London, she was at once critical of his lodgings – the Clerkenwell house had been sold in 1654 and would have to be bought back. His present rooms 'were not fit for a person of his rank and quality', a point on which she was becoming increasingly touchy. Margaret had not been improved by years of adversity. She had developed a defiant, defensive eccentricity. Now she was shocked to see her husband so little regarded in this altered England. She had never been one to compete. She instinctively avoided any situation in which she could not excel. 'Wherefore,' she says, 'out of some passion I desired him to leave the town and retire into the country.' He 'gently reproved' her for her 'rashness and impatience', but clearly her mood was not unsympathetic to his own. He was anxious to see what had happened to Welbeck and Bolsover, but his London business must be finished first. He conciliated her by moving into Dorset House, but as they had only part of the mansion she was not completely mollified.

Their relationship, in some respects so close, was in others curiously detached. Margaret, immersed in her 'fancies' and impatient of practicalities, was not an easy person with whom to discuss the future. Newcastle, too, was a seventeenth-century husband, a great nobleman used to making arbitrary decisions, and thirty years her senior. She had begged him, had she not, to retire to the country? So without further debate he completed his business, ordered the baggage waggons to be loaded, and was then 'pleased to tell' her that they were leaving for Welbeck.

The King's permission to quit the court was a mere formality. Charles, though always retaining kindly memories of his boyhood mentor, was not sorry to be relieved of a continual visible reminder of his own ingratitude. He made Newcastle Gentleman of the Bedchamber for life on 21 September and Lord-Lieutenant of Nottinghamshire ten days later. At their parting Newcastle expressed himself with his usual dignity:

Sir, I am not ignorant that many believe I am discontented, and 't is probable they'll say I retire through discontent. But I take God to witness that I am in no kind of ways displeased, for I am so joyed at your Majesty's happy restoration that I cannot be sad or troubled for any concern to my own particular. Whatsoever your Majesty is pleased to command me, were it to sacrifice my life, I shall most obediently perform it, for I have no other will but your Majesty's pleasure.

Soon the coaches and waggons were rumbling up the Great North Road. 'I observe', said Margaret tartly, 'your gracious master does not love you so well as you love him.' Newcastle did not care, he assured her, whether his love was returned or not.

TWENTY-TWO

Homecoming

DELIGHT in homecoming was mingled with dismay. Both houses were in a sorry condition. And Sherwood Forest in general was fast approaching the stage when, as Defoe declared, 'Robin Hood would hardly find shelter for a week'. Of Newcastle's own eight deer parks his brother had managed to save only Welbeck itself. At Clipstone, his favourite woodland, the oaks were cut down, the palisades gone, the deer vanished. Margaret describes his grief when he saw the devastation, with 'not one timber-tree left for shelter'. He said little, but gave orders to replace the fences and, obtaining deer from various friends, patiently began to build up the herd again.

It was one thing to get his bill through Parliament, quite another to translate its smooth phrases into fact. It would take years to bring farms back to their pristine condition. Thorny questions of ownership remained. Some confiscated lands, for example, had passed into the possession of regicides – and now, by forfeiture, to the Duke of York. Other property had been legally sold. It could not simply be taken back. Parliament had accepted the King's return on the understanding that there could be no complete return to the *status quo*. 'The Act of Oblivion', said Margaret bitterly, 'proved a great hindrance', and her husband faced a protracted struggle. The Duke of York acted well in relinquishing his part of the estates. Others were harder to deal with. Parliament had sold Bothal to a London merchant, Barnabas Trembett, in 1652, and it had now to be recovered from a subsequent owner, George Lawson. Ogle had been bought by James Moseley and, when regained, was much plundered. Newcastle could not afford to restore Bothal, but it seems that in due course he modernised Ogle as a suitable home for Henry. It took years of vexatious litigation to get back the Clerkenwell house.

Tantalisingly, while he was up to his ears in all these difficulties, Nottingham Castle was put on the market by Buckingham, who had inherited it from his mother, daughter of the Earl of Rutland. The castle had been demolished by Hutchinson, but the site, long ago admired by his father, tempted Newcastle irresistibly. He sold land in Derbyshire and bought it. One day he would build another Bolsover on that superb acropolis. For the presenth e could only fence and re-stock the small deer park that stretched below the precipice.

In that autumn of his homecoming he was nearing sixty-seven, an age at which most modern men have retired and most seventeenth-century men were dead. He was, however, blessed with usually good health and unquenchable spirit. He still looked forward, was as interested in long-term plans as in immediate problems. He believed in land drainage, 'for drowned lands are only fit to maintain and increase some wild ducks'. He planted trees, holding that there was 'none of such a temper as our English oak' and that 'in shipping consists our greatest strength, they being the only walls that defend an island'. Horse-breeding, much encouraged by the Stuarts, had decayed under the Commonwealth. He bought the best mares he could find and began to breed from them. Though he had never previously taken any interest in racing, he knew that racehorses – 'running horses' as they were termed – offered most gentlemen the strongest stimulus to apply their minds to the subject. Accordingly he laid out a five-mile course at Welbeck, held meetings six times a year, and invited his neighbours to compete for a silver cup. He devised his own rules and announced good-humouredly that 'though this be not the Law of the Medes and Persians' he would 'alter nothing in it'. If anyone wanted other rules, let him establish his own and race elsewhere. Not surprisingly, the gentry flocked to Welbeck.

Margaret gives a pen-portrait of her husband six years after his return home, when the worst difficulties had been surmounted. We see a 'neat and cleanly' man, 'sparing and temperate' of habit, 'somewhat long in dressing, though not so long as many effeminate persons are', following fashion when it did not restrict his activities. Active he still was. She emphasises that, changing ordinarily once a day, he changed oftener after exercise. He had cut down on the more strenuous equestrian feats, which caused him to get over-heated and catch cold, and was usually content merely to supervise in the riding-school. He still rode regularly through the park, however, and practised fencing daily.

His breakfast was bread with a small glass of sack. He took another glass at dinner and two good-sized ones of small beer. Supper was light, an egg usually, with more small beer. Presumably he still enjoyed his pipe, for in 1661 Francis Topp, an English merchant who had been very helpful at Antwerp and had eventually married Margaret's maid, Elizabeth Chaplain, was sending him tobacco and wine from Bristol. At Welbeck Topp's business acumen was still at his disposal, supplementing the more limited experience of his agent, Andrew Clayton, and his secretary, John Rolleston.

Much time was occupied with estate business in those first years. We may imagine the miles covered, on horseback or with Margaret in their coach, to revisit well-loved scenes, inspect conditions and discuss remedies. There were endless encounters with old neighbours, tenants and servants, or their descendants. 'To the meanest person he'll put off his hat,' wrote Margaret, 'and suffer everybody to speak to him.' He was always 'courtly' and 'civil', 'without formality or constraint', yet his manner had 'something in it of grandeur', which impelled respect. Many of his old soldiers or their widows sought his help. He did what he could, but, as he had to explain to one woman, he had not the means to help all who had been loyal to the late King.

He was wryly philosophic about his own treatment. Riding across the park he came on workmen sawing up a sound tree that had been blown down in a gale. 'I have been at that work a great part of my life,' he said. Seeing that his companions looked puzzled, he added that he was not jesting. He had been toppled by misfortune and had had to make the best of it, using 'the chips of my estate'. He once told an aggrieved friend: 'States do not usually reward past services. Those men are wisest that will be paid beforehand.'

Margaret, more resentful, began to think of a book that would vindicate his record and reveal the magnitude of his sacrifices. It could not be written hastily. She had to deal with facts, not fancies. Rolleston could give her his first-hand memories of the Civil War and the details from which she could estimate what her husband's loyalty had cost him in cash alone. His annual rent-roll from his estates in Nottinghamshire, Derbyshire, Staffordshire, Yorkshire, Lincolnshire, Northumberland, Somerset and Gloucestershire had been £22,393 10s. 1d. She reckoned the loss of this over eighteen years, with compound interest at six per cent, at £733,579. Adding further items, like devastated woodlands, and resisting the rhetorical attraction of a round million, she arrived – with a precision quite out of character – at £941,303. Accurate or not, it looks a fair figure.

It was some years before this *magnum opus* was completed. First she published her plays. Though she once confessed to an ambition to see them staged, she was realistic enough to admit that their chances were minimal. She wrote in her preface: 'Some of my scenes have no acquaintance or relation to the rest of the scenes, though in one and the same play, which is the reason many of my plays will not end as other plays do.' They were also far too long and might 'tire the spectators . . . bound by the rules of civility to sit out a play, if they be not sick'. She need not have worried. In the Restoration theatres the gallants came, went and chattered without inhibition. She had more grounds for fearing hurtful criticism. 'It would have made me a little melancholy to have my harmless and innocent plays go weeping from the stage, and whipped by malicious and hard-hearted censurers.'

This 1662 volume contained fourteen pieces, written at Antwerp. She wrote four more at Welbeck, published with another unfinished, in 1668. One of these later plays, *The Sociable Companions; or, The Female Wits*, had as theme the plight of the old Cavaliers who had lost everything for the cause and were forced to emigrate to the new American plantations. This piece shows signs of construction, with development, suspense and climax. The dialogue is more to the point and farcical humour is introduced for relief. Scholars suspect the hand of Newcastle. The theme would certainly have engaged his sympathy.

Between these two volumes several others appeared, first *Orations of Divers Sorts*, then in 1663 *Philosophical and Physical Opinions*, and a year later *CCXI Sociable Letters*, addressed to an unnamed – but some think from their naturalness an actual – correspondent. Though these letters cannot be accepted unreservedly as documentary evidence, they contain many obviously autobiographical elements extending back to the Antwerp period. Also in 1664 she published *Philosophical Letters: or, Modest Reflections upon some Opinions in Natural Philosophy, maintained by several famous and learned Authors of this Age*. She was reading much more – that year, Rolleston paid out £39 14s. in book purchases for her. She attempted philosophy, 'of purpose to learn those names and words of art that are used in schools', but she still found it easier to pick up ideas in conversation. She remained convinced of her own originality, claiming in *Philosophical Letters* that her opinions were 'new and never thought of, at least not divulged by any, but myself'. The Oxford scholar, Joseph Glanvill, who had ominously written *The Vanity of Dogmatizing*, pointed out that some of her ideas were remarkably like those of the platonists. There is no evidence that she had ever read any Plato, but this did not deter her from devoting a whole chapter of *Observations upon Experimental Philosophy* (1666) to explaining the difference between his views and her own. Research has revealed a limited number of platonic ideas in her work, apparently acquired superficially and at second hand, and frequently recycled. Contemporary critics, except for a few like the robustly honest Glanvill, treated her publications with flattering respect. The Master and Fellows of St John's, Cambridge, thought that they would 'not only survive our University, but hold date even with time itself', adding the hope that 'this age, by reading of your books, will lose its barbarity and rudeness, being made tame by the elegance of your style and matter'. They may, of course, have had another hope in mind. Her husband had once been a member of their college.

Meanwhile Newcastle's own cultural interests were as keen as ever. 'The rest of his time,' says Margaret, after mentioning the horses and fencing, 'he spends in music, poetry, architecture and the like'. One of his first appointments on returning to Welbeck had been that of a violinist at thirty pounds a year. As soon as funds enabled him to proceed beyond the urgent repairs at Bolsover he embarked on the last great phase of building there, which, Girouard suggests, covered about 1665–70 or even later, and included new and grander apartments and private rooms at the south-west corner of the great courtyard and the lofty, tie-beamed riding-school, ninety-two feet by thirty, which with its forge and harness-room runs the length of that southern side. Nor, though he had left London, did he forget the playhouse.

His prewar piece, *The Country Captain*, was soon revived at the theatre which Killigrew converted from a tennis-court in Vere Street. Pepys, on 26 October 1661, thought it 'so silly a play as in all my life I never saw, and the first that ever I was weary of in my life'. Surprisingly, he went to it again a month later, and in 1667 and 1668, with equal displeasure, but Pepys as a critic was not infallible and was equally rude about far better plays. Years later Thomas Shadwell wrote a prologue for another production, declaring:

> A good play cannot properly be said
> To be revived, because it ne'er was dead.

Shadwell was hardly impartial. Newcastle, he testifies elsewhere, had noticed him while he was still unknown and helped him for 'several years before you saw me at Welbeck, where (when I arrived) I found a respect so extremely above the meanness of my condition, that I still received it with blushes; having nothing to recommend me (but the birth and education, without the fortune, of a gentleman) besides some writings of mine, which your Grace was pleased to like.' Newcastle he pronounced 'the only Maecenas of our Age', and Welbeck 'the only place, where the best poets can find a good reception'. It is easy now to smile at these fulsome tributes, but such patronage was then almost indispensable to the flowering of much literary talent. No patron, wrote the American scholar, Perry, 'was more influential than Newcastle'. He was 'a vital factor in shaping the course of English literary history'.

Another visitor was the Irishman Richard Flecknoe, an old acquaintance from Antwerp days, whose lean and hungry look contrasted strikingly with the massive Shadwell. The man was a wanderer, with tales of lands as far off as Brazil, uncontrollably fond of reciting his own verses. Like Margaret, he wrote unactable plays – only his pastoral tragicomedy achieved performance, being dedicated to Newcastle – but he optimistically provided lists of the actors he would have cast for the parts. After his death, Dryden wrote of him mordantly that he:

> In prose and verse was owned, without dispute,
> Through all the realms of nonsense absolute . . . ,

but the Newcastles suffered him tolerantly and were rewarded with more dedications. If Flecknoe sang for his supper at least it was a good supper. In *Euterpe Revived* he remembered Welbeck:

> Whose cellar and whose larder seem t' have been
> Of ev'ry foreign land the magazine.

He is another witness to Newcastle's lack of pompousness, calling him 'a nobleman indeed' who does not always look for doffed hats and reverence from afar:

> Nor take exceptions, if at every word
> You call him not *his Grace* or else *my Lord;*
> But does appear a hundred times more great
> By his neglect of 't, than by keeping state.

Dryden could be acid about Shadwell and Flecknoe. More socially secure, with a small private income, an earl for father-in-law and a regular contract to write for the Theatre Royal, he had no need to crawl for patronage. He was, however, conscious of his own deficiencies as a writer of comedy – which his audiences demanded – and as Newcastle's modest gifts included a certain flair for broad humour and low-life characterisation there was a genuinely fruitful element in their association. He wrote gracefully of him in the dedication of *An Evening's Love:* 'now . . . happily arrived to the evening of a day, as serene as the dawn of it was glorious, but such an evening as, I hope, and almost prophesy, is far from night. 'T is the evening of a summer's sun, which keeps the daylight long within the skies.' In 'your excellent lady' Newcastle had found 'not only a lover, but a partner of your studies . . . equal with the Sappho of the Greeks'.

It is most likely that Newcastle supplied Dryden with the idea for *Sir Martin Mar-All*, believed to be Newcastle's play on its first production in 1667 but now generally accepted as Dryden's. Probably Newcastle made him the rough translation of Molière's *L'Etourdi* (itself a by no means original work) on which the piece was based. Collaboration with contemporaries, like plagiarisation of predecessors, was so common that it is now often difficult to disentangle the respective contributions. Long before, Newcastle had accepted help from Shirley. Now he found himself most in tune with Shadwell, a Jonsonian disciple like himself. Shadwell is thought to have helped him with *The Humorous Lovers*, also first performed in 1667. He clearly discussed his own work in progress with Newcastle, for he writes, in the dedication of *The Virtuoso*, 'when I first showed your Grace some part of this comedy at Welbeck, being all that I had then written of it . . .'. He professed a high regard for Newcastle's opinion as 'the greatest master of wit, the most exact observer of mankind, and the most accurate judge of humour, that ever I knew'. Though Shadwell was hardly impartial, his assessment has some support from Gerard Langbaine, fifteen years after Newcastle's death, when there was no point in flattery. 'Our English Maecenas', he declared, had a 'perfect knowledge of what was to be accounted true humour in Comedy.'

It had been face-saving to plead advancing years as an excuse to retire from court, but these manifold activities are scarcely consistent with decrepitude. Newcastle did not journey to Windsor for his long-delayed installation as Knight of the Garter on 15 April 1661. Henry, himself now Master of the Robes, was his father's proxy and heard the sonorous recital of his career, concluding, 'he now pleaseth himself in his old age in a private life, in his country, honoured and esteemed by all men'. Presumably he also excused himself from the coronation eight days later. His fourteen-year-old grandson John, Lord Brackley, eldest of Elizabeth's five boys, had a part in the ceremony.

Newcastle remained Lord-Lieutenant of Nottinghamshire till he died, and in July 1661 he was given a similar life appointment as Chief Justice in Eyre north of Trent, an ancient office concerned with the obsolescent forest laws. His lord-lieutenancy was no sinecure. In October 1663 he was dismayed to receive a letter from Buckingham, now increasingly powerful at court, instructing him to arrest his old adversary, Colonel Hutchinson, on suspicion of complicity in a plot. Newcastle and Hutchinson, though differing in politics, had always highly respected each other. Hutchinson had been expressly removed from the list of regicides and Newcastle felt sure that he was living harmlessly in retirement. Previously, when Hutchinson's house had been raided and his personal arms and armour confiscated, he had ordered instant restitution. He could not now ignore Buckingham's instruction, but took pains to receive the Colonel with the utmost courtesy. 'They say you desire to know your accusers,' he said, 'which is more than I know.' He showed him Buckingham's letter and sent him home on parole for a week, confident that the Privy Council would acknowledge his innocence. In a few days came a further letter. Buckingham admitted he had no real evidence, but 'hoped' to 'bring Mr Hutchinson into the plot'. He was to be put under close arrest, without pen, ink or paper. Newcastle wrote to Hutchinson that he still believed him innocent and 'was sorry he could not pursue that kindness he intended'. He even enclosed a copy of Buckingham's letter. Hutchinson was sent to London for interrogation, and, though never charged, died within the year from the rigours of his imprisonment. Newcastle's private feelings are not hard to guess.

The year 1663 opened happily with the birth on 19 January of Henry's first son, another Henry. Newcastle now had seven grandsons and seven granddaughters, but this was the first boy in the male line, continuing the succession. That summer, however, brought sorrow. Elizabeth's husband, the Earl of Bridgwater, had accepted a challenge from the Earl of Middlesex and was in custody at Black Rod's house in Westminster. While visiting him there she fell into premature labour and died on 14 June. Of all the ten children Newcastle had fathered only Henry, Jane and Frances survived. Nor, to his distress, did they get on well with their stepmother. She tried hard, but her oddities – people called her 'Mad Madge of Newcastle' – did not help. No Cavendish, with the family's inbred concern for property, could be expected to welcome even a childless stepmother. They resented the influence of her former maid, Mrs Topp, and her pushing husband. The grandchildren visited Welbeck, but it was never quite the family home Newcastle would have liked to make it, or the one his son and daughters remembered from long before.

Otherwise, as he entered his seventies, he was almost contented. Ambition, never an all-consuming passion, was spent. He wanted nothing more – except perhaps to leave a dukedom to his posterity. He intimated as much to the King, who was perfectly amenable. He still owed Newcastle thousands of pounds lent to his father in 1639, not to mention four thousand unpaid pension as Gentleman of the Bedchamber, so it seemed an easy way to postpone the day of reckoning. He answered affably: 'Send me therefore word what title you desire to have, or whether you will choose to keep your old and leave the rest to me. . . . I am glad you enjoy your health for I love you very well.'

So, on 16 March 1665, he turned the Marquess into the Duke of Newcastle-upon-Tyne, and Henry moved up to become Earl of Ogle. This justified a visit to London. The new Duke and Duchess set off with an appropriately impressive entourage and were welcomed on arrival by a great gathering of friends, who escorted them in triumph to Clerkenwell. On the morrow they drove in 'great state' to Whitehall and expressed their thanks in person to the King.

TWENTY-THREE

'All the Town-talk. . . .'

THE COURT in 1665 was very different from the one they had both known under Charles I. The old decorum had given place to a raffishness which, while not sinking to the excesses of James I's time, appealed to neither of them. 'Go among those women?' demanded the outspoken old Lady Anne Clifford. 'Not unless I can wear blinkers!' Though the Newcastles did not adopt the same uncompromising moral stand, they could not have been fully at ease in this new Whitehall.

Margaret had always disliked the scandalmongering and insincerity of court life. Her strongly autobiographical play, *The Presence*, depicts the hurtful ridicule experienced by an unsophisticated girl. This was not published until 1668, and her early feelings may have been revived by her more recent visits, though by then she had changed from a tongue-tied innocent to a voluble, almost aggressive, eccentric. Newcastle, for his part, could not have been unaware of the malicious amusement aroused by her dress and mannerisms. Count Grammont, arriving for a palace masquerade, described to Charles II the extraordinary apparition he had seen as he stepped from his sedan chair. 'I bet', said the King, 'it is the Duchess of Newcastle.' 'And I will bet it is another fool,' said Lord Muskerry, 'for I am very much mistaken if it is not my wife.' It was not, in fact, Margaret – but Grammont's anecdote indicates the reputation she had acquired. There was additional prejudice against her because of her writing, which no one resented more than her fellow-women. Only a few, like Katherine Philips, 'the matchless Orinda', expressed the gratitude she deserved for her pioneering courage, and young Mrs Philips had died the previous year.

Having paid his respects to the King, Newcastle had little temptation to linger in town. Charles, though as civil as ever, had nothing in common with the older generation, and even Hyde, now Earl of Clarendon, was being undermined by Buckingham and the younger set who were so much more amusing. Many of Newcastle's friends, like Endymion Porter, were dead. Outside Whitehall, he could find some pleasure in the theatre and the company of literary men, and had he been younger and more often in London his scientific curiosity might have drawn him into the newly founded Royal Society; but Welbeck and Bolsover had a stronger pull. In any case, London would soon be emptying for the summer. He started for home with Margaret, and it was as well, for on 7 June Pepys was noting the first ominous signs of the plague that was soon to spread panic through the capital.

In August, when King and court had taken refuge at Oxford, the Duke and Duchess of York passed through Nottinghamshire on their way northwards. Both had enjoyed Newcastle's hospitality in Antwerp, where the Duchess, then Anne Hyde, the Chancellor's eldest daughter, had lived in the city for some time with her family. Now, following her controversial marriage to the King's brother, she had the two small daughters who would both one day reign as queens of England. On this occasion there was time only for a roadside greeting near Clipstone Park, but the royal couple accepted an invitation to stop at Welbeck on their return journey. Margaret's behaviour, recorded Sir Charles Lyttelton, was 'very pleasant, but rather to be seen than told'. Instead of curtseys she 'made legs and bows to the ground with her hand and head'. It was as though, having invaded the men's territory by publishing books, she was impelled to imitate them in other ways. A month later James, summoned urgently to join his brother at Oxford, sent apologies from 'your most affectionate friend', but his wife paid her visit to Welbeck as promised.

That year and the next, while London endured plague and fire, the Newcastles resumed their quiet country existence. Margaret was busy writing the life of her husband, her one work of intrinsic interest and also a milestone not only in women's writing but in biography generally. She inspired an immediate successor in Lucy Hutchinson and influenced many later authors. The subservient Flecknoe, dedicating to her *A Farrago of Several Pieces* in 1666, described her study – to which now, apparently, books were admitted:

> What place is this? looks like some sacred cell
> Where ancient hermits formerly did dwell . . . .
> Is this a lady's closet? 't cannot be,
> For nothing here of vanity we see . . . .
> Scarcely a glass, or mirror in 't you find
> Excepting books, the mirrors of the mind.

He prophesied that future generations would make pilgrimages as to 'Homer's shrine, or Virgil's tomb'.

In fact, it is another room in the Abbey which, though not open to the public, is still remembered for its literary associations. Still identified on the old-fashioned bell indicator as 'the Horsemanship Room' it is the one in which, about this time, Newcastle was occupied with his second book on that subject so dear to his heart. It was, he explained, 'neither a translation of the first, nor an absolutely necessary addition to it', adding hopefully, 'both together will questionless be best.' Again he emphasised that, though he had studied all the authorities: 'my book is stolen out of no book, nor any man's practice but my own; and is as true as it is new; and if any man do not like it, it is a great sign he understands it not. . . . If it be not good, I am sure it is the best that hath been written yet.' For all his blunt self-confidence he never denied that other opinions were tenable, even if he refused to accept them. 'I find fault with no man's delights, and do only vindicate (with truth) my own.' Let others disagree. 'I shall sleep never the worse.'

This book, *A New Method and Extraordinary Invention to Dress Horses, and Work them, according to Nature*, was published in London in 1667, and so, later that year, was Margaret's *Life of the Thrice Noble, High and Puissant Prince William Cavendish* – her full title runs to a dozen lines. It was pointedly dedicated to his neglectful sovereign and buttressed with prefatory epistles (her own to her husband, Rolleston's to herself) along with a selection of Newcastle's sage remarks, 'some few notes of the authoress' and 'a true relation' of her 'birth, breeding and life'. On 18 March 1668 Pepys, never very charitable to her, 'stayed at home reading the ridiculous history of my Lord Newcastle wrote by his wife, which shows her to be a mad, conceited, ridiculous woman, and he an ass to suffer her to write what she writes to him and of him'. Posterity has not supported Pepys. It would have been a sad loss if it had been burnt, unpublished, by an embarrassed husband. It has given much pleasure and, for all its omissions and inaccuracies, has preserved a wealth of information.

It was in the spring of the previous year, before the *Life* was published, that the Newcastles came to London again. Newcastle's comedy, *The Humorous Lovers*, was to be put on for the first time by Davenant and the Duke of York's Men at the playhouse in Lincoln's Inn Fields. The action was set in London, in Covent Garden, the Mulberry Garden and other fashionable haunts. The influence of Jonson was still dominant in Newcastle's writing, and by introducing a masque into the third act –

although masques were now despised as hopelessly old-fashioned – he revealed how firmly rooted he was in the theatrical traditions of his younger days. That his earthy gusto had not deserted him is shown by one lyric which has not fallen, with the rest of the play, into justifiable oblivion. 'Faith,' declares Colonel Boldman, 'I could never meet with such a piercing beauty, and yet I love the Sex well,' which is the cue for his song, the sentiments of which – whatever its literary shortcomings – must have chimed well with those of Charles and his courtiers:

> I love the fat, I love the fair,
> The lean, that's nimble, full of air. . . .

> I love the black, I love the red
> Upon a couch, or on a bed;
> She that is dull, and will not stir,
> The active wench too, I love her.

> I love the frolic, the precise,
> The reverend lady, that is wise;
> The wife, the maid, the widow too,
> All that is Woman, and will do.

On 30 March 1667 Pepys wrote (under a misunderstanding about the authorship, since writers' names did not appear on the bills): 'with my wife's knowledge and leave, did by coach go see the silly play of my Lady Newcastle's, the most silly thing that ever came upon a stage; I was sick to see it, but yet would not but have seen it, that I might the better understand her'. He was much intrigued by Margaret. On 11 April he went to Whitehall:

thinking there to have seen the Duchess of Newcastle's coming this night to court to make a visit to the Queen, the King having been with her yesterday to make her a visit since her coming to town. The whole story of this lady is a romance, and all she doth is romantic. Her footmen in velvet coats, and herself in an antique dress, as they say; and was the other day at her own play *The Humorous Lovers*; the most ridiculous thing that ever was wrote, but yet she and her lord mightily pleased with it, and she at the end made her respect to the players from her box and did give them thanks.

Newcastle, for whatever reason, was clearly taking a back seat, and on some occasions did not even think it necessary to accompany Margaret.

Pepys was not alone in his eagerness to see Margaret's arrival at the palace – the crowd, he noted, was as big as if Christina of Sweden had been expected. They all had their trouble for nothing. She did not come that evening. Not until 26 April could he catch a glimpse of my lady Newcastle, going with her coaches and footmen all in velvet; herself (whom I never saw before) as I have heard her often described (for all the town-talk is nowadays of her extravagances), with her velvet cap, her hair about her ears, many black patches because of pimples about her mouth, naked-necked, without anything about it, and a black juste-au-corps; she seemed to me a very comely woman – but I hope to see more of her on May Day.

At the traditional fashion parade, however, he encountered

a horrid dust and number of coaches, without pleasure or order. That which we and almost all went for was to see my Lady Newcastle; which we could not, she being followed and crowded upon by coaches all the way she went, that nobody could come near her; only, I could see she was in a large black coach, adorned with silver instead of gold, and so with the curtains and everything black and white, and herself in her cap. . . .

After half an hour he despaired of a closer view and drove off towards Clerkenwell with Sir William Penn, hoping to catch her as she came home, but they stopped for a drink – understandably after all that dust in Hyde Park – and missed her. Ten days later, after a hard day at the office, Pepys sighted her again in her coach, with a hundred boys and girls running after her. He gave chase, but, though driving hard, could not overtake her. 'But,' he vowed, 'I will get a time to see her.'

John Evelyn had a long-standing acquaintance with the Newcastles, having married the daughter of the Brownes who had facilitated their own wedding in Paris. He called on 18 April and was invited to bring his wife to dinner the following week. On that first visit he was 'much pleased with the extraordinary fanciful habit, garb and discourse of the Duchess', and, on the second, with his host and hostess's insistence on seeing him and his wife down to the courtyard. This suggests that, if Newcastle did not accompany Margaret on all her excursions, it was not due to ill-health. It is likely therefore that he went to the Garter ceremonies and banquet on St George's Day, two days earlier, and to the 'sumptuous supper in the banqueting-house at Whitehall' the night before that. Evelyn states that 'all' the members of the Order were there, and it would have been markedly discourteous if Newcastle had stayed away. On 6 May the King came to see his comedy, and he was at the theatre with Margaret to do the honours.

Following their dinner-party at Newcastle House, the Evelyns paid an afternoon call on Margaret, who welcomed Mary 'in a kind of transport, suitable to her extravagant humour and dress, which was very singular'. On 11 May Evelyn went alone and dined with Newcastle, but after the meal 'sat discoursing with her Grace in her bedchamber', a quite proper social procedure at that date, 'till my Lord Marquis of Dorchester with other company came in, when I went away'. The Newcastles, especially Margaret, were getting full value from their rare visit to town.

If the Duke had many common interests with Evelyn, the Duchess had a special motive for cultivating him. She was dying to attend a meeting of the Royal Society, in which he was prominent, and had extracted an invitation from that all-male institution, 'after much debate pro and contra' (says Pepys), 'many being against it'. Both diarists were present on 30 May when she entered 'in great pomp' with her waiting women, but significantly without her husband. She was welcomed by the Lord President with great deference, and Pepys was able at last to get a good look at the living legend. She had been, he conceded, 'a good comely woman' – she was now in her mid-forties – 'but her dress so antic and her deportment so unordinary, that I do not like her at all, nor did I hear her say anything that was worth hearing, but that she was full of admiration, all admiration'. She had the seat of honour next to the President and watched several scientific experiments. Then, still exclaiming that she was 'full of admiration', she was escorted out by several titled Fellows. Evelyn himself handed her into her coach. We may imagine her enthusiastic, if incomprehensible, attempts to describe to her husband, on her return to Clerkenwell, the demonstrations of chemistry and magnetism she had just witnessed.

That Royal Society meeting is the last recorded event of a visit that had already lasted nearly two months. A week later Pepys was recording a more alarming invasion – the Dutch fleet's entry into the Thames. If the Newcastles had not already left, it is unlikely that Margaret, with her nervous disposition, would have stayed in the threatened city. That scare passed, but they seem not to have come south again, even for the first performance of *Sir Martin Mar-All*, which was put on at the Duke's playhouse on 15 August to a full house including the King and court. Pepys went the next day, the house again sold out, and noted: 'a play made by my Lord Duke of Newcastle, but as everybody says corrected by Dryden. It is the most entire piece of mirth, a complete farce from one end to the other, that certainly was ever writ. I never laughed so in all my life.' Two days before, at the King's playhouse, he had been to yet another revival of *The Country Captain*, from which (Pepys never learned) he had 'no pleasure . . . at all'. *Sir Martin Mar-All* was entered in the Stationers' Register as Newcastle's work, and enjoyed a long popularity. Dryden never claimed it until fifteen years after his patron's death.

He may have had a hand too in *The Heiress*, a vanished comedy which the King went to see on 29 January 1669. Pepys thought it 'an indifferent play – wrote they say by my Lord Newcastle'. Mary Evelyn, more likely to have certain information, refers to the piece as 'one of my Lord Newcastle's' and to a collaborator, 'Briden', otherwise unknown and perhaps a faulty transcription of 'Dryden'. There has been some conjecture that his lost play was an earlier version of the already-mentioned *The Triumphant Widow*, which was not performed until 26 November 1674 (when Nell Gwyn was in the audience), though it incorporated the scenes Newcastle had written at Antwerp and called *A Pleasant and Merry Humour of a Rogue*. But the balance of opinion is against connecting this with *The Heiress*. In *The Triumphant Widow* it was Shadwell who probably contributed the main plot and Newcastle the sub-plot, where his humour and observation of low life had full scope.

Whatever the proportions of collaboration in these two plays, it is unlikely that he embarked on any sustained writing after his second horsemanship book. In 1668 Dryden's dedication of *An Evening's Love* had gracefully suggested that his patron's own 'evening' was 'far from night', but Newcastle, now seventy-five, could recognise a compliment. For Margaret, thirty years younger, he had arranged an annuity, charged on his Northumbrian estates, as long ago as 1662. Bolsover was settled on her for life. Now the London house was made over to her. In the servants' hall at Welbeck, where she was not universally popular, it was supposed that eventually she 'would break up the family and go to rant at London'. If the Duke caught any of these mutterings he gave no sign.

He could not fail to notice that the privileged position of Francis and Elizabeth Topp was resented. He owed much to Topp's business ability, but the tenants, as Sir Thomas Williamson told the steward, Andrew Clayton, had 'suffered much through the crossness . . . of Mr Topp, for I perceive my Lord Duke leaves the managing of his concerns chiefly to him'. Newcastle's children suspected that, in view of Mrs Topp's former situation as Margaret's maid, their stepmother's interests were likely to prosper at the expense of their own. Henry disliked his extravagant expenditure scrutinised by eyes less tolerant than his father's. 'Sweet Jane', less sweet than usual, complained to her sister-in-law of meeting the upstart Mr Topp in his coach in Hyde Park, and learning 'the thousand pound my father was pleased to give me is not yet due;

truly, I expect nothing he can keep from me. I am of your opinion, he intends none of my Lord's children any good, and am very sorry he should so much waste the estate as you mention; methinks there might be some means contrived to hinder him; I would assist in anything I could.'

Jane obstinately refrained from referring to him as 'Sir Francis', though a year previously, after persevering efforts, he had acquired a baronetcy – and, thanks to Newcastle's influence, without paying the customary fee. Whether he now felt ready to move on, or whether the family somehow contrived his removal, a friend was soon congratulating Henry's wife, Lady Ogle, 'that the Lady Topp and her daughter is gone from Welbeck, I hope never to return thither any more'. Now, it might be hoped, the Ogles would be 'more firmly fixed in my Lord Duke's favour and affection'.

For poor Jane, however, the solution came too late. She died on 8 October 1669, aged forty-seven, leaving a twelve-year-old son, William. It was a sad loss for Newcastle, to whom in earlier days she had been particularly close, sharing his literary interests. The elegy composep by the indefatigable Flecknoe can have brought scant consolation.

Now only Henry and Frances remained. Newcastle tried hard to remove the estrangement, of which he was painfully conscious. Frances, now Countess of Bolingbroke, was childless, but Henry had a little son, Henry, and four daughters, Elizabeth, Frances, Margaret and Catherine. These grandchildren came to stay at Welbeck in January 1670, and the boy's seventh birthday was celebrated there. Newcastle wrote to his son the next day to assure him that the children were all well. Young Henry, he reported with transparent emphasis, 'loves my wife better than anybody, and she him I think'. It may be doubted whether this assurance mollified the Earl of Ogle. Only two days later Margaret's settlement was augmented by the assignment of all the Duke's 'waste' land in Sherwood Forest. For years now she had been taking a keen interest in the running of the estates, scrutinising the rentals and generally keeping an eye on everything. With the Topps gone, and Newcastle ageing, she was taking over to a degree that the heir found alarming. Nor did it please those who had spent their whole lives in Newcastle's service.

A crisis occurred on 2 November 1670, a few days after Margaret's jointure had once more been increased with the addition of Clipstone Park and the manor of Sibthorpe. John Proctor, the Duke's personal servant, brought in a letter. It had been sent from Grantham but was unsigned. As Lord-Lieutenant, Newcastle was probably used to anonymous letters. This one began with a tribute to his popularity in the good old days, but went on to suggest that of late this had diminished, thanks to the behaviour of his second wife. Then came the startling allegation: she had had an affair with Francis Topp.

It is unlikely that Newcastle doubted Margaret for a moment. They had a close relationship which had survived disappointments and difficulties. Whatever follies she committed, a sexual misdemeanour was the least probable. He showed her the letter.

Who could have written it? Margaret suspected Clayton, with whom she had had more than one difference over estate business. Or perhaps another servant, Gilbert Eagle? Or the pair in collusion? Newcastle felt sure of their innocence, but sent for Clayton, who was out. Personally, he suspected 'that acute rascal, the parson of Mansfield'. Whoever it was, he would 'have his ears'. The fellow must be a fool as well as a knave if he thought to influence him by such libels.

By evening Clayton was back. Newcastle summoned him from his supper. Was the letter in verse, the steward inquired, perhaps some scurrilous doggerel? No, said Newcastle, a serious thing in prose. It 'abused Peg abominably'. Clayton protested that he knew nothing of it, and withdrew.

For the next eight months the Newcastles had to live with the unsolved mystery in the background. There was no further letter. By their demeanour they demonstrated their contempt for the libel. But it was unpleasant, and unforgettable.

On 16 May came a very different communication: the King had graciously granted Newcastle's request for burial in Westminster Abbey. The Dean, John Dolben, promised to arrange it when the time came. He wrote that he was 'glad to see the King do that which is so decent and worthy of him', but added that Newcastle had himself prepared a more lasting monument 'in the fame of your heroic actions', which Dolben had witnessed as an ensign of eighteen, wounded at Marston Moor.

Six weeks later one of the Welbeck servants, John Booth, came to Newcastle. He could no longer live with his guilty secret. He and Clayton had conspired with one of the Northumbrian tenants, Francis Liddell, at Ogle, in the hope of discrediting Her Grace and furthering certain transactions in which Clayton and Liddell were involved. Clayton, the prime mover, had told them that he had 'studied all ways in the world to give her Grace a dead blow', for she was planning to marry again, 'well knowing his Grace could not live long'. Clayton had suggested a specific allegation against Sir Francis Topp, and Liddell had supported him.

The game was up. Within four days, on 3 July 1671, Newcastle had the written confirmation still preserved:

Memorandum that I, Francis Liddell Esq., have perused this confession written in three sheets of paper and I do hereby acknowledge that all and every matter and thing therein contained against Andrew Clayton, myself and John Booth mentioned and expressed to be acted against their Graces the Duke and Duchess of Newcastle are really true and I will be ready to attest every of them upon my corporal oath whenever I am thereunto called before any lawful authority. . . .

It seems that no legal proceedings followed. Clayton, it must be assumed, lost his position but kept his ears. Life went on much as before at Welbeck, and relations between Margaret and her stepson grew a little warmer. He paid a visit himself in 1673 and expressed himself cordially on leaving. He took back a letter to young Harry from Margaret. Soon afterwards, when writing to Lord Ogle, she expressed humorous sympathy over the boy's bumping his forehead.

That autumn Newcastle attained his eightieth birthday. Truly, as Clayton had warned his accomplices, 'his Grace could not live long'. But to everybody's amazement, on 15 December it was Margaret who suddenly died.

TWENTY-FOUR

The Castle on the Cliff

THE NATURE of Margaret's last illness is not recorded. Her health had caused anxiety before, and neither her dislike of exercise nor her habit of dosing herself was calculated to improve it. But she is as likely to have been struck down by some affliction demanding surgery or other emergency treatment unavailable in the seventeenth century. Although the long-delayed funerals of the aristocracy required the urgent postmortem ministrations of surgeon and apothecary, the former often bequeathing to posterity a gruesome survey of the internal organs, no such document survives for our information in this case.

Newcastle's reaction is equally unknown. It would be reasonable to deduce shock and grief, but borne with his usual dignity. He did not travel to London for the splendid Abbey burial. Nearly a hundred and fifty miles in the depth of winter, and the road conditions of that age, might have been too much for him. He made his private farewells to his Peg at Welbeck. Then her embalmed body was sealed in wax, according to the custom with one of her quality, and laid in a leaden coffin moulded to her form, after which the cortège made its departure for London.

Newcastle House was being made ready for the lying in state. The rest of the family were gathering. The funeral, fixed for the evening of 7 January, was in the hands of two old friends, Dolben as Dean of Westminster and Sir Edward Walker as Garter King of Arms. When the time came, Newcastle could only sit in the sombre house of mourning, deep in the leafless January woodlands, picturing the torchlight procession with the Earl Marshal of England, the black-cloaked mourners, the rumbling coaches of the nobility, the hearse and coffin all black velvet and escutcheons, an Officer of Arms carrying the coronet on its little cushion.

It must have been easy to see it all in his mind's eye, to traverse pace by solemn pace the road from Clerkenwell that he had first known as a hopeful courtier, bound for the elegant new court of the young Charles I. Then, just as the London houses crowded closer and closer in the rosy lambency of the torches, so the memories thronged, ever thicker. The Strand, along which he had ridden in James's time with all those other youths, now dead as Prince Henry himself, to their investiture as Knights of the Bath. . . . The Strand, with Arundel's great house, all that talk of Italy and art, all those discussions over Uncle Gilbert's will . . . and, on the other side of the street, the house where he had been wont to visit Endymion Porter and Olive, both now at rest in St Martin-in-the-Fields close by. Now the procession would be entering Whitehall, passing the tiltyard where St Antoine had introduced him to the intricacies of the *haute école* – what, sixty-five years ago? And now passing the banqueting house, a reminder enough to convulse the features with a wince – Charles stepping out through the window to meet the headsman, a thought to blot out all happier memories of masques and feastings under the glorious Rubens ceiling . . . Westminster, the Abbey and the Parliament House looming against the night sky, and next to the Abbey, squeezed between it and St Margaret's, the house where Jonson had lodged in his final years, writing for the King's entertainments at Welbeck and Bolsover. . . .

Once inside the great church, all would be ordered according to his wishes. Had he not, with characteristic thoroughness, conveyed his 'express desire and direction' for the marshalling of the family? Margaret's two surviving sisters behind the coffin as the Dean and Chapter, having met them at the west door with the choir, led the way to the allotted resting-place in the north transept . . . then Frances and Henry's wife, and the other ladies . . . Henry next with the Earl Marshal, followed by his widowed son-in-law, Bridgwater, and other titled relatives . . . poor Elizabeth's boy, Lord Brackley, would be in front as one of the pall-bearers . . . everyone would be there except himself – and of course the many, the all too many, who were long ago in their own graves. Now the coffin would be vanishing from sight, the sonorous voice of the herald rehearsing her titles . . . 'Thus it hath pleased Almighty God to take out of this transitory life to His divine mercy the most high, mighty, and most noble Princess Margaret, Duchess of Newcastle, late wife of the most high, mighty, and most noble prince, William, Duke of Newcastle, now living.'

'Now living.' But not, reason told him, for long. He would soon be laid beside Peg. He took his pen – he still preferred to do important things himself – and composed the inscription that would be placed over them. Here it is, in the original spelling, as it can still be read beneath their effigies:

Here lyes the Loyall Duke of Newcastle and his Dutches, his second wife, by whome he had noe issue; her name was Margarett Lucas, youngest sister to the Lord Lucas of Colchester; a noble familie, for all the Brothers were valiant and all the Sisters virtuous. This Dutches was a wise, wittie and learned Lady, which her many Bookes do well testifie; she was a most Virtuous and a Loving and carefull wife, and was with her Lord all the time of his banishment and miseries, and when he came home never parted from him in his solitary retirements.

People, he knew, could be cynical about epitaphs. Margaret had suffered sufficiently in her lifetime from their covert smiles. So, he would buttress his simple words with impressive witnesses. In the months that followed he began to collect for publication everything that had been written in her praise – letters from famous philosophers, academic addresses, dedications, valedictory elegies. The volume came out in 1676, *Letters and Poems in honour of the Incomparable Princess, Margaret, Duchess of Newcastle.*

One elegy came from the assiduous Shadwell. Over the years he produced no fewer than six of those 'northern dedications' which Dryden derided, after the poets had quarrelled, in his savagely satirical *Mac-Flecknoe*. One was to Margaret, four to Newcastle himself and one to his son. Shadwell clung to the Cavendish connection. Later in the Duke's year of mourning he arranged for the staging of their joint effort, *The Triumphant Widow*, and after Newcastle's death he was to publish it. A lesser playwright, Elkanah Settle, attacked Shadwell in 1675 and tried, with the dedication of a tragedy, *Love and Revenge*, to supplant him in Newcastle's favour. But to the old man at Welbeck the petty jealousies of the London playhouses meant little. Dryden might assail Shadwell from one side and Settle from the other, but he continued the easy-going, uncritical generosity he had always shown to men of letters, whatever their faults.

It is evident, however, that advancing years and bereavement had not impaired his old mental alertness. The repairs and extensions at Bolsover must have been completed well before Margaret's death – a 1670 inventory conjures up a picture of the castle splendid again with tapestries and crimson taffeta and cloth-of-silver chairs – and he turned now to his long-cherished dream of building a new castle on the rock at Nottingham. The site had first attracted William the Conqueror, who had planted a motte-and-bailey fortress there within two years of Hastings. Successive medieval kings had developed it into one of the principal royal strongholds, that 'Castle of Care' from which Richard III had ridden out to his doom at Bosworth. Thereafter the place had decayed. Tudor townsmen had quarried it for masonry. In the late war Hutchinson had made it defensible again, then demolished it for fear Cromwell would use it to sustain a dictatorship. Now Newcastle ordered the ruins to be cleared and the summit of the rock levelled for an entirely new building, although excavations from 1976 onwards suggest that some of the earlier walls were retained as boundaries and that large quantities of the medieval dressed stone, being of good quality, was used again elsewhere. The massive fourteenth-century gatehouse was left at the foot of the slope, facing the town below.

Some twenty years later the tireless Celia Fiennes was to stand on the leaden roof of the new castle and admire the 'very fine prospect of the whole town and river', the Trent, that is, a mile away across the meadows, not its little tributary, the Leen, which washed the actual base of the precipice. Celia could see for more than twenty miles, 'plains and rivers and great woods, and little towns all in view'. She could pick out the Earl of Rutland's castle at Belvoir, the Holme Pierrepont seat of the Earl of Kingston, and, closer at hand, the great mansion at Wollaton which Robert Smythson had completed in the Armada year. It was a prospect that must have appealed even more strongly to Newcastle, so fully packed was it with the memories of a lifetime.

This time, he resolved, he would be his own architect. Though Robert Smythson's great-grandson was still at Bolsover, carrying on the family profession, he was not brought into the new project. Newcastle had been passionately interested in architecture all his life and had learnt much from the preceding three generations he had employed. With a trustworthy clerk of the works he could build this new Nottingham Castle himself. It would give him a fresh interest. He engaged a Lincolnshire man named March, of whose other building experience nothing is now known.

The castle – a house really, almost a palace – should be a rectangle, looking down over the town, with two wings at the rear projecting towards the edge of the sandstone cliff. It should have a noble frontage, with nine broad bays, columns and pilasters dividing them. Mullioned windows, small square ones on the upper storey, with the Flemish-style architraves he remembered from Antwerp . . . a balustrade above, going all round the roof . . . an impressive front door, reached by a double

staircase, and over it his own statue, mounted of course . . . balconies . . .
bold rustication. . . . When Pevsner saw it about 1950, he wrote:
'Everything is done to increase life and movement in the way in which
the Continental Baroque tried to do it everywhere. Yet the English
accent can nowhere be mistaken. The comparison that comes to mind at
once is with . . . Bolsover.'

As usual, Newcastle knew just what he wanted. Realistically he
accepted the likelihood that he might never see the completion, but he
could see it in his mind's eye as Celia Fiennes saw it in 1697:

The Castle, which is a fine thing stands very high on a hill . . . you ascend 40
steps to the Court and Hall, the rooms are very lofty and large, 6 or 7 state
rooms, and a long gallery hung with fine pictures of the family, the wainscoat
is most of cedar; some rooms are hung with good tapestry, the chamber of
state is hung with very rich tapestry, so much silver and gold in it that the 3
pieces that hung the room cost £1500; the bed was rail'd in as the presence
chamber used to be – the bed was damask; the floor of the room was inlay'd
with ciphers and the coronet, here the Princess Anne lay when she fled in
King James's time when the Prince of Orange was coming over. . . .

That time Newcastle was not to see. The 'Loyal Duke' was spared the
sight of his castle seized in his son's absence by the Whigs – the Chatsworth Cavendishes among them – and used as a refuge for Hyde's
grand-daughter, until the success of the Glorious Revolution gamble
was assured.

While the building operations proceeded steadily at Nottingham, it
is evident from shakily written verses among the Portland Papers that
the old man's imagination was still active in other directions. There are
randy rhymes inspired by observation of the female staff at Welbeck as
they flitted about their duties. *Of a Chambermaid* and *Of a waiting
Gentlewoman* are among the titles, while *The Sweepers* who, though
'being young lusty wenches', were prudently nervous of unwanted
pregnancy, were reproved:

> What shift do you make since flesh you refuse,
> Your broom staff for a dildo then you use.

A starcher in the laundry wins more commendation:

> You're nimble at your trade, with any hand,
> You love to starch, to make it stiff to stand.

In a slightly more ambitious effort, *An Epigram of Age and Love*, he
faced facts with philosophic self-mockery:

When periwigs come on, spectacles woo,
And on the wrong side of his forty, too,
With a dry palm and crow's feet in his eyes,
Stoops in his back, and nothing by his thighs,
Increasing belly, and decreasing member,
And no wits left, but past sins to remember.
If he then look for Love, his brain is stupid.
As Cupid hath paid him, he must pay Cupid.

These verses bear no date, but a long series of short poems, numbered, dated, and described as 'Songs', suggests that he was 'looking for Love' almost to the end of his life – and something like real love, not senile gropings with complaisant women of the household. *Song 8th*, dated '30 Sept 75', declares:

When I look on thee 't is with such delight,
The joy is such, as sure 't is more than sight.
When thou dost whisper, music then I hate,
'T is more than hearing, it's a higher rate.
Thy breath is sweeter than all sweets to me,
Spanish perfumes, or sweetest flowers can be,
And when I steal a kiss methinks 't is taste.
Oh, breathe again, thy breath thus will not waste.
Touch is beyond expressions joy, therefore
Repeat it often, and I'll ask no more.

These ardent sentiments are expressed in so tremblous a hand that there is a fair copy, probably made by the faithful and discreet Rolleston.

Two days later comes *Song 9th*, six lines beginning:

Cupid, I've served thee this many a year . . . ,

an echo of the previous *Epigram. Song 11th*, on 8 October, runs:

Your eyes two suns to me appear,
Which makes it summer all the year,
Those eyes of yours do shine so bright
Makes it perpetual day not night.
Except your eyelids curtains drawn
That's night, although they're white as lawn.
But when they're open all may say
Your eyes are then the break of day.

There is no indication by whom these verses were inspired – no certainty indeed, only a strong probability, that they were addressed to an actual woman. If so, was it more than a sensual old man's pathetic attempt at a flirtation – or was he, as someone has suggested, toying with the idea of a third marriage? Such a hypothesis is by no means incredible. He might well, in some moods, have convinced himself that he was still capable of begetting children, and there was a strong motive for trying – Henry had had no more sons, and the continuance of the male line depended solely on young Harry, still a boy. He had married Margaret in hopes of a second family, and been disappointed. If he had considered, even at this late hour, another venture into matrimony, it would have been quite in keeping with the dynastic obsessions of his class and century.

If he was indeed wooing some young woman, the course of love did not run smoothly. *Song 12th*, 16 October, suggests a rift:

> When frown thou it makes dark clouds aspire,
> To lightning's flashes of great fire . . .

and the next poem three days later, *A Song of Money*, is cynical:

> Money does all things in this world as King,
> Yet of itself can not do anything.
> Money, great monarch of this earthly ball,
> Love it doth much, but money it doth all.
> Virtue, nor Vanity, nor Vice can be,
> Without thy help, then money give to me.
> There's nothing then that can be done without thee,
> And that's the cause, that makes such stir about thee.

In the following weeks it would seem that the Duke was finding more comfort in the bottle:

> Give me the Canary, the wholesome sherry,
> The radical Malaga makes us merry,
> Sometimes the claret, the Rhenish, the white . . . ,

and so on to the warning that too much Lacrima Christi 'will make your eyes misty'. He had never been an excessive drinker by the standards of his time, and another poem, dated 22 November 1675, shows that he still acknowledged the value of moderation:

> Then give me the glass to heighten my fancy,
> Witty repartees, not lying romancy.
> I'll drink up to wit, not beyond it. Then
> We should all turn beasts, lose the title of men.

There were still times when he turned to more exalted themes. In February of the next year his mind must have gone ranging back, as an old man's will, to that other February thirty-three years earlier when Henrietta Maria had landed on the Yorkshire coast and he had sped to ensure her safety. Then he recalled their parting at Pontefract when he saw her on her way to join the King. The memory prompted him to write *A Song of the Queen's Departure out of the North*, and then a second and a third poem on the same subject, as if that moment in the war had left an indelible impression.

The dated poems run from 30 September 1675 to the sixty-second 'song' on 27 October 1676, and if their poetic quality is not high their sheer number and subject-matter throw some interesting light into the growing shadows of his last years. Three weeks before that final poem he made another will, on 4 October. 'I have begun to carry up a considerable building at Nottingham Castle,' he wrote, 'which I earnestly desire may be finished to the form and model by me laid and designed.' He appointed March, Mason, his lawyer from Newark, Richard Neale, one of his stewards from Mansfield Woodhouse, and a certain Thomas Farr as joint trustees to ensure that it was done. He thoughtfully set aside two thousand pounds a year to cover the remaining work. The total cost, when the castle was completed in 1679, came to £14,002 17s. 9d.

He was leaving yet another splendid seat to his successors – and, as he signed his will that autumn day, he could only hope that the succession was safe. He was not to know that young Harry would die 'of the new fever' at seventeen, and that the male line would end with Henry's death in 1691. Subsequent Dukes of Newcastle would be of a new creation. Most of the family estates, passing through the female line, would come to the future Dukes of Portland.

All this was mercifully hidden. The wet signature sanded, the will was put away, and for a little while longer he could turn his pen to songs again. Soon it was his birthday. Eighty-three. Then the anniversary of poor Peg's death, 15 December, three years ago. Christmas next, one of the good old festivals he approved of, 'carols and wassails, with good plum porridge and pies'. The usual preparations went forward in the great house at Welbeck and on the estate. But if he knew the joy of Christmas morning he certainly did not see the end of the day, only at last the end of his own long day, for at some time on 25 December 1676, the details unrecorded, the old man slipped into the silence. A month later, on 22 January, the nobility and quality crowded round the re-opened vault at Westminster, heard the herald recite his high-sounding titles for the last time, and saw 'the loyal Duke' – an apter title than any of them – laid to rest beside his eccentric, infuriating, beloved Peg.

Notes on Sources

Chapter 1   For an approximate birth-date I have followed the Handsworth parish register, which is consistent with the age given on the Duke's tomb, and seems to dispose of the last lingering doubt in *The Complete Peerage*. Other contemporary authorities are the Portland Papers, Hardwick MSS, Calendar of State Papers (Domestic) (CSPD) and Chamberlain's *Letters*. Among modern writers I am particularly indebted to David N. Durant's most fully documented *Bess of Hardwick* for the general life of the Cavendish family at this period, and to Roland Bibby's *Bothal Observed* (especially the description quoted from *The Bothoole Booke* of 1576) for the Northumbrian background.

Chapter 2   For the boyhood years we have the Duchess's *Life* of her husband, published with his approval. Other early authorities are Oldys (*Biographia Britannica*, 1747–1760) and Arthur Collins. Durant is again useful for Cavendish and Talbot family background. For the wider world of court there is Agnes Strickland's *Lives of the Queens of England* and Akrigg's *Jacobean Pageant*, while for specialist equestrian matters there is Lady Apsley's *Bridleways through History*.

Chapter 3   The Savoy journey is documented by Wotton's dispatches and references in Chamberlain and in the Calendar of State Papers (Venetian), all in Logan Pearsall Smith's *Life and Letters of Sir Henry Wotton*. The Duchess, half a century later, preserved one or two further details.

Chapter 4   Besides the Portland Papers, the CSPD and the Duchess, the main contemporary sources are Chamberlain and the House of Commons Journals. The weather record by the anonymous Youlgreave churchwarden will be found in Thomas Moult's compilation, *Derbyshire in Prose and Verse*, 1929. For Bolsover Castle I have relied mainly on Mark Girouard and P. A. Faulkner, though they do not invariably agree on building dates.

Chapter 5   Again the contemporary sources are the Portland Papers, Chamberlain, the Calendar of State Papers (Foreign as well as Domestic), the Duchess (*CCXI Sociable Letters* as well as the *Life*), Lords Journals now for parliamentary attendance, and the Ben Jonson poems in his *Underwoods*, with a Harleian MS reference to the baptismal Interlude at Blackfriars. Modern authorities consulted have been mainly Girouard and Faulkner on the buildings, Turberville, and for general Jacobean background Akrigg, with John Nichols (1828) for the royal progresses.

Chapter 6   The events of this chapter are fairly fully covered by the CSPD, the Lords Journals, *The Complete Peerage* and the *Dictionary of National Biography*. The poems are from the Portland Papers (PwV26) at the University of Nottingham Library. Lady Rutland's visit to Welbeck is recorded by Turberville, citing the Rutland MSS. I have used T. Carte's collection of contemporary letters for the changes at court, Girouard and Faulkner for the continuing building operations, and, for militia matters, L. Boynton's *The Elizabethan Militia 1558–1638*, published in 1967.

Chapter 7   The scanty surviving information about Newcastle House comes mainly from W. J. Pinks' *History of Clerkenwell* (2nd edn, 1880) and older histories of London, plus undated and unidentifiable newspaper cuttings preserved in the local library; and Mr Neil Burton thinks the architectural evidence consistent with a date in the 1630s. The rest of this chapter is based on the Portland Papers, CSPD and Ben Jonson's letters. I am indebted to Bentley for some theatrical details and to Gervas Huxley for the glimpse of Endymion Porter's home.

Chapter 8   Besides the Portland Papers and the Duchess we have the letters of Wentworth (later Strafford), Ben Jonson and Hobbes, and from now onwards there is Clarendon's *History of the Rebellion*. On the literary side I have consulted Perry, Allardyce Nicoll, and Maurice Hussey's *The World of Shakespeare and His Contemporaries*.

Chapter 9   The continuing life-line of the Portland Papers, CSPD and Lords Journals is here strengthened with extra strands of contemporary documentation from *Strafford's Letters*, Ellis and Rushworth. Perry,

Bentley and Montague Summers have been helpful for theatrical information, and Aylmer for the staffing of the royal household.

Chapter 10   The Duchess's narrative has been checked, expanded and where necessary corrected by reference to the CSPD, Lords Journals, *The Complete Peerage* and Clarendon, with the *Thomason Tracts* for events in the Newcastle area.

Chapter 11   With the start of the Civil War we enter a positive blizzard of contemporary documents. This chapter is based not only on the Portland Papers and Harleian MSS, the Duchess's biography (with Firth's editorial notes) and Clarendon, but on the *Fairfax Correspondence*, the recollections of Slingsby and Philip Warwick, and the Royalist newspaper, *Mercurius Aulicus*, as well as Ellis, Thomason and the York City Archives. In the next century Drake's *Eboracum* was written in time to save many details from oblivion. Among modern authorities I have relied mainly on Young and Holmes's *The English Civil War*.

Chapter 12   For the Queen's adventures there are her letters, edited by M. A. E. Green, and Agnes Strickland's *Lives*, as well as topical reports in *Mercurius Aulicus* and the *Weekly Intelligencer*, and the Duchess's own account. For this chapter in general we have Bulstrode, Clarendon, Warwick, and the Commons Journals. I am indebted to Huxley for details of the Porter family and to R. H. Hodgkin's *Six Centuries of an Oxford College* for the fate of Hudson.

Chapter 13   Besides the recollections of Slingsby, Warwick, Fairfax, Lucy Hutchinson and Rolleston, the Duke's secretary, as used by the Duchess, plus the Portland Papers and all the contemporary material assembled by Rushworth, Thomason, Warburton and Green, I am particularly indebted to Newman's thesis, which has gathered and winnowed a whole harvest of lesser-known documents. The 'scurrilous Roundhead pamphlet' is cited by Bentley.

Chapter 14   The sources are much the same as in the previous chapter, supplemented by such studies as C. S. Terry's *The Scottish Campaigns in Northumberland and Durham . . . 1644* (Archaeologia Aeliana, 1899). Again Newman has smoothed my way, and Wenham is of course invaluable.

Chapter 15   The contemporary documentation is too massive to be listed here, but much will be found set out in Newman's separate Borthwick Paper, *Marston Moor*. I have compared this with the interpretations of Burne, Young and other modern writers, in trying to reconstruct Newcastle's personal experiences that day.

Chapter 16   The Portland Papers and CSPD are here supplemented with evidence from Ellis, Rushworth, Strickland and Warburton. For theatrical references I have used Hotson, and, for Jane and Elizabeth's writings, Harbage's *Annals of English Drama.*

Chapter 17   Margaret's letters were first published by Goulding, 'from the originals at Welbeck Abbey', in 1909. Newcastle's MS poems are in the British Library. Both were combined, edited in their original spelling, and published by Grant in 1956. From this point onwards I have also made grateful use of Grant's biography of the Duchess.

Chapter 18   Contemporary sources are the letters and poems mentioned above, the Portland Papers, *Several Proceedings in Parliament, Sept. 1651* (for the intercepted letter), the Duchess, Evelyn, and news-papers cited by Hotson. Other modern authors drawn upon are Perry, Morrah, and, of course, Grant.

Chapter 19   This chapter is based mainly on the Duchess's own writings – *The World's Olio, Sociable Letters* and *Nature's Pictures* – but I have consulted Bentley on Newcastle's plays and Pierre Cabanne's *Rubens* for further details on the house.

Chapter 20   I have used the Duchess's various publications, as cited, the Duke's horsemanship writings, the Portland Papers, the CSPD, and *The Nicholas Papers* (ed. G. F. Warner), with Lady Apsley as a twentieth-century commentator on the Duke's equestrian activities.

Chapter 21   Besides the Duchess's own account, the Portland Papers, the Lords Journals and *The Complete Peerage,* I have used *Prepara-tions for the Coronation of H.M. Charles II,* published in 1820 from Sir Edward Walker's original MS. Newcastle's memorandum to Charles, in the Bodleian, was identified only after the printing of the *Summary Catalogue,* and should be inquired for by its shelf-mark, 'MS Clarendon 109', in the Department of Western MSS.

Chapter 22   The Duchess is our chief source, buttressed by Lucy Hutchinson for the treatment of her husband and *The Complete Peerage* for some family items. Dryden, Shadwell, Flecknoe, Pepys and Langbaine supply the literary background. Of modern writers I have principally consulted Perry, Turberville and Grant, with Girouard and Faulkner for the building operations.

Chapter 23   Besides the publications of the Duke and Duchess, we have the Portland Papers, CSPD, *Complete Peerage*, *Dictionary of National Biography*, Pepys, Evelyn, Grammont's *Memoirs*, and the *Hatton Correspondence*, cited by Goulding, himself a valuable authority on the Welbeck records.

Chapter 24   The Duke's verses are in the Portland Papers, catalogued at Nottingham University as PwV25 and 26. His will, and some other details on Nottingham Castle, are given by T. C. Hine. Celia Fiennes provides a contemporary description of the completed building, and Robert Thoroton's *Antiquities of Nottinghamshire* (1677) gives the cost. For the adaptation of the medieval remnants I have consulted the Trent Valley Archaeological Research Committee. Details of the Duchess's funeral are in the certificate of the College of Arms. The epitaph can be read on the tomb.

Bibliography

Akrigg, G. P. V., *Jacobean Pageant* (1962)
Apsley, Lady, *Bridleways through History* (1936)
Aylmer, G. E., *The King's Servants* (1961)

Bentley, G. E., *The Jacobean and Caroline Stage* (1956)
Bibby, R., *Bothal Observed* (Newcastle-upon-Tyne, 1973)
——, *Northumbriana*, Nos. 3–6 (Morpeth, 1975–6)
Bulstrode, R., *Memoirs and Reflections upon the Reign and Government of King Charles I and King Charles II* (1721)
Burne, A. H., *The Battlefields of England* (1950)

Calendar of State Papers (Domestic) (1858–97)

Carte, T., *Collection of Original Letters . . . 1641 to 1660* (1739)

Cavendish, M., Duchess of Newcastle, *Poems and Fancies* (1653)

——, *Philosophicall Fancies* (1653)

——, *The World's Olio* (1655)

——, *Philosophical and Physical Opinions* (1655)

——, *Nature's Pictures drawn by Fancies Pencil. . . .* (1656)

——, *Playes* (1662)

——, *Orations of Divers Sorts* (1662)

——, *CCXI Sociable Letters* (1664)

——, *Philosophical Letters: or, Modest Reflections. . . .* (1664)

——, *Observations upon Experimental Philosophy . . . The Description of a new Blazing World* (1666)

——, *The Life of the thrice Noble, High and Puissant Prince William Cavendish. . . .* (1667)

——, *Grounds of Natural Philosophy. . . .* (1668)

——, *Plays, never before Printed* (1668)

(*Some of these titles reappear with additions and revisions in subsequent editions.*)

Cavendish, W., Duke of Newcastle, *A Declaration made by the Earle of Newcastle . . . for his resolution of marching into Yorkshire* (1642); *A proclamation . . . for bringing in of arms* (1642); *A Proclamation* (York 1643)

——, *The Country Captaine, and The Varietie, Two Comedies* (1649)

——, *La Méthode Nouvelle et Invention Extraordinaire de dresser les Chevaux* (Antwerp, 1658)

——, *A New and Extraordinary Method to dress Horses* (1667)

——, *The Humorous Lovers* (1677)

——, *The Triumphant Widow* (with Shadwell) (1677)

——, *A Pleasant and Merry Humour of a Rogue* (1933)

——, *The Phanseys addressed to Margaret Lucas and her Letters in reply* (ed. D. Grant, 1956)

——, *The Cavalier and his Lady* (selections from the Duke and Duchess's works) (1872)

Chamberlain, J., *Letters* (ed. N. E. McClure 1939)

Clarendon, Earl of, *History of the Rebellion* (ed. Macray, 1888)

Cocking, H. M., *Originality and Influence in the Work of Margaret Cavendish* (thesis, University of Reading, 1972)

Collins, A., *Historical Collections of the Noble Families of Cavendish, &c.* (1752)

Commons Journals

Complete Peerage (ed. H. A. Doubleday and Lord Howard de Walden, 1936)

Dictionary of National Biography (1882)
Drake, F., *Eboracum: or the History . . . of York* (1736)
Durant, D. N., *Bess of Hardwick* (1977)

Ellis, H., *Original Letters Illustrative of English History* (1824–46)
Evelyn, J., *Diary and Correspondence* (ed. E. S. de Beer, 1954)

Faulkner, P. A., *Bolsover Guide* (1975)
Fiennes, C., *The Journeys of Celia Fiennes* (ed. C. Morris, 1947)
Firth, C. H., *see* Cavendish, M., *The Life*, 1886 edn

Girouard, M., *Robert Smythson and the Architecture of the Elizabethan Era* (1966)
Goulding, R. W. (ed.), *Letters written by Charles Lamb's 'Princely Woman . . .' . . . from the originals at Welbeck Abbey* (1909)
Goulding, R. W., *Margaret (Lucas) Duchess of Newcastle* (Lincoln, 1925)
Grant, D., *Margaret the First* (1957)
(*see also* Cavendish, M., *The Phanseys*, 1956 edn)
Green, M. A. Everett, *Letters of Queen Henrietta Maria* (1857)

Hine, T. C., *Nottingham Castle* (1876)
Hotson, L., *Commonwealth and Restoration Stage* (1928)
Hutchinson, L., *Memoirs of Colonel Hutchinson* (1806)
Huxley, G., *Endymion Porter: The Life of a Courtier* (1959)

Johnson, G. W., *Fairfax Correspondence* (1848–9)
Jonson, B., *Works* (ed. C. H. Herford and P. Simpson, 1925–52)

Knowler, W., *The Earl of Strafford's Letters and Despatches* (1739)

Longueville, T., *The First Duke and Duchess of Newcastle* (1910)
Lords Journals

Markham, C. R., *Life of Fairfax* (1870)
Morrah, P., *Prince Rupert of the Rhine* (1976)

Needham, F. (ed.), *A Collection of Poems by Several Hands* (Welbeck Miscellany No. 2) (1934)

Newman, P. R., *The Royalist Army in Northern England 1642–5* (thesis, University of York, 1978)
——, *Marston Moor, 2 July 1644: The Sources and the Site* (Borthwick Paper No. 53, University of York, 1978)
Nichols, J., *The Progresses, Processions and Magnificent Festivities of King James the First* (1828)
Nicoll, A., *Stuart Masques and the Renaissance Stage* (1937)

Ollard, R., *This War Without an Enemy* (1976)
Oman, C., *Henrietta Maria* (1936)

Pepys, S., *Diary* (ed. R. C. Latham and W. Matthews, 1970–6)
Perry, H. T. E., *The First Duchess of Newcastle and her Husband as Figures in Literary History* (1918)
Pevsner, N., *Nottinghamshire* (1951)
Portland Papers

Rushworth, J., *Historical Collections* (1659–1701)

Slingsby, H., *Diary of Sir Henry Slingsby* (ed. D. Parson, 1836)
Smith, L. P., *Life and Letters of Sir Henry Wotton* (1907)
Stone, L., *Crisis of the Aristocracy 1558–1641* (1965)
Strickland, A., *Lives of the Queens of England* (1840–8)
Summers, M., *The Restoration Theatre* (1934)

Thomason Tracts (1641–62)
Turberville, A. S., *Welbeck Abbey and Its Owners* (1938)

Warburton, E., *Memoirs of Prince Rupert and the Cavaliers* (1849)
Warwick, P., *Memoires of the Reigne of King Charles I* (1701)
Wedgwood, C. V., *The King's Peace* (1955)
——, *The King's War* (1958)
Wenham, P., *The Great and Close Siege of York, 1644* (1970)

Young, P., *Marston Moor 1644: The Campaign and the Battle* (1970)
Young, P. and Holmes, R., *The English Civil War* (1974)

Index

I. Persons

Index

II. Principal Places